Indigenous Educational Models for Contemporary Practice

Volume II

The book challenges teachers, researchers, educational leaders, and community stakeholders to build dynamic learning environments through which indigenous learners can be "Boldly Indigenous in a Global World!" Three days of focused dialogue at the 2005 World Indigenous Peoples Conference on Education (WIPCE) led to the charge to create Volume II of *Indigenous Educational Models for Contemporary Practice: In Our Mother's Voice*. Building on the first volume, Volume II examines these topics:

- Regenerating and transforming language and culture pedagogy that reminds us that what is "Contemporary is Native"
- Living indigenous leadership that engages and ensures the presence, readiness, and civic work of our next generation of leaders
- Indigenizing assessment and accountability that makes certain that native values and strengths lead this important work
- Highlighting the power of partnerships that begin with the child-elder, which is then nurtured in community and institutions to cross boundaries of cultural difference, physical geography, native and non-native institutions and communities

Indigenous Educational Models for Contemporary Practice: In Our Mother's Voice, Volume II honors the wisdom of our ancestors, highlights the diversity of our indigenous stories, and illuminates the passion of forward-looking scholars.

About the Editor: **Maenette Kape'ahiokalani Padeken Ah Nee-Benham**, Kanaka Maoli, is a Professor in the Department of Educational Administration at Michigan State University.

Sociocultural, Political, and Historical Studies in Education

Joel Spring, Editor

For additional information on titles in the Studies in Sociocultural, Political and Historical Studies in Education series visit www.routledgeeducation.com

Indigenous Educational Models for Contemporary Practice

In Our Mother's Voice

Volume II

Edited by

Maenette Kape'ahiokalani Padeken Ah Nee-Benham
Michigan State University

Routledge
Taylor & Francis Group
NEW YORK AND LONDON

First published 2008
by Routledge
270 Madison Ave, New York, NY 10016

Simultaneously published in the UK
by Routledge
2 Park Square, Milton Park, Abingdon, Oxon OX14 4RN

Routledge is an imprint of the Taylor & Francis Group, an informa business

© 2008 Taylor & Francis

Typeset in Goudy by
Swales & Willis Ltd, Exeter, Devon
Printed and bound in the United States of America on acid-free paper by
Edwards Brothers, Inc.

Library of Congress Cataloging in Publication Data
A catalog record has been requested for this book

ISBN10: 0–8058–6402–4 (hbk)
ISBN10: 0–8058–6403–2 (pbk)
ISBN10: 1–4106–1855–2 (ebk)

ISBN13: 978–0–8058–6402–1 (hbk)
ISBN13: 978–0–8058–6403–8 (pbk)
ISBN13: 978–1–4106–1855–9 (ebk)

In memory of Beatrice Medicine for lighting our way!
To the champions of our indigenous schools: teachers and leaders.
To our native children and youth, today and seven generations hence.

Hoe aku i kou wa'a!
(Paddle your canoe forward!)

Contents

Series Editor Foreword

Dr. Joel Spring, Choctaw

This second volume of *Indigenous Educational Models for Contemporary Practice: In Our Mother's Voice* provides more models of indigenous forms of education. The volume gives concrete meaning to Article 14 of the 2007 United Nations Declaration on the Rights of Indigenous Peoples:

> Indigenous peoples have the right to establish and control their educational systems and institutions providing education in their own languages, in a manner appropriate to their cultural methods of teaching and learning.[1]

The legacy of colonialism and genocide has made it difficult to fulfill this right. Many educational traditions and practices have been lost or only remain in the memories of survivors of the indigenous peoples' holocaust while other educational traditions have remained active. *Indigenous Educational Models for Contemporary Practice* provides educational models that affirm the vitality of these traditions and their adaptability to contemporary times.

[1] United Nations General Assembly (2007) *Report of the Human Rights Council: United Nations Declaration on the Rights of Indigenous Peoples*, Article 14. New York: United Nations, p. 6.

In a broader context, the world's people should pay close attention to indigenous educational models as alternatives to current global standards that link economic development to educational practices. These dominant models are focused on training workers for an economic system that produces environmental destruction, unhappiness, and an empty spirit. Speaking before the United Nations in 1992, Thomas Banyacya, the last of the four Hopi messengers sent by the Great Spirit Maasau'u, Guardian of the Earth, to warn that the earth was out of balance and headed for destruction, described a rock drawing found in Hopiland.

> This rock drawing, shows part of the Hopi prophecy. There are two paths. The first with high technology but separate from natural and spiritual law leads to these jagged lines representing chaos. The lower path is one that remains in harmony with natural law. Here we see a line that represents a choice like a bridge joining the paths. If we return to spiritual harmony and live from our hearts we can experience a paradise in this world. If we continue only on this upper path, we will come to destruction.[2]

It is my hope and belief that the educational models described in this book will help put students, teachers, and the world on the path to harmony and hope. In closing I offer the following gift to the spirit of this book.

Cleansing the Blood of My Ancestors
My father's father and his father's father were all chiefs,
but not the type that brought good to their people.
Born from the joining of a Frenchman and Pushmataha's daughters,
they preached that forgetting the old ways would end the genocide,
but they were wrong.
One signed a treaty of destruction,
another built schools to teach English—of all things, Latin and Greek.
Forget the old ways, they proclaimed,
forget your mother's tongue,
forget the stories of tribal birth and of your links to the scared hoop of life,
forget it all,
we now have a better way to teach and learn,
this new way will make you rich and strong.

[2] Thomas Banyacya, "The Hopi Message to the United Nations General Assembly," http:www.alphacde.com/banyacya/un92.html (February 15, 1999), pp. 4–5.

But the riches turned out to be mere paper and coin,
poor sustenance for those seeking joy and life.
The strength turned out to be power to destroy,
to destroy mother earth.
So now I must cleanse my ancestors' blood,
restore the lost good.
I must find the lost ways of teaching,
because what we have now has surely failed.

Preface

Maenette Kapeʻahiokalani Padeken Ah Nee-Benham

It is difficult to talk about the importance of language and culture without telling stories. In Hawaiʻi, we "talk story." That is we sit together—we are present with each other—and we share our stories, which range from day-to-day activities to our hopes and dreams. We "talk story" with our young people, sharing stories about people and places, about relationships, about possibility. I have found that if you begin with the stories that are shared with young people, you will learn a good deal. For example, in Hawaiʻi we have ʻōlelo noʻeau, wise sayings that give insight into how one thinks and behaves. Likewise, other indigenous cultures have stories, told over and over again, that teach values and world views. So, in this book, our second *In Our Mother's Voice* volume, we will tell you stories.

In the fall of 2005, at the World Indigenous Peoples Conference on Education (Hamilton, Aotearoa, New Zealand), more than 200 indigenous scholars from around the globe participated in three days of intense discussion on the topics of educational leadership, research and inquiry, and learning and teaching. As a result of that generative process, the framework for this second volume was developed. The authors of this book gathered in the fall of 2006 to think together about how to translate the volumes of transcripts we had collected in Aotearoa into a coherent volume. We remembered that we were writing for a broad audience of Native and non-Native teachers and soon-to-be teachers, school leaders and the next generation of educational leaders, policymakers, parents, and educators of teachers and leaders. Most of all, we remembered the power of song, of story, of joy, and of passion that permeated our sessions in 2005.

With that spirit, our elder Sam Suina (Cochiti Pueblo) helped us to weave a basket to hold the many stories we had been charged to tell. Hence, the basket Sam weaves for the *In Our Mother's Voice* project entwines each of the four main parts of the book, braiding them around the core of love: love for our children and love for our families. The authors bring to this writing the voices of their ancestors, the wisdom of their own professional and scholarly knowledge, and the passionate reflections they have gathered from colleagues and friends. And to honor the sacred path that we travel, we present (where appropriate) prayers, poetry, and wise sayings to light our way.

The text begins with a focus on language and culture through which we present the ontological foundation of the "Go to the Source" model and the challenges and realities of "living-into" the theme "The Contemporary Is Native!" This is followed by a generational view of leadership that uses the metaphor of the *kiha* (spirit dragon) to illuminate stories shared by our next generation of Native leaders. A focus on the tensions of accountability and assessment follows the leadership section. The co-authors of this section remind us that Native peoples always have had accountability standards and methods of assessment that are rigorous, relevant, reciprocal, and respectful of relations. They charge the reader-practitioner to make these standards and processes visible. The final section of the book brings stories of partnerships—from family to institution—to the center of the conversation. Authors worked with mentors to develop their stories, and scholar-practitioners commented on those tensions within the story that teach us important lessons. A unique part of this process was the conversation between the mentor and mentee as they thought through the dilemmas of the case story. A part of their conversation is presented. Each section of the book stands on its own and can be read separately and out of sequence with little confusion. Appropriately, the book ends with the voice of our elder Henrietta Mann.

It is my prayer that the *aloha* that fills the pages of this book—the aloha for ʻōhana as the core partnership, the aloha for children and youths as life-long learners, and the aloha for teachers and educational leaders as keepers of our language and cultural treasures—will help the reader make this work of indigenous models for contemporary practice reachable, valuable, and most of all possible. This preface concludes the same way our first volume ended. Jeannette Armstrong, Okanagon educator, emphasized learning in her passionate words, "We cannot afford to lose one Native child!" Indeed, Native peoples, like the individual flowers entwined lovingly into a fragrant lei, must value our interconnectedness and work collectively to ensure that our unique histories, languages, and traditions are preserved. This book is an offering to the personal responsibility and commitment each of us has to look within and reach out.

E hoe wa'a me ka akahele . . . paddle your canoe carefully.
Journey well in the breath of life. Aloha.

Acknowledgements

Mahalo to the spirited and courageous scholars who joined our talking circles in the fall of 2005 at the World Indigenous Peoples Conference on Education (WIPCE), Hamilton, Aotearoa, New Zealand. And *Mahalo* to Katie Cherrington, Bentham Ohia, and all the organizers of WIPCE, who made it possible for *In Our Mother's Voice* to have a presence at this global gathering. A very special, heart-felt *Mahalo nui loa* to the co-authors of this volume for their strength, their expertise, and their lifelong commitment to education. *Mahalo* to Dr. Valorie Johnson and the W. K. Kellogg Foundation, without whom this work and other work for Native communities would not have been realized. My thanks to our dear friend, Sue Miller, who graciously read each draft of our manuscript. A very special *Aloha* to our editors, Joel Spring and Naomi Silverman, whose continued support of *In Our Mother's Voice* has helped to transform lives!

I give thanks to my loving family, to Bob Benham and our two children, Kaimi and Kiana, who love me unconditionally; I love their spirit and hope—they light my path. As always, speaking for all the authors of this volume, we give thanks to our elders who love us on both our good and bad days, and who never refuse us their wisdom and hope.

Maenette Kape'ahiokalani Padeken Ah Nee-Benham

A NOTE ABOUT THE HAWAIIAN LANGUAGE

The Hawaiian language has two unique characters: the okina (a glottal stop), which appears as a reversed apostrophe, and the kahako (macron).

ʻōlelo noʻeau
Hawaiʻi
ā ē ī ō ū

PART I

NEW HORIZONS FOR LANGUAGE AND CULTURE

Basket as Metaphor:
The Base of the Basket

Samuel Suina

Before we start to weave a basket, we call upon our relative spirits to walk with us, to guide us. They lead us to the materials we will use to weave our basket. For the *In Our Mother's Voice* basket, I began with the willow. Many people bring willows into the house or plant them right next to the house because of their medicinal value; for example, the outer layer of the branch is used for aspirin, and the inside is ground down and applied to sores and can extract the poison from bee stings. The leaves of the willow are used for tea. And the willow tree itself keeps the bugs away!

Before we take the willows from Mother Earth, we pray. Then we separate the branches of the willows and select the strongest ones for the base of our basket. Next we lay the branches to create our base, moving from north to west to south to east.

> *From the North, Yellow Cornmaiden brought corn in her basket;*
> *With a loving heart this was her gift for the people.*
> *From the West, Blue Cornmaiden brought animals in her basket;*
> *With an open heart she set it out for the people.*
> *From the South, Red Cornmaiden brought plants, vines, and*
> *watermelons in her basket;*
> *With a caring heart she fed the people.*
> *From the East, White Cornmaiden brought cotton in her basket;*

3

With a tender heart she provided clothes for the people.
These are the gifts and directions of elders.
This, our history, language, and culture, are the foundation
of whom we are as indigenous people.
The base represents all creation; the gifts for people.

We lay two branches on the floor in each of those directions, interweaving them to create a sturdy web.

The Base of the Basket

Ganönyö:k

Lawrence E. Wheeler
(edited by P. Eileen Williams Bardeau)

In the Haudenosaunee (Iroquois) tradition, each gathering of individuals commences with the recitation of a thanksgiving address. The following address is a "short" version that contains stanzas that are considered to be the essential elements for which we as Ögwe'öweh (Real People) are instructed to give thanks.

Da:h onëh dih, nigë:johgwi:yo:h ögwaya'dayei:oh. Ne'hoh näh ganö:kshä'. Dëdwadë:nö:nyö' gagwe:göh sgëno' heh swënö:hdonyöh. Da:h ne'ho niyo'dëh näh ögwa'nigöë'.

And now, then, we have gathered as a group of good people. We have gathered in love. We will give thanks for the good health and good-mindedness of us all. Now our minds will be together.

Da:h onëh, dëdwadë:nö:nyö' Hojë:nokda'öh hotga'wëh neh yoëja:de'. Da:h ne'ho niyo'dëh näh ögwa'nigöë'.

And now, we will give thanks to the Creator who provided us with the earth. Now our minds will be together.

Da:h onëh, dëdwadë:nö:nyö' Hojë:nokda'öh hotga'wëh neh ha'deyogeo'dza:ge:h. Da:h ne'ho niyo'dëh näh ögwa'nigöë'.

And now, we will give thanks to the Creator who provided us with the grasses of all sorts. Now our minds will be together.

Da:h onëh, dëdwadë:nö:nyö' Hojë:nokda'öh hotga'wëh neh oneganos. Da:h ne'ho niyo'dëh näh ögwa'nigöë'.

And now, we will give thanks to the Creator who provided us with the water. Now our minds will be together.

Da:h onëh, dëdwadë:nö:nyö' Hojë:nokda'öh
hotga'wëh neh gë:jöh shö'öh.
Da:h ne'ho niyo'dëh näh ögwa'nigoë'.

And now, we will give thanks to the Creator who
provided us with the fish.
Now our minds will be together.

Da:h onëh, dëdwadë:nö:nyö' Hojë:nokda'öh
hotga'wëh neh onöhgwa'shä' shö'öh.
Da:h ne'ho niyo'dëh näh ögwa'nigoë'.

And now, we will give thanks to the Creator who
provided us with the medicines.
Now our minds will be together.

Da:h onëh, dëdwadë:nö:nyö' Hojë:nokda'öh
hotga'wëh neh shesah ojisdöda'shä'.
Da:h ne'ho niyo'dëh näh ögwa'nigoë'.

And now, we will give thanks to the Creator who
provided us with the wild strawberry.
Now our minds will be together.

Da:h onëh, dëdwadë:nö:nyö' Hojë:nokda'öh
hotga'wëh neh ha'deyoji:yage:h.
Da:h ne'ho niyo'dëh näh ögwa'nigoë'.

And now, we will give thanks to the Creator who
provided us with the berries.
Now our minds will be together.

Da:h onëh, dëdwadë:nö:nyö' Hojë:nokda'öh
hotga'wëh neh gäi:da'shö'.
Da:h ne'ho niyo'dëh näh ögwa'nigoë'.

And now, we will give thanks to the Creator who
provided us with the trees.
Now our minds will be together.

Da:h onëh, dëdwadë:nö:nyö' Hojë:nokda'öh
hotga'wëh neh wahda'.
Da:h ne'ho niyo'dëh näh ögwa'nigoë'.

And now, we will give thanks to the Creator who
provided us with the maple tree.
Now our minds will be together.

Da:h onëh, dëdwadë:nö:nyö' Hojë:nokda'öh
hotga'wëh neh ganyo'shö'öh ta'jo'dë'.
Da:h ne'ho niyo'dëh näh ögwa'nigoë'.

And now, we will give thanks to the Creator who
provided us with wild animals of all kinds.
Now our minds will be together.

Da:h onëh, dëdwadë:nö:nyö' Hojë:nokda'öh
hotga'wëh neh ji'dë'öh shö'öh ta'jo'dë'.
Da:h ne'ho niyo'dëh näh ögwa'nigoë'.

And now, we will give thanks to the Creator who
provided us with birds of all kinds.
Now our minds will be together.

Da:h onëh, dëdwadë:nö:nyö' Hojë:nokda'öh
hotga'wëh neh Jöhehgöh.
Da:h ne'ho niyo'dëh näh ögwa'nigoë'.

And now, we will give thanks to the Creator who
provided us with the Three Sisters.
Now our minds will be together.

Da:h onëh, dëdwadë:nö:nyö' Hojë:nokda'öh
hotga'wëh neh deyë:wënye:h.
Da:h ne'ho niyo'dëh näh ögwa'nigoë'.

And now, we will give thanks to the Creator who
provided us with the winds.
Now our minds will be together.

Da:h onëh, dëdwadë:nö:nyö' Hojë:nokda'öh
hotga'wëh neh hadiwë:nodaje's.
Da:h ne'ho niyo'dëh näh ögwa'nigoë'.

And now, we will give thanks to the Creator who
provided us with the thunder beings.
Now our minds will be together.

Da:h onëh, dëdwadë:nö:nyö' Hojë:nokda'öh
hotga'wëh neh ëdeka'gähgwa'.
Da:h ne'ho niyo'dëh näh ögwa'nigoë'.

And now, we will give thanks to the Creator who
provided us with the sun.
Now our minds will be together.

Da:h onëh, dëdwadë:nö:nyö' Hojë:nokda'öh hotga'wëh neh soëka'gähgwa'. Da:h ne'ho niyo'dëh näh ögwa'nigoë'.

And now, we will give thanks to the Creator who provided us with the moon.
Now our minds will be together.

Da:h onëh, dëdwadë:nö:nyö' Hojë:nokda'öh öikiohwih onëh Ganyödaiyo'. Da:h ne'ho niyo'dëh näh ögwa'nigoë'.

And now, we will give thanks to the Creator for the Prophet Handsome Lake told us.
Now our minds will be together.

Da:h onëh, dëdwadë:nö:nyö' Hojë:nokda'öh öikiohwih onëh Ge:ih hadiöya'geö:nö'. Da:h ne'ho niyo'dëh näh ögwa'nigoë'.

And now, we will give thanks to the Creator for the Four Messengers told us.
Now our minds will be together.

Da:h onëh, dëshedwanö:nyö:' ha:ho' Hojë:nokda'öh hehjohe'. Do:ges hotga'wëh yoëja'geh oiwagwe:göh deyögwa:dawë:nye:h. Da:h ne'ho niyo'dëh näh ögwa'nigöë'. Da:h ne'ho.

And now, we will give thanks to he himself, the Creator. It is true that he provided everything on the earth for us.
Now our minds will be together.
That is all.

Chapter 1

Go to the Source: The Contemporary is Native

Ke hoʻi aʻe la ka ʻōpua i Awalau.
The rain clouds are returning to Awalau.

This *ʻōlelo noʻeau* presents an important lesson; that is, it literally means "a return to the source." For those of us who work to ensure that our language and culture guide the learning and teaching of our children and youths, the lesson is about *intention*. That is, because all of our actions reveal intention, we must ensure that that intention comes from a good source, because if it is good, then it will lead to *hoʻolōkahi* (bring to unity), *poʻokela* (excellence), and *aloha* (love and care).

In our first volume (2000) we introduced the *Go to the Source* model (see p. 10) as a vision that placed the sun, our learners, at the core of a ring of fire that illuminated the passion, power, and partnership of everyone in our community. This model is grounded on four principles:

1. Native spiritual wisdom that is guided by the heart-stories, the blood-stories of our grandmothers and grandfathers.
2. Critical development of the intellect that intersects Native ways of seeing and doing with contemporary ways of seeing and doing.
3. Promotion of a healthy body and healthy environment.
4. Preservation and revitalization of Native languages, arts, and traditions.

These four principles presented in the model (see model below) function collectively to bridge the individual, the institution(s), and the community in such a manner that creates opportunity for the regeneration of ritual (knowledge and ceremony), responsibility (position and role in time/history), and reciprocity (the indigenous education movement in action that creates sustainability and legacy).

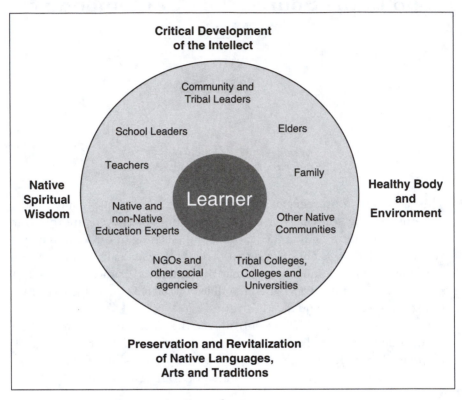

Go to the Source

To further deepen our understanding of this model, we have come to believe that "intention" to do good work requires an understanding of the premise that the *Contemporary is Native!* We would like you to consider that to do good work that weaves *na pua, na lei, na mamo* (past-present-future), we must reawaken to the origins of our place (physical place, metaphysical place, spiritual place) and learn to live-into this truth. Tarajean Yazzie addresses this regeneration in "Creating Culture in the Here and Now," laying an ontological pathway, and both Teresa Magnuson and Jeremy Garcia present honest accounts of their personal and professional challenges to live-into this truth. In the end, what we know is that if there is a core group of individuals who are able to educate and motivate and create a critical movement that opens a gracious space to live-into the *Contemporary is Native* truth, then the work of indigenous educational models for contemporary practice will generate a sustainable legacy. The work to actualize this is presented by the team of Silva, Kawai'ae'a, Alencastre, and Housman in "Generating a Sustainable Legacy: Teaching Founded Upon the *Kumu Honua Mauli Ola*." Keiki Kawai'ae'a concludes this section with a call to action, "Ho'i hou i ke kumu!" that reawakens our soul to the work ahead.

Chapter 2

Creating Culture in the Here and Now: Regenerating Rituals in Purposeful Epistemologies

Tarajean Yazzie-Mintz

Of origins I have full knowledge . . .
Of Earth's origin I have full knowledge.
Of plant origins I have full knowledge.
Of various fabrics' origins I have full knowledge.
Now of long life's, now of happiness's origin I have full knowledge.
Of Mountain Woman's origin I have full knowledge.
Of Rain Mountain's origin I have full knowledge.
Of various jewel's origin I have full knowledge.
Now of long life's, now of happiness's origin I have full knowledge, of their origin I
    have full knowledge.
Of Water Woman's origin I have full knowledge.
Of collected water's Woman's origin I have full knowledge.
Now of long life's, now of happiness's origin I have full knowledge.
Of Corn Woman's origin I have full knowledge.
Of pollen's origin I have full knowledge.
Now of long life's, now of happiness's origin I have full knowledge. [1]

---

[1] This is a Navajo song referring to the hogan (home) in which ceremonies and daily life routines take place. I use only the first stanza for the opening of this section. This information is published on the following website: http://www.hanksville.org/voyage/navajo/chief.html (retrieved May 29, 2007). I use only the first stanza for the opening of this prayer to open this essay.

Indigenous peoples have theories that articulate origins of knowledge, and we have ways of purposefully regenerating these origins within our contemporary technological societies. This section was opened with a version of a Navajo song, a planning song that is sung when a hogan is to be constructed. The song provides the knowledge and paves the direction in which the structure is to be built. According to a Navajo epistemology, the Navajo home is constructed. The hogan is central to my existence as a Navajo woman, and this centrality of the home in the maintenance of knowledge is the reason why I am particularly drawn to these words: "I have full knowledge." Knowledge is connected to *knowing* origins, earth, plants, and fabric because it is these entities that provide the locality, the appropriate context, in which knowledge is created and validated. Knowledge generated about culture and about language, and their purposes for Navajo people, can be traced in this song to the home—the hogan. Some believe that the very act of voicing the song's words—the act of giving breath to the song—is, in and of itself, a re-creation of the first hogan, making the home a reconstruction of the entire cosmos. Although the song has a much larger and complex story, I used the beginning of the song to open this section on creating culture in the here and now, for I believe that in order to construct meaning (create knowledge) about indigenous lifeways, values, education, and ways of thinking, we must return to the home, a place wherein the origins of knowledge and order can be appropriately placed.

For traditional Navajo people the hogan is a space of daily life routine and a place of ceremonial purpose and creation. To complicate my point, not all Navajo people believe that the hogan is the context of all knowledge. For those who have taken on other world epistemologies and religious practices, the hogan might not serve any purpose in their belief systems. Whereas many of our indigenous communities have been powerfully transformed by non-Native belief systems, I find that many indigenous individuals and communities continue to refer to origin stories, which articulate the context in which Native knowledge is constructed. Genevieve Gollnick (Oneida educator) and Linda Aranga-Low (Māori educator) both share their knowledge, tracing the pathways of understanding to ceremonial spaces: the three baskets are the focus for Linda Aranga-Low, and for Genevieve Gollnick the Longhouse plays a significant role in ceremonial connection through the telling of oral histories.

As scholars and practitioners of education, we are curious about the role that indigenous languages and cultures play in our contemporary educational contexts. Inherently, when we discuss culture and indigenous languages, we are transported to considerations of the ancient past, of a time long ago. I wonder whether thinking about culture as a representation of *what used to be* means that what we do now is merely a reenactment of the past. Can ancient knowledge, practices, and theories have a place in contemporary schools of thought?

I believe it is our hope among and within indigenous educational contexts that we can expand our notion of indigenous culture by examining the transformations that Native cultures have made in contemporary society. A well-noted example is the phenomenon in our communities wherein the mother tongue is no longer taught in the home. Transformation in language acquisition for Navajo, Cherokee, Seneca, Crow, Hawaiian, and numerous Native communities is now located in schools that serve Native nonspeakers of these languages. Conceptualizing language instruction outside the routines of daily life and cultural action in homes, families, and the community is a challenge for Native communities in their efforts to revitalize and maintain language use and cultural practices. Moreover, for the many families and individuals living away from our homelands, the challenge is vast and connections to our tribal nation's knowledge and context are lacking. The distance we live from our homelands may be a reason for the need to create new conceptions of culture and engage in new discourses about purposes and use of Native languages.

I wonder how these processes and the answers to these questions influence the ways in which we might imagine the roles of languages and cultures in the schooling and educational experience of indigenous youths. How do we make explicit the necessary links between indigenous identities and knowledge—ways of being—without the continued use of indigenous languages and practice of cultural traditions within the geographic milieu of Native epistemologies and structures? The fact is, we are able to generate necessary connections for the perpetuation of Native culture. In order to make visible our efforts, we are required to witness the numerous and powerful ways in which culture lives and is born in spaces away from our ancestral homelands. Take, for example, our music. Our Navajo songs and chants are now mixed with the rhythms of jazz and the resonance of Western classical influences. Navajo musicians compose and sing songs of contemporary social and political resistance in the traditions of rock and roll or rap, reaching youths of all ages and people of varying cultural backgrounds. These examples serve to highlight the ways in which Native peoples and their knowledge are recreated in new contexts for, perhaps, new purposes. I am impressed with the evolution of our knowledge—the ability to see in written form Navajo words in a computer program or on a website accessible to millions of people around the world, or to see email correspondence take form in the Hawaiian language. Native knowledge and existence are shaped by and themselves shape contemporary Native society and cultures in powerful ways. Our contemporary existence emerges from Native origins.

While these important strides take place, I continue to experience the static notions of indigenous culture when it is revealed to non-Natives that I am a Navajo (often their first racial and cultural filter is to recognize me as Native American; then I layer onto their existing knowledge my distinct tribal affiliation). Staying the course of the norm, these people often share with me that they feel shame for *the* plight of the American Indian. They say, "It is sad that the Native Americans lost their lands," "Do your people still practice their traditions?" and, with respect to culture, "It's a shame that many of your people do not have their culture." These statements reveal to me that many non-Native people (and I include Native people in this example, as well) do not recognize the complexity of our many indigenous cultures and languages, or know of the multidimensional aspects of our different and distinct social contexts within and across tribal nations. The assumption of "the lost culture" expresses the sentiment that Native people are subordinate, have little power, and lack self-determination to maintain or change cultural traditions and livelihoods in contemporary society.

In contemporary society, it is rare to witness discourse in which indigenous ways of knowing are referenced as occurring in the here and now. Often references to Native peoples and ways of being are articulated or imagined as events or rituals of the past. The expectations for our Native societies are so low that there are few expressions of expectations beyond extinction. Perhaps these examples demonstrate the ways in which non-Native and Native peoples operate with a one-dimensional definition of Native culture that keeps us from imagining the possibility of cultural representations being truly dynamic and alive in the here and now.

There is something about the past, "the ancient," that forces us to recognize that culture is contextual, socially defined, and intricately connected with the past. When I ask my parents about Navajo culture, they often attempt to speak about how things used to be and then say something about how we do things now. Even if my parents have not explicitly stated it, I am learning that Navajo culture, for instance, is in the here and now. If I am Navajo in the here and now, and not in the past when our ancestors lived and practiced the traditions within their geographic spaces, isn't it reasonable to consider that culture and cultural enactments are going to reflect the changes of geography, philosophy, and society? If culture is created in the here and now, and not solely in the past, can we, as Navajos, consider changing the way we see ourselves as indigenous peoples who have the possibility to flourish in contexts that no longer represent just the past, but represent *this* moment and the future? I must push the point by stating that although I appreciate and honor the past and the representations and traditions inherited from my ancestors, I also wonder how it is that we keep those traditions intact if our lands do not remain integral or if we, as a people, become migrants across multiple boundaries. Isn't Navajo culture contextually situated within physical boundaries as well as rich social and cultural boundaries? There is a reason why the Navajos believe that we are who we are because of the place from which we emerged—the lands within the four sacred mountains. Our connection lies in where we come from, although our culture is continually shaped by our present contexts. I believe there are reasons for our continued return home for ceremonial purposes and renewal.

If we are only enacting the past, might reenacting the past leave little room for people like me to be a part of the culture that reflects the diversity of experiences of *being Native*, and being Native in multiple social, political, cultural, and linguistic contexts? For example, if my perceived identity is shaped by the indicators of language, participation in tribal customs, traditions, and ceremonies in the geographic spaces of the Navajo, my own people might not recognize me as culturally and linguistically Navajo. How can this be?

A recent question about challenging traditional notions of being and contemporary interpretations of being is illustrated by the conundrum witnessed in the 2006 tribal elections, in which a woman ran for president of the Navajo Nation. Can a woman lead the nation just as men have in the past? I pose this question, not being influenced by the feminist movement but shaped by the need to ask, *How can we, as Navajo people, define leadership within our own social and cultural context?* If we can recreate Navajo culture, values, and language in the here and now, can a Navajo woman lead the nation into a new conception of leadership among the Navajos? In the world today, we have Navajo people living in the here and now, and sometimes the here and now takes place and extends beyond the four mountains. Sometimes the here and now reshapes and recreates the cultural practices of our ancestors. In this essay I pose the possibility of conceptualizing culture beyond what some might consider "traditional" culture based on what is witnessed and experienced as culture in contemporary society.

This line of thinking about temporal contrasts and cultural connections shapes the questions I ask in my work in the field of education. I am drawn to wonder about how teachers—who teach our Native youths—conceptualize culture in their various classrooms, across geographical and tribal nations, and across generations. Some people believe that culture is the reenactment of past traditions; I believe that culture is a dynamic entity, created and recreated in each new "here and now." For example, when Genevieve Gollnick teaches Oneida prayers in their language in schools, by their very action in reciting the thanksgiving address, the Oneida youths regenerate rituals, which redefine the spaces of schools into powerful spaces in which origins of indigenous knowledge can unfold. When we are able to see beyond Western paradigms also shaping our views of ourselves, we may be able to regenerate rituals and the origins of our indigenous knowledge systems in new cultural, political, and epistemological spaces. Our work as educators, in the here and now, is to create opportunities for the cultures of our people to be generated and renewed. *Indigenous peoples have theories that articulate origins of knowledge, and we have ways of purposefully regenerating these origins in our contemporary technological societies.*

In closing, I share the Blessing Way closing song recited to and translated for me by my father. This song offers appropriate expressions of forward motion, beauty, and regeneration in our work to revitalize our Native cultures and languages in the here and now.

In beauty I walk
With beauty before me I walk
With beauty behind me I walk
With beauty below me I walk
With beauty above me I walk
With beauty all around me I walk

It has become beautiful again
It has become beautiful again
It has become beautiful again
It has become beautiful again

Chapter 3

Transforming the Self: Living-Into "Contemporary is Native"

Language Promise

Kina go ndo nowemaaganak.
All my relations.

Anishnaabe ndoo aaw.
I am Anishinaabe.

Ndo wiikodjitoon wii Anishinabemo yaan.
I am trying to speak my Anishinaabe language.

Ndoo giyetinaamendam wii ni Anishinabemo yaan.
I am determined on my language path.

Ndoo miigwechawendam kina gegoo maampii akiing e temigak.
I am thankful for everything here on Earth.

Ndoo miigwechawnedam se anishinaabewi yaan.
I am thankful to be Anishinaabe.

Nga niganawendaan maanda gdo noweninaan.
I will take care of our language—keep it going.

Mii wi.
That is it.
(Ziibiwing Cultural Center)

BECOMING AND BEING
Teresa Magnuson

When I was a young lady, my grandmother gave me the spirit name *Kwe Bidasmose*, Woman Walking Forward. During my naming ceremony she explained the origin and meaning of my name. From her prayers, *Gizheminido* (the creator) showed her the person I was to become. In her vision, she saw me as a grown woman walking toward her as a person who was doing good for the people. She did not know what I would be doing for my community, nor how, but that it would be good and meaningful. Recently, I returned to my grandmother to inquire more about how my name came to her. For the first time, she told me that her mother, my great-grandmother, and I share the same name.

My grandmother told me that, before realizing my name, she had been praying and thinking of me all the time. She saw me approaching womanhood, about to embark on the world—a woman walking forward. I reminded her of her mother's spirit. Knowing the English translation of our name, my grandmother researched its true meaning in Potawatomi. On my grandmother's side, we are citizens of the Pokagon Band of Potawatomi. (My relatives have not spoken the Potawatomi language for several generations, back to my great-great-grandmother's generation.) First my grandmother asked her mother how to pronounce our shared name, but when it was spoken, other Potawatomi speakers were not able to recognize or understand the name. She then sought out a few of the remaining fluent Pokagon Band Potawatomi speakers and asked for their translation. This is where my name, *Kwe Bidasmose*, and my journey with the language began.

I am Thankful to be Anishinabe

Over the years, numerous people, experiences, and opportunities have influenced my life. Through my journey, I have continually been drawn to Anishinabemowin, the language of my ancestors. Anishinabemowin is the language of the Anishinabek people who comprise the Three Fires Confederacy—the Potawatomi, Odawa, and Ojibwe Nations. Potawatomi is a dialect of Anishinabemowin. I have been a language student for many years and am a graduate of the Anishinabewmowin Language and Instructors Institute at Bay Mills Community College, a tribal college. Being introduced to the language as an adult felt like becoming reacquainted with an old friend. My studies at Bay Mills proved to be a transformative learning experience, one that nurtured Anishinabe ways of thinking and knowing. Through the language, I found the roots of my identity as an Anishinabe *kwe* (woman). My passion for learning developed into an ambition to help revitalize the language. This passion and ambition have proven to be influential in my career and life choices.

I am Trying to Speak my Anishinabe Language

As a language student, I have decided to focus my graduate education on indigenous and adult education to advance my own and my community's thinking and knowledge of Anishinabemowin language education and programming. My goal is to use the knowledge and skills I have learned to develop meaningful language-learning opportunities in order to preserve our language and culture, to encourage and support teachers and students, and to contribute to the existing knowledge of indigenous language programming.

I am Determined on my Language Path

As an emerging scholar in indigenous education, I have been closely observing and listening to established language professionals. I have heard stories of their struggles and successes. Being a leader in the language community is an extremely demanding position that requires heart, diplomacy, and enduring commitment. There are many different views and opinions about how language should be spoken, taught, and written—if written at all. As emerging leaders, we need to not be afraid to ask questions of our elders and mentors. We need to be active listeners and learners. To the seasoned language professionals, *miigwetch* (thank you) for your dedication to the struggle, for your leadership, and for your spirit! You are our mentors and our teachers. You inspire those of us who follow in your footsteps.

I will Take Care of our Language—Keep it Going

My journey with the language began with a name and continues with a dream. At a recent solstice gathering, a speaker shared with us the teaching that our ancestors, the spirits, are with us and are guiding us. We need to take an active role in listening to what they are trying to share. By doing so, we will help the spirits do their job. It is important that we listen to our ancestors' guidance; they will help lead us into the future seven generations. They will help lead us back to being a community of mother-tongue first-language speakers. To reach that dream, teachers and students alike in the language community need to practice patience, balance, and understanding both with themselves and with others. This will help us develop our thinking on language education and determine our community's language goals.

As Anishinabek, we know that we have become the people we are because of the guidance and support of our grandparents and ancestors. I believe that my attention keeps returning to the language because my ancestors are calling. As *Kwe Bidasmose*, I believe that my contribution to the community is through language revitalization.

For all my relations.

HONORING OUR ROLE AS FATHERS

Jeremy Garcia

"Thank you, dad, for providing food for me"
"When you go to the ranch and field, I am going to make you lunch"
"When I get big, I am going to cook, so I can feed the katsinas"

It was October 31, 1998, during my first semester as a graduate student at Michigan State University, at 5:00 a.m., when my wife and I rushed to the hospital. This would be our first child. Our exhaustion and impatience disappeared when our daughter, Nawinmana, was born at 11:00 p.m., November 1, 1998. The calls from family living at Hopi in Arizona conveyed their excitement, as well as specific requests for honoring the Hopi tradition. We would have to save certain things, shelter her from the sun for 20 days, and plan for her naming ceremony. Although she was born away from home, we did what was necessary to fulfill our parents' and grandparents' requests to honor tradition. As emotions began to settle, I asked myself, "How will I know what to do? How do I care for my daughter? What are the roles and responsibilities of a father? How do I teach her to walk proudly as Hopi in a contemporary world?"

I found strength and courage as I reflected on my own childhood and how my father, uncles, and grandfathers raised me. I was taught that children, like our animals, crops, and nature, should be treated with respect, honor, faith, and pride. We pray, talk, and sing among and with them. We find laughter and beauty in observing their growth. In particular, I remembered Nawinmana's Qwa-ah (great-grandfather) showing patience with his crops, giving each one time and attention, and handling them with care, thereby ensuring that his touch enriched their growth. I also reflected on how my family approached the harvest. We nurtured and honored our crops by acknowledging, through prayer and dance, their growth and beauty. Lessons and experiences like this guided me at the moment of Nawinmana's birth, to ensure that she would grow to be strong, healthy, and blissful.

Knowing Ourselves Through Our Children's Questions

We returned to southern Arizona so that Nawinmana could be closer to our family and the place of our relatives. We would make regular visits to the Hopi villages of Hotevilla and Sichomovi. It didn't take long for Nawinmana to discover that we made the long four-hour drives home to attend cultural ceremonies such as ceremonial dances, weddings, and baby namings, as well as to plant and be with family. I was pleased that we could attend the ceremonies, but I knew that simply being present was not enough. On each trip to our Hopi villages, my daughter would ask, "Daddy, can you tell me a Hopi story? How come Hopis do this? Why do they believe that? How come other people don't do that? Why are *pahanas* [Whites] different?" So many, many questions!

Although I answered her questions, neither she nor I was entirely satisfied with the response. I came face-to-face with the limits of my own cultural knowledge as I began to teach Nawinmana to be Hopi in our contemporary society. Her inquiries have led me to engage in conversations with my extended family members and elders that have opened up new learning and knowing. I have also become a more careful observer, learner, and practitioner of our cultural ways of knowing and doing. Just as I have reached out to learn from my elders, Nawinmana has begun to seek knowledge from her uncles, aunts, and grandparents. It was through

Nawinmana's questions that I became more committed to learn and define my cultural roles and responsibilities as a Hopi father.

Our Roles and Responsibilities as Fathers

Learning and then accepting my important cultural roles and responsibilities as a Hopi father began, for me, at Nawinmana's birth. On the surface, I understood that fatherhood, and in particular Hopi fatherhood, would require me to take stock of my beliefs, values, identity, and roots, in an effort to transform myself into a person who could guide, in a sincere and culturally appropriate way, children and youths through the labyrinth of the twenty-first century. No trivial task! I was reawakened to this important challenge when I realized that what our children know and do is dependent on what I know, how I live, and what I teach in both a contemporary and indigenous context. Today, it is important that I, and my fellow indigenous men, become fully cognizant of the world around us and work hard to understand the differences and similarities between our home, cultural context, and the contemporary pathways of a global community. Learning more about how to balance the three—home, cultural context, and pathways—although it is a lifelong journey for us all, is key to how we can better nurture and prepare our children to walk multiple pathways.

I continue to contribute to Nawinmana's cognitive development and affective-social well-being, but I also make certain that she understands and participates in those activities that make us uniquely Hopi. Through stories, prayer, ceremony, and experiential learning, I share our epistemologies with her at various times. Nawinmana often recounts moments she has spent with family members and me. Recently she shared,

> Dad, remember that time we went to the ranch? We rode the horses with Tay-tay (grandfather, Tewa). I had so much fun that time, when we were taking care of the cows. We have to take care of our cows because they help us by feeding us. It was funny that the baby calf wanted to be my friend. He kept following us when we were riding back home. I think he wanted to go home with us. Tay-tay was silly when he put the calf on the horse to carry him back to his mom.

Spending time with Nawinmana in both work and celebration of our people's daily lives, I believe, is key to teaching her how to walk proudly as Hopi in a contemporary world.

Children Guide Us

Culturally knowing our roles as sons, fathers, uncles, and grandfathers will provide an increased awareness of what is expected, but even more, it will furnish an opportunity to share in the happiness and humility that children offer. I encourage my fellow indigenous men to embrace their position with dignity and a sense of worth, while raising their children within their own cultural, social, and academic contexts. I encourage each of us to take pride in understanding our relationship with our children and families. What stories will your children, nieces, and nephews remember of time spent together?

There is much hope and promise as Nawinmana and I explore who we are, where we came from, and where we are going.

Chapter 4

Generating a Sustainable Legacy: Teaching Founded Upon the Kumu Honua Mauli Ola

Kalena Silva, Makalapua Alencastre, Keiki Kawaiʻaeʻa, and Alohalani Housman

In early 1998, a year before the graduation of the first class of Hawaiian-medium high school students, a group of Hawaiian-language educators met to assess what had been, and what remained to be, accomplished in Hawaiian-medium education. Despite the graduation milestone that was about to take place, the group of educators strongly believed that there remained a need for an articulated vision of what Hawaiian-medium education at all levels should seek to accomplish over the long term. Having learned how valuable the Māori educational philosophy statement, *Te Aho Matua*, was to Māori language-revitalization efforts, the group was inspired to develop a Hawaiian statement that would serve as a conceptual framework to guide Hawaiian revitalization efforts. To ensure a wide representation of ideas, the group comprised both Native and non-Native speakers of Hawaiian, spanning three generations of Hawaiian-medium educators from prekindergarten through tertiary levels, and representing—through residence and family ties—every inhabited Hawaiian island except Lānaʻi.

Early in our group retreats, held over a period of several weekends, we agreed that, although absolutely essential, Hawaiian language revitalization is but one of several major, interrelated elements. By March 1998, the group developed the first draft, in Hawaiian, of its philosophical statement, *Ke Kumu Honua Mauli Ola* (The Foundation for Nurturing the Hawaiian Way of Life). The statement abounds with language and terms rich in Hawaiian cultural meaning and nuances not easily explained in another language and beyond the scope of this chapter. Without question, a full understanding of the statement can be attained only from the original Hawaiian. Nonetheless, because it provides a philosophical template for the future direction of Hawaiian-medium education and contains universal elements that might be useful in other cultural contexts, we present a summary here. The summary is followed by a brief description of the challenges and benefits of the philosophy as applied to three educational contexts: prekindergarten through secondary education, teacher preparation, and literacy development.

At the core of this philosophy lies the *mauli Hawai'i*, the unique way of life that is cultivated by, emanates from, and distinguishes a person who identifies him- or herself as a Hawaiian. If tended properly, this *mauli*, like a well-tended fire, can burn brightly. If left untended, like a neglected fire, it can die out. Four major elements of an individual's life-giving *mauli* are identified below in relation to the parts of the body where they are tended.

1. *Ka 'Ao'ao Pili 'Uhane*—the spiritual element, that is, the spirit with which we are all born which is seated in the head, the most sacred part of the body, that recognizes right from wrong, good from bad, and creates a relationship with everything in the universe, both seen and unseen.
2. *Ka 'Ao'ao 'Ōlelo*—the language element found in the ears, the mouth, and the tongue. Language can be used in many different ways and may be soft, rough, gentle, harsh, forthright, or secretive, but perhaps its greatest strength lies in its ability to transmit *mauli* to future generations.
3. *Ka 'Ao'ao 'Ike Ku'una*—the traditional-knowledge element seated in the intestines, where knowledge and emotions lie, which is expressed in traditional values and practices like the hula, poetry, and prayer. Such practices have creative aspects and, like language, can reflect misrepresentations. Thus, the true power of traditional knowledge lies in authentic practices carried out by mature people

who recognize their cultural responsibility to others who share their *mauli*.

4. *Ka ʻAoʻao Lawena*—the physical-behavior element found in the limbs of the body, in gestures, in the way one stands or moves the feet while walking, in a facial expression, in a smile. This element of one's *mauli* usually is learned at a young age through unconscious imitation and is easily recognized and appreciated by those who share the same *mauli*.

In addition to the four elements of *mauli* tended within an individual's body, three elements of *mauli* connect a group of people to the divine, to preceding generations, and to generations to come. Found in the three centers of the body, they are the

1. *Piko ʻĪ*—the fontanel or soft spot at the tops of our heads when we are babies and through which we became physically connected to the spiritual beliefs of our people.
2. *Piko ʻŌ*—the navel, attached to the umbilical cord and placenta, which connects us to our ancestors, and is closest to the *naʻau*, the seat of our knowledge and emotions.
3. *Piko ʻĀ*—the reproductive organs, which create future generations and, by extension, all that we create and establish.

Through these three centers, we exist in relation to one another as members of a group of people who share the elements of spirit, language, traditional knowledge, and physical behavior. This sharing occurs in *honua*—places where we may freely express our *mauli*. Life can be seen to have three major *honua* as follows:

1. *Honua ʻĪewe*—the highly protected placenta, representing the close ties of family that are the foundation of one's *mauli*.
2. *Honua kīpuka*—the gardenlike area where a lava flow has left a patch of uncovered forest representing the ties of community—an extended, protected environment in which one develops the *mauli* brought from the family.
3. *Honua Ao Holoʻokoʻa*—the world-at-large, where an adult who has been raised with a strong *mauli* expresses and shares the distinctiveness of that *mauli* with others from diverse backgrounds.

Even as the Hawaiian *mauli* has been weakened greatly over the years, we can seek to create *honua* with our families, among friends, at school, at work, and in other places where the fires of our *mauli* may be rekindled and once again burn brightly. We present below the challenges and benefits of using the *Kumu Honua Mauli Ola* philosophy in three specific areas of education.

Prekindergarten Through High School

The principles embodied in the *Kumu Honua Mauli Ola* are embraced by three unique prekindergarten-secondary school programs: Ke Kula 'O Nāwahīokalani'ōpu'u (Hawai'i island), Ke Kula 'O Kamakau (O'ahu), and Ke Kula Ni'ihau O Kekaha (Kaua'i). Indigenous laboratory schools of Ka Haka 'Ula O Ke'elikōlani College of Hawaiian Language of the University of Hawai'i at Hilo, these Hawaiian-medium programs were established as extensions of the successful family-based Pūnana Leo prekindergarten programs and subsequently chartered as New Century Public Charter Schools by the Hawai'i Board of Education. Each of these programs has been created and is being implemented by and for Hawaiians to meet the distinct needs of their communities.

The verdant windward side of the island of O'ahu is home to Ke Kula 'o Samuel M. Kamakau, where 90 youths, ages 3 to 18, are educated in a total Hawaiian language-immersion setting. In the midst of an increasingly westernized island community, Ke Kula 'o Kamakau was created as a *honua mauli ola*, a *kīpuka* where being Hawaiian is considered to be a positive attribute of one's life, where Hawaiian is the primary language of communication and learning, where children learn the traditional wisdom of the past in order to pass it on to the future, and where academic success is founded in the connections made between Hawaiian and contemporary world knowledge. Needless to say, these qualities are not otherwise available to children in the vast majority of Hawai'i's schools.

With a desire to cultivate a sense of cohesiveness, staff, students, and family consider the *Kumu Honua Mauli Ola* beliefs and values essential elements of the program. In order to ensure the care and transmission of the Hawaiian *mauli Hawai'i*, a conscious effort is made to apply *Kumu Honua Mauli Ola* in all aspects of Ke Kula 'o Kamakau, and this is reflected in the daily activities, protocols, and pedagogy. This deliberate focus is important to maintaining the integrity of

Hawaiian-medium educational initiatives as schools are continuously challenged to conform to state and federal educational policies and mandates.

"Becoming a Practitioner of my Culture Makes me Feel Alive."—Eleventh Grader

Spirituality is recognized as an integral element of *mauli* explicitly interwoven into all aspects of life and necessarily evident within the domain of Hawaiian education. By fostering an awareness of the quality and depth of interdependent relationships, the traditional values of *aloha* (love) and *mālama* (care) are relied on as a framework for life and supportive of healthy, respectful interactions. Symbolic of these connections and as a means to clear the way and center the energy for learning to occur, staff and students gather together at the *piko* (center) of the school to begin and end each day with chants, songs of praise, and thanks.

"If we don't Speak Hawaiian, Kupuna [Grandma] will be Sad."— Kindergartner

With the exception of the small Native-speaking community of Niʻihau, most Native Hawaiians throughout Hawaiʻi have not been speaking Hawaiian for two or more generations. Sadly, many people considered Hawaiian to be a dying language and worthless to modern society. However, the commitment of the ʻAha Pūnana Leo, nā kūpuna and educators to reversing this trend has created a revival of the Hawaiian language and culture through Hawaiian-medium educational programs. It is the children who have been educated in Hawaiian for the past two decades who are bringing Hawaiian back into their homes and inspiring family and community members to learn and use Hawaiian.

With the seeds of a Hawaiian-language resurgence planted, growing numbers of students and families now speak Hawaiian as the primary language of their homes. Yet the majority of students continue to rely exclusively on schools such as Ke Kula ʻo Kamakau as the major source for Hawaiian language learning, which is limited by the confines and contexts of a school program. Students ranging in age from toddlers to young adults are educated in total-immersion settings that are designed to optimize language acquisition. As the quality and quantity of learning that occurs is dependent upon the level of teachers' expertise, there is a continuous focus on professional development, including Hawaiian language and culture, content, and pedagogy. For the most part, teachers in Hawaiian-medium schools themselves have learned Hawaiian as a second language by relying on the precious few Native speakers and university language courses. The Kahuawaiola Indigenous Teacher Education Program has been instrumental in providing extensive training in these areas and assisting teachers to fulfill the criteria required for teacher licensure.

Although costly, small class sizes intentionally are maintained in order to support a low speaker-to-speaker ratio and provide extensive opportunities to actively use language while learning academic content. Teaching through traditional songs, chants, stories, dances, and the arts engages learners to apply and strengthen their language skills in ways that are culturally appropriate and provides a critical wholeness to formal language learning. For students to attain high levels of Hawaiian language proficiency, language instruction occurring in authentic situations and functions should begin as early as possible and be sustained for as many years as possible, with a focus on the development of both oral and written competence.

Although this current generation of students continues to be raised in predominantly English-speaking homes and communities, cultural and social activities are extremely important in supporting and extending Hawaiian-language usage beyond the classroom and the school. These opportunities are especially significant to encourage families to learn together and to involve middle and high school students, who are especially vulnerable to the onslaught of messages from the media and wider community that directly conflict with and weaken the *mauli Hawai'i*.

"This is Valuable to me Because the Land is Always Giving me so Much. Now I Have a Chance to Give Something Back."—Fifth Grader

Educational innovation is highly visible throughout Ke Kula 'o Kamakau's curriculum. Teachers work in teams to create schoolwide thematic units of study that incorporate the *Nā Honua Mauli Ola* guidelines and the state content and performance standards. Experiential learning is a highly successful instructional methodology that is being employed to engage all learners and allows for the integration of direct learning from our culture and environment.

"We're not Just Planting Seedlings, We're Planting the Desire to Care." —
Teacher

Although surrounded by the magnificence of the Koʻolau Poko mountain
range on one side and the tranquil ocean on the other, much of the
community suffers from neglect, overdevelopment, and pollution. In
applying the wisdom and teachings of our nā kūpuna (elders) about the
importance of *mālama ʻāina* (caring for the land), substantive lessons in
environmental health, stewardship, resource management, conservation,
and sustainability serve as a major focus of the curriculum. Work at a *ma
uka* (upland) site includes removing alien plants, revegetating the lowland
forest and wetlands, and restoring the watershed area. *Ma kai* (seashore)
site efforts focus on endemic-plant restoration as students plant hundreds of seedlings of endemic species along shoreline areas that were
once covered with rubbish. Experimental plots at both sites are helping
to determine the most efficient means to propagate seedlings and to control alien weeds. These projects are integrated into various areas of academic study and research, including science, language arts, social studies,
art, and music, and are recognized and appreciated as a valuable contribution to the community. By paying attention to the needs of the *ʻāina*,
reconnections are being made with the environment, and a realization of
the significance and beauty of these areas among students, their families,
and the wider community is growing.

*"Someone will Help You if You Don't Know How. We Help and Take Care
of Each Other."* —Third Grader

Ke Kula ʻo Kamakau is a multiage program in which two or more grade
levels are intentionally grouped together. Multiage grouping is seen to
strengthen learners' interpersonal relationships, develop their leadership
skills, and increase their ability and willingness to collaborate and share
responsibility. Depending on the type of activity, multiage groupings of
learners may include prekindergarten through high school students, or a
variety of subgroupings within that range. Modeled after the traditional
value placed on *kuleana* (responsibility) found in Hawaiian families,
kaikuaʻana (older siblings/students) regularly assist and are expected to
model positive behaviors for *kaikaina* (younger siblings/students) of the
school. Individual and group *kuleana* is emphasized as students cultivate

taro in the mountains, raise fish and seaweed at the fishpond, design web pages, research current issues, compose and illustrate stories, and make multimedia presentations.

By adopting the traditional beliefs and values set forth in *Kumu Honua Mauli Ola*, genuine educational reform in Hawai'i is being realized in Hawaiian-medium schools. The true effect will be made apparent by the successes of the generations of youths who will carry the language and knowledge of their ancestors into the twenty-first century.

Teacher Preparation

The *kumu* (literally, "source"), or teacher, holds an honored place in traditional Hawaiian culture, revered as both a source of knowledge and an exemplar. In contemporary Hawai'i, where a highly multicultural base reflects strong American influences, a *kumu* in a Hawaiian-medium educational setting serves students best when he or she has also been prepared to be an able Hawaiian cultural leader. The Kahuawaiola Indigenous Teacher Education Program—a total Hawaiian-medium, postbaccalaureate program of Ka Haka 'Ula O Ke'elikōlani College of Hawaiian Language at the University of Hawai'i at Hilo—aims to prepare such educators.

The *Kumu Honua Mauli Ola* educational philosophy has shaped and guided the development of the Kahuawaiola program. The original philosophy statement in Hawaiian led to the development of *Nā Honua Mauli Ola Hawai'i Guidelines for Culturally Healthy and Responsive Learning Environments* by the statewide Native Hawaiian Education Council in partnership with Ka Haka 'Ula O Ke'elikōlani College. Endorsed by more than 30 different Hawaiian organizations, these cultural guidelines shape all aspects of Kahuawaiola, in concert with state and national teacher education requirements.

Kahuawaiola faculty strive to provide meaningful and engaging first-hand Native experiences that nurture the *mauli ola Hawai'i* (Hawaiian way of life) of teacher candidates to deepen their own personal understanding of the educational philosophy and its application for learners' success. During all phases of the program, teacher candidates observe *mauli Hawai'i* teachers in action; analyze and discuss approaches, methods and practices; design *mauli*-based curriculum; and teach Hawaiian-medium students.

With the exception of a few Hawaiian-medium education graduates, the majority of teacher candidates are themselves products of the English-medium American educational system. The teacher training experience is challenging but necessary for students to experience authentic Hawaiian-medium learning situations that support the transition to a Native paradigm. The new candidates discover that it is entirely possible (and preferable, for those with a Hawaiian cultural base) to successfully deliver a modern, twenty-first-century curriculum through a strong Hawaiian world view supported by activities carried out completely in Hawaiian and emphasizing traditional cultural perspectives, knowledge, behaviors, and spiritual connections grounded in the *piko* (centers) of group relationship.

Teacher candidates begin the year-long, three-semester program during the summer in an intensive, six-week experience held at Keʻelikōlani College's laboratory prekindergarten through secondary school, Ke Kula ʻo Nāwahīokalaniʻōpuʻu. Foundation coursework is delivered through a live-in immersion experience in which academics are infused within a curriculum that supports the spiritual, physical, emotional, intellectual, and social growth of the candidates with other teachers, practitioners, and K-12 learners, both in and out of the classroom, for a balance of theory and applied-learning situations.

Traditional Hawaiian beliefs about learning, teaching, leading, and evaluating are embedded within strategies guided by old understandings found in proverbial sayings like ʻO *ke kahua ma mua, ma hope ke kūkulu* (The foundation first and then the building), *Ma ka hana ka ʻike* (Knowledge comes from direct experience), and *Ma mua ka hana, ma hope ka walaʻau* (Direct experience comes first, discussion comes second). Teacher candidates are immersed in a learning process that requires the development of a wide variety of new skills and the strengthening of old skills, completely in Hawaiian.

The summer experience is followed by two semesters of teacher practicum, seminar coursework, and workshops that help teacher candidates bridge the reality of the classroom environment with the profession as culturally based educators. Through a team effort with mentor teachers and university faculty, teacher candidates continue to strengthen newly acquired skills and the disposition needed to sustain them as *mauli Hawaiʻi* educators. The transformational process empowers and builds the skills and endurance needed to foster *mauli Hawaiʻi* educators.

Kahuawaiola is an important component of the larger movement toward a fully realized P–20 Mauli Ola Hawaiian-medium educational system. The recent approval and/or implementation of other components of this system—including an early childhood certification program, an M.A. in Indigenous Language and Culture Education, and a Ph.D. in Hawaiian and Indigenous Language and Culture Revitalization—means that although the P–20 program pieces are now in place, the flow between and among them remains to be strengthened to form a seamless whole. Using the *Kumu Honua Mauli Ola* as our driving philosophy, we strive for excellence at all levels to build healthy communities through strong and healthy *mauli*.

Literacy Development

Native Hawaiians have a proud history of education and high literacy through the Hawaiian language. In the mid-1800s, King Kamehameha III established the Hawaiian language public school system and publicly proclaimed, "*He aupuni palapala ko'u* (Mine is a nation of writing)." Before annexation to the United States in 1898, Hawai'i's well-developed Hawaiian-medium public school system produced an exceptionally high rate of literacy, enabling and inspiring Native Hawaiians to create the world's largest repository of written literature by an indigenous people. Much of this early literature was created at Lahainaluna, established in 1831 as both a Hawaiian-medium high school and a teacher preparation college, and the oldest school in the U.S. west of the Rocky Mountains. The Hawaiian literacy rate in the late 1800s was higher than that in the U.S., with 84 percent and 91.2 percent literacy, respectively, for full-blooded Hawaiians and part-Hawaiians over the age of six. In fact, the Hawaiian literacy rate at the time exceeded that of any ethnic group in Hawai'i, including Whites. Although Hawaiian was an oral language until the first Hawaiian alphabet was printed in 1822, within a short time, literacy soared to high levels. This was possible because literacy was taught through the Hawaiian language and deemed important at all levels of Hawaiian society.

After the overthrow of the Hawaiian government in 1893, a subsequent legislative ban on Hawaiian-medium schools followed three years later. Students were severely punished for speaking their native tongue in the school setting. Hawaiian language use dwindled in the home and the community. Surveys in the late 1980s showed that, after nearly a century of English-only schools, the Hawaiian language was nearly extinct, and 30 percent of the Native Hawaiian population were at the lowest level of English literacy for all ethnic groups in Hawai'i.

The movement to revitalize Hawaiian language use and to regain high literacy began in 1983 with the establishment of the nonprofit 'Aha Pūnana Leo, Inc. ('APL) and its first Hawaiian immersion prekindergarten program in 1984. When this effort began some 20 years ago, only 35 children under the age of 18 were fluent in Hawaiian. Today, more than 2,000 students have acquired fluency in Hawaiian-medium programs that are articulated from infant-toddler to a recently approved doctoral program.

In 1987, after the law banning Hawaiian-medium schools had finally been repealed, the Hawai'i State Department of Education (DOE) agreed to start Hawaiian immersion kindergarten and first-grade classes in the public school system. However, not wanting to provide the necessary curriculum development resources, the DOE erroneously judged Hawaiian to be a solely oral language and indicated that any literacy-development materials would have to be provided by the 'APL. The 'APL had already begun to teach beginning literacy in Hawaiian and worked in cooperation with the UH Hilo Hawaiian Studies Department to produce elementary-level materials. In 1989, after much lobbying by families, the state legislature established the Hale Kuamo'o Hawaiian Language Center at UH Hilo, which includes among its several goals the provision of Hawaiian-language materials to the state's public and private schools.

In the early days of the public schools' Hawaiian-language immersion program, when children's reading books were sorely needed but scarce, Hawaiian translations were cut and pasted into English-language books. Such books, however, generally were not grounded in a Hawaiian world view. Rich in culture and language, traditional stories convey important Hawaiian values and perspectives—an integral part of Hawaiian education. Thus, the Hale Kuamo'o is presently creating a model system of literacy development for Hawaiian-medium education called *He Aupuni Palapala*, after the famous proclamation of King Kamehameha III. The system is based on the *Kumu Honua Mauli Ola* educational philosophy, with guidelines and benchmarks from the Native Hawaiian Education Council's *Nā Honua Mauli Ola Hawai'i Guidelines for Culturally Healthy and Responsive Learning Environments* and the DOE's *Hawai'i Content and*

Performance Standards. The ultimate goal is to develop a curriculum model for Hawaiian-medium education that strengthens students through traditional ways of teaching and learning found in storytelling, reciting oral histories, giving speeches, memorizing, chanting, singing, and hula. These traditional methods have proven to be valuable and effective agents of literacy.

For example, the traditional *Hakalama*, an approach to teaching reading developed in the nineteenth century, is now used to teach beginning reading in the *He Aupuni Palapala* model. The *Hakalama* is made up of Hawaiian consonant–vowel clusters: 40 clusters with, and 40 clusters without, the *kahakō*, or macron. This traditional teaching approach has proven very successful, helping young children learn to read Hawaiian quickly and fluently. Students move from fluency to understanding with emphasis placed on comprehension strategies and vocabulary, which enable students to discover and to understand important concepts of Hawaiian language, culture, and perspectives.

Another important part of the *He Aupuni Palapala* model is the *meiwi*–traditional elements of both oral and written Hawaiian poetry, songs, storytelling, oratory, and narration. Examples of *meiwi* are embraced in all areas of literacy. A major goal is for students to recognize, understand, and utilize *meiwi* in their own oral and written language creation of stories, poetry, songs, and so on.

Native Hawaiians once held the prestigious position of being one of the world's most literate peoples. Through the development of the *He Aupuni Palapala* literacy model, we hope to make that position a reality once more. We believe that this can be achieved by fully utilizing the wisdom found in the *Kumu Honua Mauli Ola* educational philosophy. The language, the culture, the spiritual connection to our ancestors, and our behaviors must be a vital part of the literacy program that we provide for our children and future generations.

In summary, the foundational *Kumu Honua Mauli Ola* continues to shape evolving P–20 programs focused on revitalizing the Hawaiian language. The successful outcomes seen thus far in the programs described above provide hope that the dream of fully revitalizing the Hawaiian language will someday become a reality.

Chapter 5

"Ho'i hou i ke kumu!" Teachers as Nation Builders

Keiki Kawai'ae'a

Echoes of voices from our ancestral past remind us that our Native languages and cultures define who we are, where we come from, and whom we become as Native peoples. They are a call that beckons to us to return to the source—*ho'i hou i ke kumu*—because the answers that build strong nations are within us and need only to be reawakened. The call resonates in the words of our languages. It is seen in the practices of our traditions and beliefs. It is connected through our spirituality. It is felt within the center of our *na'au* (gut), that place from which wisdom flows and we become enlightened—*na'auao*—as cultural beings. This gift passed on by our *kūpuna* (elders), through our parents, to us, and on to our children and grandchildren is our cultural legacy.

Through the lessons of our *kūpuna*, we are reminded that tradition, genealogy, history, and place are important parts of our connection to language and culture. Language is the core, the code that maintains our cultural world view and is perpetuated through our actions, beliefs, spirituality, practices, and traditions. Genealogy and history trace our stories of family, tradition, and origin, and they connect us to a place and a people. These understandings are built on timeless wisdom and provide valuable insights useful for our modern-day contexts.

Our *mauli* (life force) is the living spirit within us, the fire that is fueled

41

by the people and places that surround us and tend to our welfare and development. Education in the Native mind is holistic and a lifelong process that is nurtured through spiritual and emotional connection, intellectual inquiry and challenge, social-cultural maturity, and physical development. By looking through the window of our ancient past, we can reconnect to lifelong lessons that have positive implications for educating the Native child—a continuum of our Native legacy in progress.

What, then, are these lessons that foster our ability to internalize our place and build an understanding of our role as responsible, capable, caring, and healthy human beings? The lessons begin early in life, teaching who we are and how we are connected to the world that surrounds us. Developing our cultural identity and a sense of belonging is the underpinning that begins to develop our personal integrity as Native peoples and as cultural beings. Proficiency in academic and life skills strengthens our ability to contribute to our families and communities. Thinking critically through challenges that allow us to make *pono* (proper) decisions and provide us avenues to give back and share with others is innate within the Native sense.

The *kumu* (literally "source") or teacher plays a critical role in our ability as learners to see, feel, experience, and understand the connection to the things around us; our interdependence on each other and with our place; and finally, our role and responsibility as Native, community, and world citizens. Preparing educators as cultural leaders and community and family partners adds a new twist to teacher preparation. It requires us to REconsider the needs of our communities and people, and to REcreate a vision for education based on the wisdom of our culture as the foundation. Such basic understandings include love of our people, love of our homeland, love of our language and culture, and love of knowledge and wisdom as the cornerstones that build a conceptual framework for teacher development. The task is a call to action, a journey to REgenerate our languages, cultures, and traditions. It is a time to REthink our current practices and REclaim our traditional wisdom and practices from within which Native pedagogy and practice have always existed.

The Native language and culture provide the foundation. The vision provides a direction for preparing a new kind of culture-based educators. These educators can serve as change agents in the restoration of healthy Native and culturally oriented communities. Beginning first with the children, and working together with the families and community, these teachers will prepare the generations of future families, workers, and leaders. Teachers are nation builders. Preparing teachers as cultural and educational practitioners requires abilities from a new skill set aligned with, yet different from, mainstream practices. Language, culture, community, pedagogy, dispositions, and content are the components of a Native-based teacher education program. These six major components constitute a rigorous program that contributes to the preparation of teachers as culture-based educators—teachers as nation builders.

1. *REvitalize—Use the Native language and teach through the Native language.* Teachers who have the gift of the Native language have a richer perspective and understanding of the culture than those who do not. Speaking in the Native language demonstrates the importance of the language and culture and provides a living example for learners. Teachers as nation builders perpetuate the use of the Native language to ensure cultural survival and foster learners' cultural identity.

2. *REnew—Instill knowledge of Native pedagogy and natural learning processes that build meaningful connections through the culture.* Traditional methods of child rearing, vocational training, life-skills preparation, cultural practices, arts, traditional stories, and folklore (oral and written) provide the foundation for Native teaching and instruction. The language also provides the critical context for understanding Native pedagogy through such venues as traditional wisdom passed down through wise sayings, riddles, and stories. Building on Native ways of learning, teaching, reflection, and leadership provides best practices that complement learners' culture. Understanding the naturalness of human development and the innate qualities inherent in our humanness—in relation to place and culture—gives teachers the tools to address the diversity of learners. It also provides teachers with strategies to nurture learners' wholeness. Teachers as nation builders understand the cultural and natural process of learning and incorporate their skills with the needs of learners.

3. *RElevance—Foster inquiry and passion for learning.* Teachers need to know how to stretch and engage students in purposeful ways that make meaningful connections to their lives. Teachers as nation builders foster inquiry and passion for learning. They help students see that language and culture ground a sense of identity and broaden the ability to see the world through multiple perspectives.

4. *REsponsible—Deliver curriculum that cultivates identity and belonging and develops critical thinking, academic proficiency, responsible behavior, and generosity of heart.* Teachers as nation builders must have a core sense of purpose that is driven by a set of values, goals, mission, and vision. The preparation of teachers also entails helping them to develop their philosophy and voice as educators. Teachers who teach with purpose are driven to touch the lives of students differently. Teachers who empower students to apply their knowledge, skills, and talents with humility and grace encourage responsible citizenry.

5. *RElationship—Cultivate relationships and develop partnerships among the school, family, and community.* At the heart of the Native world is an understanding of the symbiotic relationship between people and their environment. Relationships are valued—self to others, family, community, place, and natural and spiritual world. Therefore, education is a school, family, and community affair. Teachers as nation builders create respectful partnerships with families in the education of learners. They help learners value the importance of family and community as contributors in real and responsible ways.

6. *REsponsive—Participate as culturally responsive educators.* Culturally responsive educators know the learners, families, and community. They highly value the well-being of the learners. Likewise, responsive educators are observant, alert, disciplined, engaging, and supportive. Teachers as nation builders shape the dynamics of the learning community and are responsive to the needs of the one in addressing the needs of the many. Responsive educators work collaboratively with the learners, families, schools, and community to ensure the success of the learners and learning community.

Ka mo'opuna i ke alo (literally, "grandchild in the presence") is a traditional Hawaiian expression that places the child in a place of importance. Great efforts were made to ensure that the grandchild developed straight and tall in stature, and strong in character, and that the youngster was skilled in the family vocation and knowledgeable about the family's history, place, and genealogy. The perpetuation of the family legacy continued through the well-prepared child. Both the nuclear and extended family participated to ensure that the child attained the family's standards of competency because the success of the child brought honor to the family.

We can build on such examples and draw from the richness of traditional practices for application in the learning environment. Return to the source—*ho'i hou i ke kumu*. The answers are contained in the Native culture, language, beliefs, and practices. These best practices provide a pathway for educating strong and healthy children—the hope for tomorrow. Indeed, teachers are nation builders.

Recommended Resources

Ah Nee-Benham, M. & Cooper, J. E. (eds) (2000) *Indigenous Educational Models for Contemporary Practice: In our Mother's Voice*. Mahwah, NJ: Erlbaum.

Aranga-Low, L. (2000) "Grounding vision on the three baskets of knowledge 'Kia ora ai te iwi Māori.' " In M. Ah Nee-Benham & J. E. Cooper (eds), *Indigenous Educational Models for Contemporary Practice: In Our Mother's Voice*. Mahwah, NJ: Erlbaum, pp. 45–50.

Gollnick, G. (2000) "Creating a ceremony: 'Nature's model from the Longhouse people.' " In M. Ah Nee-Benham & J. E. Cooper (eds), *Indigenous Educational Models for Contemporary Practice: In our Mother's Voice*. Mahwah, NJ: Erlbaum, pp. 101–111.

Hawai'i General Superintendent of the Census (1897) *Report of the General Superintendent of the Census, 1896*. Honolulu: Hawaiian Star Press.

Ka Haka 'Ula O Ke'elikōlani & 'Aha Pūnana Leo (In press) "Ke Kumu Honua Mauli Ola." Unpublished philosophical doctrine written in 1998. University of Hawai'i at Hilo.

Kawai'ae'a, K. (2000) "Teacher candidate language, culture and values standards." Unpublished teacher education program standards document for the Kahuawaiola Indigenous Teacher Education Program. University of Hawai'i at Hilo.

Kawai'ae'a, K., DeMorales, P., Akana, K. K., Chun, K., Garma, M., Kim, M., *et al.* (2002) *Nā Honua Mauli Ola: Hawai'i guidelines for culturally healthy and responsive learning environments*. Hilo: Native Hawaiian Education Council and Ka Haka 'Ula O Ke'elikōlani, University of Hawai'i at Hilo.

Kōmike Hua'ōlelo, 'Aha Pūnana Leo, & Hale Kuamo'o (eds) (2003) *Māmaka kaiao: A modern Hawaiian vocabulary* (3rd edn). Honolulu: University of Hawai'i Press.

Mataira, K. T. H. (1997) "Te Aho Matua o ngā Kura Kaupapa Māori: An interpretation of the Māori language document." Unpublished [photocopied material, 14 leaves, in Māori and English. Section 1 is a document written by the pioneers of kura kaupapa Māori as a foundation document for their kura. Section 2 is an interpretation by Kāterina Mataira.].

Pease-Pretty on Top, J. (2003) "Native American language immersion: Innovative Native education for children and families [Electronic Version]" Retrieved April 9, 2005, from http://www.collegefund.org/pdf/ImmersionBook.pdf.

Pukui, M. K. (1993). ʻŌlelo Noʻeau: Hawaiian Proverbs and Poetical Sayings. Honolulu, HI: Bishop Museum Press.

Pukui, M. K. & Elbert, S. H. (eds) (1986) Hawaiian Dictionary (6th edn). Honolulu: University of Hawaiʻi Press.

Pukui, M. K., Haertig, E. W., & Lee, C. (1972). Nānā i ke kumu (Look to the source) (Vols. I & II). Honolulu, HI: Queen Liliʻuokalani Children's Center.

Silva, K. (2000) "Revitalizing culture and language: 'Returning to the ʻāina.' " In M. Ah Nee-Benham & J. E. Cooper (eds), Indigenous Educational Models for Contemporary Practice: In Our Mother's Voice. Mahwah, NJ: Erlbalm, pp. 72–80.

State of Hawaiʻi Department of Education (1994, May) Long Range Plan for the Hawaiian Language Immersion Program Papahana Kaiapuni Hawaiʻi. Honolulu, HI: Office of Accountability and School Instructional Support/School Renewal Group.

PART II

LEADERSHIP IS LIVING INDIGENOUS IN A NEW WAY

Basket as Metaphor:
The Shaping of the Basket

Samuel Suina

First we pray and ask for the blessing of our elders. The weaving of a basket is a sacred task because baskets are used to carry dance clothing and other sacred objects that dancers or singers use during our ceremonies. Baskets are used to hold our oven bread, tortillas, and fruit. The way of the Cochiti is to pray—dance and sing—because all of nature is our church.

> *From the base we have four branches sticking out in the directions of north–west–south–east.*
> *They are strong and flexible. These four willows form our family, our leaders.*
> *Although four separate branches, they will work together to shape and form the bowl of the basket; they will not break.*
> *We start with the north willow and begin adding branches to form the bowl.*
> *As each leader branch is pulled-up, the west—then the south—then the east, branches are added that begin to add more directions.*
> *The lattice strengthens the basket.*

Our leaders gather our people together; like the spines of the basket, they work together to find a direction and a course that we will travel together. They may find different pathways to journey, but the vision is the same. We must strengthen our culture and tradition, our language and ceremonies, through our children. The leaders need to stand up, and ensure that the gifts of our grandmothers, the Corn maidens, are taught to our children.

The Shaping of the Basket

Chapter 6

Living Leadership

Maenette K.P. Ah Nee-Benham

Lawe i ka maʻalea a kūʻonoʻono
(To take wisdom and make it deep)
(Hawaiian ʻōlelo noʻeau)

The power of the many indigenous philosophical and spiritual stories that are being shared in public (in both indigenous and non-indigenous venues) and that appear throughout this volume reaffirms our "ah-hah" (see Benham with Cooper, *Indigenous Educational Models of Contemporary Practice: In Our Mother's Voice*, 2000) that a healthy and engaging learning environment requires that we live "in," that we walk "in," leadership that is rooted in our stories and traditions, our homeland (place), and our mother-tongue language. But we also have learned that we need to know, more deeply, who we are—that is, where we have come from, what our stories are of our indigenous peoples, and "own" the stories. We need to know our mother-tongue language and "use" it so that we can advance a clearly articulated cluster of guiding principles for framing rigorous, dynamic, hopeful, and culturally appropriate learning environments and practices.

One way to understand the meaning of leadership for indigenous peoples is through metaphor or story. In this case, I would like to use the metaphor of the *kiha* or spirit dragon (*moʻo* or lizard) to explain an ontology of the Kanaka Maoli shared with the *In Our Mother's Voice* (IOMV) scholars by our *kumu* Sarah Keahi and our scholar Kalena Silva.

The *kiha* embodies the values of strength and tenacity, and the stories of what has passed, what is present, and what will be our future. Here are the key principles:

- The head, moving forward into tomorrow, *i kēia mua aku*, represents the future promise and potential of all indigenous peoples.
- The front legs are the beginnings, *na pua*, of new generations. These front legs are always exploring and taking important steps forward.
- The body is the maturing *ʻopio* (youth) that represents a period of growth, of focusing and refocusing, of constancy and stability.
- The hind legs are *mākua*, the parents and teachers who both support and ground the head, front legs, and body to *ka ʻāina* (the land).
- The tail is where *kūpuna* (elders) reside (both past and present). Here, in the tail, is where the stories of our experiences, our ancestry, and our rootedness exist.
- The tip of the tail is *akua* (God by any name). It is important to know that all decisions and directions come from the tail.

Now, our elders teach us that the *kiha*, our being in the world, can grow or languish, depending on how we embrace our stories and employ them to live a good life. For the Kanaka Maoli it asks that we live the values of *aloha*, *ʻohana*, *ʻāina*, *mana*, and *lōkahi*.

- To live in *aloha* means that one's embrace of self (*alo*) holds firmly to (*hā*), the breath of life, which is the cordage that connects all life. *Aloha* is a spiritual embrace that is shared graciously with others. This is an essential principle of how we, as educators, generate knowledge (our epistemology) and construct pedagogy.
- *ʻOhana* literally means to spread as vines and to grow lush. To value *ʻohana* means we know that, because we are all related, we are responsible for and accountable to one another. In addition to one's present relations, there is a link between the individual and the world of the ancestors and the world of relations yet to come. This connection maintains our bond to the sacredness of traditions and ceremonies. We must remember, then, that every effort we make as educators must support our extended family, the primary social unit of our indigenous communities. It is only through this commitment that we can prepare a prosperous future for our *ʻohana* yet to come.

- To value 'āina is to recognize the complexities of life, and challenges each person to live within the balance of three places: the physical 'āina, the psychological 'āina, and the spiritual 'āina. When we develop policies and practices, when we do our research, we must ask ourselves whether our work honors (a) the physical 'āina, our ancestral homeland, which provides us roots, home; (b) the psychological 'āina, the place of our thoughts and feelings that we need to nourish continually with positive and productive convictions; and (c) the spiritual 'āina, our personal relationships with ke akua—our traditional source of sustenance.
- Mana is what defines the unique spirit of an individual, and it is the core of one's volition to act in a self-determined way. If this bond, mana, is frayed or broken—the tail of our kiha is cut—the individual/the community becomes disconnected from hā, 'āina, and 'ohana. Learning and teaching in our indigenous communities, therefore, requires that we, who are privileged to be in this space, are courageous and make visible the importance of honoring this sovereign spirit.
- Valuing lōkahi means that we honor the interconnectedness and interdependence that characterize our relationships. It means that we live our lives to create unity and to build bridges within our own community and across many communities. Within this concept of individual generosity and collective action lies the soul of social justice, as our elder Henrietta Mann reminds us, "When the least of us is first."

In short, if educational leadership is rooted in fundamental cultural values, then what does it look like? Returning to our metaphor of kiha, the head represents forward-looking work that contributes to building healthy communities of diverse peoples who have the capacity to sustain healthy schools. The front legs are the beginnings of new ideas, new places, and new energy; this is where our passion begins. This is the place where we think deeply about the impact of educational policy on indigenous peoples and their communities; where we explore the role of school leadership to create a socially just learning environment; where we discover and learn more about how indigenous models of learning, leading, and teaching in preK–16+ settings make a difference; and where we consider how models of engaged communities of learning create and sustain collective will and individual volition that support substantive change. The body of the *kiha* reflects the power of our ideas through development, advocacy, and action. It is a place and time of doing, of focusing and refocusing, where connections, bridges, are built across ideas, people, and diverse communities. The hind legs are the supporting teams of people, expert in diverse fields (e.g. governance structures, legal and fiscal teams, and so on), that are essential to healthy educational institutions. The power of these hind legs is dependent on the expert knowledge of the *mākua* and the integrity with which they translate core principles from our ancestors (the tail) and *akua* (tip of the tail) into practice.

Therefore, the core of an educational leadership team is located in the hind legs of the *kiha*. The obligation of this dynamic team is to ensure that the vision and the mission of the organization are achieved every day. What, then, are the principles of indigenous educational leadership?

- Leadership that is culturally based *and* administratively effective;
- Leadership that invites contributions from all stakeholders to engage in the life of learning and teaching in a manner that is locally relevant and globally responsive;
- Leadership that engages in processes of inquiry that regenerates and generates knowledge and practices, which enhance the quality of life;
- Leadership that necessitates an awareness of and skill to navigate the political, organizational, and symbolic dimensions of and across organizations;
- Leadership that draws on and engenders human qualities of caring, ethical awareness and judgment, generosity of interpersonal style and skill, and introspection and self-knowledge;
- Leadership that provides direction and inspires commitment.

We know that the march to make visible the power of our indigenous stories, which began with our *kūpuna* who have passed and those who are still with us and that rally us to step up, is alive and well on its way. We know this because there is much going on today in our indigenous communities. For example, there are more indigenous immersion in preK through post-secondary schools, there is more attention on the unique needs of indigenous learners in public schools, young people are collecting oral histories from their elders in order to retain cultural knowledge and mother tongue language, and there is an increase in research and evaluation that focuses on indigenous ontologies (to name a few activities). Indeed, if we look to our young people, oh, what inspiring passion and good works we see.

This section presents the stories of leadership work, grounded in the power of our stories, from the next generation of indigenous educational leaders. Each tells a story of good works that remind us of the compassion and spiritual knowing that are essential to the work of learning and teaching, and each helps to build a vision for lifelong learning, in school and in community, that is grounded in self-determination, homeland (place), and wholeness (interconnectedness of family, community, and nature). We begin our journey with Edyael Casaperalta's piece because it powerfully represents the voices in this section. We end with Lai-Lani Ovalles's story, which challenges us to learn and to engage in transformative change. She asks, "If not you, then who? If not now, then when?" Between these two stories, emerging scholars share their stories of leadership—that is, how and why they have come to engage in leadership, the challenges and dilemmas they have faced, and the work they are doing to sustain themselves. In the end, we want you, the reader, to add your story of emerging leadership and take your voice to a higher level!

Chapter 7
The Stories Inside

Edyael Casaperalta

For my *familia* there is no designated story-telling time; it is *always* story-telling time. We talk-story while the *tortillas* warm up, we segment them across commercials during TV shows, we sugar them with *pan dulce* on Sunday mornings, and we even scream them through walls when we are in different rooms. If you are on the phone with one of my family members, it is likely that you are not the only one hearing or telling a story; our ears are trained to listen simultaneously to the various stories being shared in the background of life. Our stories *are* our way of life.

We use stories as our basis of communication, but we don't call them stories all the time. They are the events that happened this morning at school, the gentle spreading of *masa* onto corn leaves to make *tamales*, the challenges and opportunities that shape life. Our stories are adorned with pride of being who we are, they teach us how to cure the evil eye, they are present in our college essays, and they are our education. Our stories are ours to cherish, to hear, and to share—in our own way.

I didn't always see my *familia's* stories in this way, however. Actually, there was a time when I remained silent. I thought the stories inside me should not be shared. Out of fear, I hid them.

Let me tell you a story . . .

After my parents' divorce, my mamá decided that, in order to be safe, we had to move—out of the country. So one day, Mamá, my sister, and I boarded a bus headed to the Northern-Mexico border. The house with the red and pink rosebush outside, the town square where music played every Sunday afternoon, a brother, my *abuela's* warm *jamoncillo*, an aunt, the juiciest red apples you have ever tasted all stayed in Canatlán, our home town. With the help of a *coyote*, a smuggler, we crossed the Rio Grande River. Hidden under the back seat of a truck, we arrived at Elsa, Texas. Our new life in the United States had begun, and the stories of our life in Mexico were stored, silent and deep, inside our hearts.

Getting used to a new life in a new country surrounded by a new culture was no easy task, and not speaking English and being undocumented didn't make it any easier. At school every day, insults and disapproving looks screamed, "*Mojada!* Wetback!" I wanted to tell them about how beautiful Mexico was, but I knew that I'd be told to go back. I wanted to tell them that what my *familia* had done was no crime and that Texas was actually stolen land, but by doing so I would risk being deported. Out of fear, my voice retreated in silence.

Although I understood English by the end of the school year, I was not comfortable speaking again until my sophomore year in high school, two years later. My world-history teacher, Ms. Delia Perez, encouraged us to tell our own stories as an act of rewriting history. It was in her classroom that, for the first time, I spoke to my classmates of my life in Mexico, my family in Peru, the challenges of learning a new language, and my love for salsa dancing. I spoke *my* stories. What began in high school as a class discussion flourished into admission essays for college and graduate school, scholarship applications, testimonies supporting education reform, and keynote addresses at nationwide conferences, and the inspiration and strength to achieve my professional and personal goals. I realized *my* stories were all of these. They had strength tucked away in their details, inspiration curving their beginnings, middles, and ends, and history in their meaning. And when I began telling them, *my* stories, my *familia's* stories, they resonated strongly like thunder in the air, and I discovered that my voice had echoes. I was not the only one eager to share stories.

Through Ms. Perez's class, I became involved with the Llano Grande Center for Research and Development, and there I was introduced to yet another way to tell stories—*digital storytelling*. Digital storytelling is like making your own mini-movie about your own stories. You can write a script, focus on pictures, record videos, add music, or express your story in any form that will honor it. The best part is that anyone can make a digital story! You don't have to be an expert or enroll in special courses to learn about digital storytelling. In fact, there are some free resources on-line that will teach you the details of digital storytelling.

For example, as part of an initiative on digital storytelling called *Captura*, the Llano Grande Center created a Digital Storytelling Toolkit. The toolkit is a collaborative production shared by the W. K. Kellogg Foundation, Fellows from the Kellogg Leadership for Community Change (KLCC) Series, and the Llano Grande Center. It is an easy-to-follow guide on the power and technicalities of digital storytelling. It talks about your roles as the producer, writer, director, and editor of your own story, and at the same time, it provides step-by-step technical instructions on how to make your movie. If you have access to the Internet (at school, at home, at work, at the community center, at the library, etc.) you can use this toolkit free! Simply log on to www.llanogrande.org. On the lower right-hand side of the home page, you will see a picture of a cactus; place your curser over it, and click on the word *Captura*. This will take you directly to the toolkit.

As part of the Captura Initiative, Llano Grande has conducted digital storytelling workshops with other KLCC Fellows around the country. The goal of the workshops is to guide Fellows through the process of producing their own digital stories. Through these workshops, KLCC Fellows have shared with us inspirational stories of hope, resilience, and community change. These stories, of course, are the core of the toolkit. When you access the toolkit, you can view all the digital stories produced by KLCC Fellows, people just like you! Let them inspire you.

One of the stories you will see featured in the toolkit is entitled "Organized Generations," created by youths and adults from the Lummi Cedar Project in Bellingham, Washington. Misty Oldham and Michelle Vendiola created this story as a recruiting tool to encourage youths and adults from the Lummi Nation to join Organized Generations, a group committed to engendering positive community change through inter-generational partnerships.

Another story featured in the toolkit is entitled "Edcouch-Elsa Independent School District (EEISD) Bond Election 2006." The school district wanted to apply for a $21 million loan from the state to revitalize its school facilities. A loan for which a school district applies is called a bond. If the bond is approved, the state assumes responsibility for paying a large percentage of the amount requested. However, the school district cannot apply for the bond before the constituents of the district vote in favor of it. A youth-led organization called Tomorrow's Leaders Today (TLT) learned about the issue and decided to create an educational digital story that would inform voters about the bond and how it could affect their economy and schools. In the end, the bond was approved; the EEISD was able to get the bond for $21 million, with the state paying more than $19 million of the debt.

Arthur Ray Joe from the Laguna Pueblo and Nadia Casaperalta, a Mexican immigrant from South Texas (as well as being my sister), also have stories to share about their communities and themselves. Arthur's story, entitled "Native Americans in Wars," honors the history of soldiers in his family who have proudly served in U.S. wars. Similarly, Nadia's story, entitled "Curanderismo," explores the traditional healing practices in her family and community.

More than simply making a story, digital storytelling is about providing you with an extra tool for telling the valuable stories inside you. As Nadia said, "My digital story wasn't necessarily about *curanderismo*, but about the healing traditions that have been passed from generation to generation in our culture, and how I could contribute, in my own way, to making sure that they would continue to be passed on for generations to come." After hearing the stories of the soldiers in his family, Arthur said, "I'm proud they served for their country. Now they are a part of history. And I shall pass the history and stories of them on to my children."

Digital storytelling, like other stories we tell, can be used to entertain, shape our community's future, enact social change, and rewrite and preserve our history. I have learned that my own story is the essence of my academic, professional, and personal aspirations. Digital storytelling is a tool I use to tell my stories and achieve my goals. Misty and Michelle fostered an intergenerational partnership in creating a digital story for their organization. In doing this, they became the change they wanted to see in their community. Through their digital story, the members of TLT helped their community obtain more than $19 million in state funds for the revitalization of their school district. Thanks to the bond, the construction of a brand new ninth-grade campus, a new high school gym, new science labs, and 20 new middle school classrooms, in addition to other renovations, will take place in the Edcouch-Elsa Independent School District. In the process of making their digital stories, Arthur and

Nadia not only learned about the history of their communities, but they also took an active approach to writing that history. Digital storytelling didn't bring these stories to Misty, Michelle, TLT, Arthur, and Nadia. Digital storytelling was simply the tool they used to share their stories.

So, I ask you to share. . . . What stories have life inside you?

Let your hands cradle the voices of your elders. Let your eyes be windows through which your community's history can be seen. Let your voice move the wind with songs about your *familia*. Let your feet dance the traditions that have always lived inside you. Your stories are there— waiting to make words with your hands, paint colors with your eyes, shape melodies with your voice, shake the earth with your steps. Let the stories flow, guide you, give you strength; share them in the way that best honors them. Your stories, like history books, hold power. This time, though, write the history yourself.

Chapter 8

What Does It Mean to Lead and Advocate for Our A'ani Language?

Lynette Stein-Chandler

I was made for this. I remember the struggles I endured at the beginning of my language journey, on my reservation in Fort Belknap, Montana. I was constantly in a fighting mode. I recall making this statement to my elders, spiritual people, and young adults at a community meeting:

> I believe in our ways and our A'ani language. I have been raised in my ways and had a heavy influence of my Grandfather Charles Longfox and Grandmother Naomi Stiffarm Longfox; I know who I am. I will not let anyone run me over, run me off, or stop me from what I am here to do, and that is to help bring our language back. I will not stop and fight with those who oppose this movement. I will simply go my own way. I am a tough person. I was made for this.

I had found my passion, my voice.

I remember the first person who believed in me and the dream of an A'ani language-immersion school. It was Good Strike Chandler, my father-in-law. I had told many people about my dream, but I always saw in their eyes the look of doubt or unbelief. My father-in-law sparked my hope and helped me believe in myself and my dream. In the beginning, I called on Darrell Kipp (from the Piegan Institute) to guide me. As a mentor and friend, he has seen me through many years of difficult challenges and glorious achievements. I still call him regularly because he, too, is committed to helping our A'ani language survive.

I am often asked where my passion originated. I believe my family has instilled in me the desire I have for our ways and our language, for my sense of family and for who I am. My grandpa inspired me to learn and to live strong in our ways. My grandma and mother encouraged me, yes, taught me to be tough but to have a loyal and loving heart. My father has shown me the value of having a dream, to desire to make the world a better place for indigenous peoples. My husband has supported me without hesitation as I earned my Master's degree and now as I work toward my doctoral degree. He is my partner as we work to achieve my language-immersion dream. Especially during times when I felt broken, I could count on my husband's warmth and love. Both my father-in-law and spiritual uncle helped me through life-threatening illnesses so I could continue my journey here on earth. My mother-in-law, the president of Fort Belknap College, has created the space and the place for our immersion school to grow. And, most important, my daughter, Wozek (Ghost Calf), has kept the fire alive deep inside of me. Every day as I look into her deep eyes, it reminds me how important this work that I'm doing is to making an A'ani world a possibility for all of our A'ani children. So, when I speak and when I carry out the work I'm doing, I bring with me my family.

As it has been for many of my indigenous brothers and sisters around the world who are working hard to recapture their native languages and ways of life, this journey has been difficult for a young leader like me. I have had my heart broken, suffered health problems related to stress, and have had to sacrifice precious time away from my family. I have overcome all of these trying situations. Perhaps that is a quality of leadership that goes unnoticed: the ability to persevere in the face of adversity. I have persisted because of one consideration: my love for Wozek. For her I can move mountains, for her I will persevere, for her I will survive. So, I give thanks to the Creator and to Wozek for lighting my way every day; this is where leadership begins for me.

I wrote this letter to my daughter so that she will know that leading in a native way begins with love.

Dear Wozek,

I am so blessed to have Beyhaatek bring you into my life and entrust me with raising you to be a *nee ee A'ani initaa*.

Eejaheyaats, Wozek. Thank you for everything you have given me the desire to accomplish. Because of you I chose to finish college, because of you I worked hard to complete my Master's degree, because of you I have almost completed my doctoral degree. You gave me a reason to want to better myself and provide you and *neethaw* with a nice life through education.

Gineeheyaan for making me want to stay on this earth and ask Beyhaatek, Uncle Lee, Istahook, and Neethowaak to help heal me when I was in so much pain. I could have just let go; I felt my spirit could pass on if I just let go. But one thing kept going through my mind: I don't want to leave *ni naa agis nawdawn* [my little daughter]. I love you too much to leave; you hold me here on this earth.

Gineeheyaan for giving me the desire to give you more A'ani language than I had growing up. I want you to have a nice life. For you I strive to create one world—your A'ani world. No longer will you feel you have to walk in two worlds, the *Neehawto* and the *Dowatsinitaa* worlds. You will walk in your world: the A'ani world. I started the A'ani Language Immersion School for you. Because of my love for you, our A'ani language has a place. Because of my love for you, your peers and generation will have the opportunity to make history and bring our language back and regenerate it among our people.

I want to give you all you will need to be successful and happy in life. I already see that you believe in our ways so strongly; you have always been able to communicate with the spirit world. Your belief in our ways, our prayers, and our songs will see you through anything you choose to do in life. If you truly try to do good things and keep good thoughts in your heart, Beyhaatek will bestow blessings upon you and always will be with you.

Never get discouraged and think the world is unfair. Everything happens for a reason. Sometimes the meaning of a tragedy or heartbreak might be revealed much later; sometimes we must survive these hard times to thicken our skin—there is a lesson in everything.

I want you to do what will make you happy in life. But to do so, you must pursue your higher education. This is the key for indigenous peoples today. Go into a career that will make you happy. I know whatever you decide to do in life the time will come when you will be called upon to help our A'ani language live on. Teach it to your children and your grandchildren. You are strong. Neethaw and I have raised you deeply rooted in our spiritual and cultural ways in ceremony, art, language, culture, ways of knowing, and ways of living, believing, and being. You have been given all the tools you will need in life to change the world. The change began in our people. It is in you that the tide will turn in favor of our A'ani ways and philosophies in our language.

Our language has never left us; it has always remained with us. It is merely dormant. Our prayers have reawakened the A'ani language. It has waited for the certain time, the people, the prayers, the desire, and heart to reawaken. It has reawakened to us because we believe; we are willing to work hard for good things in life. Good things are never easy to obtain, Neethaw says, and he is right. Always remain humble. Always be prosperous. Always be generous. These teachings come from Nabisiwaw Istahook and Neethaw Neethowaak. They carry these qualities on from the beginning of our time.

Dabeetow Wahnawsayhenaw.

Know that I will always be with you; no matter where I am in the world, I will live in your *initaan* [heart]. Even when I have left this physical world and go to the spirit world, call upon me and I will be with you.

Neebeedotshaan Nadawn Wozek Istahook.

Na ah Badatha

Leadership begins where we can touch the soul of our children! I live leadership in my community through my advocacy for our immersion school. We have accomplished much in a short time, due in large part to the support of our elders, the expertise of staff and faculty at Fort Belknap College, and our partnership with other indigenous immersion schools. For example, we are learning about the power of resiliency that can be found in family. Our A'ani students, in collaboration with Native American studies and science professors at Fort Belknap College, painted birdhouses with our traditional designs while listening to bird songs indigenous to our region. We then placed the birdhouses around the campus with the help of our maintenance staff in order to observe the birds throughout the coming months. Our science professors used a GPS program that plotted the location of the birdhouses using satellite technology. Unfortunately, three days later, our birdhouses were vandalized and some of them were stolen. Needless to say, our little young students were sad and upset. Liz McClain, one of our science professors, urged us to push through this incident and draw on the way of *Dowhatsinitaa initaan* (indigenous people); that is, strive to have our A'ani Nakoda Winchohage be present every day. So, we learned together how to be resilient and move forward by calling on members of our extended families at school, at the college, and throughout the community. Together we rebuilt our birdhouses and repainted them. This time we hung them higher. This was a learning metaphor that helped us to know our own strength of character to overcome obstacles. We also remembered to call upon our spirits and Bayhatek (Creator) to help us be humble in our work and have good hearts. This lesson helped our school to reaffirm the importance of being an A'ani family and of treating each other with respect and kindness.

We do have a good base of community support and families. In our Indian community, as in many other Indian communities, our families include extended family members and are far reaching. For example, early in the first year we opened our school, we had to speak with parents of a child who was having a hard time following school rules. The following day, the student's father came to school with his son and spoke to our class about how he felt. He shared his beliefs and wishes for his son and the other students. His son asked forgiveness and ceremoniously gave the elder of our classroom, *Neewah Faye*, a blanket. This was a powerful moment among our people as it followed the protocol of our ways. The father passed on our ways to his son and at the same time taught all of our students. Since that time, the student has been respectful and will grow to be a respectful young man. Our families, in our communities, teach us many things. As leaders we must listen to these voices!

Chapter 9

Life Lessons from the Land:
Loko Kuapa as Leadership Model

Noelani Lee

A *loko kuapa*, a fishpond built with *pōhaku* (rocks) forming a wall or semicircle into the sea, is a style of fishpond endemic to Hawai'i. Many of today's *loko kuapa* are found on the island of Molokai. They say that the rocks for fishponds on Molokai were passed among thousands of people. Some of the oral histories say that the fishponds were built in a day; others say that the rocks were passed along human chains from the north side of the island to the south shore. But regardless of how the *loko kuapa* were actually constructed, and although each rock wall has its own personality, one thing is sure: their foundation is strong, as many of these fishpond walls have withstood the test of weather, tides, and time for hundreds of years.

Two such ponds are licensed to a nonprofit organization called Ka Honua Momona International for their Molokai Reef Fish Restoration Project. Ka Honua Momona means "the fat earth," and in Hawaiian, fat is synonymous with sweet, fertile, or bountiful. The nonprofit's mission is to be a model of sustainability *mauka a makai* (from the mountains to the sea). Ka Honua Momona's two ponds, Kalokoeli Pond and Ali'i Pond, are located in an area of land referred to as Kamiloloa/One Ali'i Homestead.

Both of the ponds are close to 30 acres in size and were built around fresh-water *puna* (springs). Fresh water in Hawaiian is called *wai*; sea water is called *kai*. The fresh water mixing with the salt water turns to *waikai* (brackish water), which provides the nutrients for *pua* (baby fish). At two points in the rock wall of the fishpond, there are *makaha* (sluice gates) that allow the tide, as well as fish, to enter and exit the pond. The *pua* come in through the *makaha* to feed on the *waikai*, and soon they grow too fat to fit back through the *makaha*, preventing them from leaving the fishponds.

The health of a pond often denotes the health of the *ahupua'a* (section of land stretching from the mountain to the sea). What happens *mauka* affects *makai*. (What happens in the uplands affects the low lands.) Silt on the bottom of the ponds denotes mismanagement of the land above; it often is runoff from heavy rains in the mountains and results from overgrazing of nonnative animals.

Animals are not the only threat to our ponds. Mangrove, a favorite native plant of Florida, is an alien invasive species in Hawai'i. It is said that mangrove was brought in to Hawai'i to build land banks for developers; unfortunately, it often does the job it was intended to do, only in the fishponds. Besides holding unwanted silt in the ponds, while it is growing, mangrove often breaks apart the historic rock walls and also drinks up the fresh water, preventing the *limu* (seaweed) and algae from growing on the rocks. Then, instead of the fish feeding on the algae, they feed on the silt. This important cycle illustrates how every living thing affects everything else. We are all interconnected.

In this way, we have used the pond to model our project; Ka Honua Momona is built the way the pond is built. Just as the pond is built around fresh-water *puna* (springs), our program is built around a strong *kupuna* (elder). *Wai*, in Hawaiian, means fresh water, but it also, appropriately, means wealth. *Wai* is the source of our knowledge. The *wai* in our pond is a man named Mervin Dudoit. Uncle Merv, as he is called, is our source. And appropriately, the word *source*, in Hawaiian, is *kumu*, which also means teacher.

The state of our fishponds represents the state of our Native Hawaiian people and our culture. Unfortunately, most of our fishponds in Hawai'i have fallen into disrepair from nonuse. It is sad to see that they have been filled in for developers' hotels, neglected, or tangled in the red tape of bureaucracy. Fortunately, however, in some cases, like that of Ka Honua Momona, Hawaiians are reclaiming their right—their responsibility—to take care of the fishponds. Not only are they restoring the rock walls of the ponds, but also they are caring for the land and sea, which is a cornerstone of Native Hawaiians' philosophy.

Our Leadership is the *Loko Kuapa*

The stone wall of the fishpond is the foundation we lay. We have to make sure it is built strongly enough to withstand the crashing of waves and the changing of tides. In Ka Honua Momona's program, our stone wall has been built through good, old-fashioned hard work. To ensure that our *'ōpio* (youths) fully learn the value of their *'āina* and their responsibility to care for it, we ask them to get into the pond; feel the sand, the tides, the weight of the water; and know the life of the fishpond. We ask them to feel the entangled roots of the invasive mangrove, to feel the silt beneath their feet as they push the boat full of cut mangrove back to shore to unload, to feel the tide changes in the *makaha*, the eyes and the breath of the pond. They become frustrated and fatigued as they labor in the hot Hawaiian sun.

The *'ōpio* begin to know that the pull of the water through the *makaha* is as routine as the changing of the tides. They know that when we cleared out the *makaha*, the tide could run smoothly through the opening, and the pond began to change. Its circulation improved, and with its arteries unclogged, the pond could breathe again. Just like the *waikai* that attracts *pua* (baby fish) who feed off its nutrients, Uncle Merv, when he is in the pond with the *'ōpio*, provides food for their souls. As the children grow fat on the lessons Uncle Merv provides, they become attached to the fishpond. In the end, their blood, sweat, and tears go into the earth, into the fishponds, both giving the pond new life and nourishing each young person's soul.

The health and well-being of our fishpond is a reflection of the health of our *'ōpio* and our community. The *'ōpio* are learning to address the social problems of their community and generation, for example, drug and alcohol abuse. Just as they care for the health of the pond, they have begun to clear their minds, strengthen their bodies, and nurture their spirits. Just as they have grown to love the pond, they have grown to love themselves, each other, their families, and their island community. They now have a vested interest in their *'āina* and their *loko kuapa*. It is in this place that they have grounded their memories and their relationships. They are learning the important leadership values of *ha'aha'a* (humility), *lōkahi* (unity and harmony), *ahonui* (patience), and *kuleana* (responsibility). They are learning that through dedication, hard work, and a collective spirit, each person can make a difference in the world, starting with our own place. These young people who labor long hours in our fishponds will be the teachers of future generations and stewards of the land.

I have learned that our leaders must stand firmly on the land because it is always teaching us something; we just need to listen to what it's telling us. The ripples in the water tell us where the fish are, how big they are, and whether predators are chasing them. I believe that the land leaves imprints of our legacy and our ancient and contemporary generational knowledge while giving new roots to succeeding generations. Learning from, on, and with the *'āina* means that we are alive—still growing, still teaching, still learning!

Chapter 10

Leading in Relationship, Learning from Our Youths

Malia Villegas

Allriluq, Mal'uk, Pingayun.
One, two three.
Allriluq, Mal'uk, Pingayun.
One, two, three.
Allriluq, Mal'uk, Pingayun.

June and I sang these words over and over again as we wove together and the camera zoomed in on the amazing Alutiiq-style basket she was working to finish. I had been hired to be a youth program evaluator for a native basket weaver exhibit at the Smithsonian Institution's fortieth Annual Folklife Festival on the National Mall in Washington, DC.[1] Yet, I found myself being invited to participate in what would become one of the most meaningful experiences of my life. June Simeonoff Pardue is a culture bearer and one of few remaining Alutiiq basketweavers. Volun-

---

[1] *The Carriers of Culture: Native Basket Traditions* program at the 2006 Smithsonian Folklife Festival was produced by the Michigan State University Museum, the Smithsonian Center for Folklife and Cultural Heritage, and the National Museum of the American Indian. The participation of Native youth weavers and leaders in the "Next Generation" component of the program was supported by a grant from the W. K. Kellogg Foundation.

teering in the Alaska Native weavers' tent, I found myself talking with June because we are both Alutiiq. After a few rounds of "Where is your family from?" and "Do you know so-and-so?" we found that we had some family members in common through our connections to Kodiak Island. She invited me to observe her and to practice weaving with some scraps of raffia while she worked with the rye grass collected on the shores of Alaska. I did not realize she would begin to teach me the songs she had been taught and stories about how she had learned to weave, or that we would be interviewed for a documentary about the event.

The festival ended after a week, and two months later, I returned to Seattle excited to share with my mother and grandmother what I had learned. Driving to a family gathering, I shared this song and my experience with my grandmother. She was incredibly moved, but nonetheless took a moment to correct my pronunciation. She said it had been decades since she heard these words, and she was so proud that I was learning our language.

The power of the connection I experienced with June and with my grandmother through practicing the weaving, singing, and sharing stories cannot be captured by mere words because it is something intangible, yet so real—something that flowed through each of us and drew us closer together and left us wanting more. Whereas I was at the festival to learn about and document what the youths were learning, I was able to understand much more because I became a learner myself. And that learning inspired me to want to share their stories as well as my own, to seek more knowledge about my language and culture, and to become a more active part of my home community. I began to recognize these desires as attributes of leadership because I felt a new responsibility to grow in my knowledge and in my relationships. In getting to know the young people in the program, I was curious about their learning, their sense of responsibility, and their leadership. In what follows, I will share a few short stories that capture what I learned from them.

Cherish is a 17-year-old Potawatomi weaver from Michigan. She and her mother travel around the country demonstrating their weaving, in large part to share with others the dangers of the emerald ash borer. This beetle is ravaging the remaining black ash trees that provide the raw materials the Potawatomi traditionally have used in weaving. By most projections, no black ash trees will remain by the time Cherish has children. It would be easy, it would seem, to become dejected and hopeless about this situation, but Cherish has such a positive way and spirit about her. She and her mother, Kelly, have found the silver lining—or perhaps I should say the "plastic" lining. They have begun using plastic Venetian blinds, which have a texture and flexibility similar to the strips of black ash used in weaving, to continue teaching and learning the weave while preserving the remaining stock of trees. They also have begun to research the possibility of submerging remaining trees to prevent the borer from getting at the precious bark. Along with all of this innovative work and research, Cherish and Kelly continue to travel to warn other communities about the borer, discuss with other weavers ways to protect remaining stands of trees, and otherwise advocate for the preservation of culture through the conservation of natural resources. In this way, Cherish has found ways to continue to be in relationships with her culture, traditions, and community despite the dangers threatening the black ash trees and basketry.

One of Cherish's fellow festival weavers was Joseph, a 20-something Tohono O'odham weaver from a community where women traditionally have been the weavers. Joseph recreates scenes and stories through his baskets and weaving. When I asked him why he had become interested in weaving, he chuckled and said that he could not believe for how much his mother sold her baskets, and that the money initially had been a big motivator. But, as he began to learn from his mother how difficult it was to prepare the materials and weave, he gained a new appreciation for her work. As Joseph improved his skills through observation and practice, he began to have new confidence and pride in himself and in his culture. Although he uses many of the traditional weaving methods, he creates new shapes and scenes that have meaning for him and that push on the bounds of basketry. For example, one of his creations represents a scene from the Tohono O'odham rain dance and captures aspects of the dance that he finds beautiful and special. Joseph explained that becoming a weaver saved his life because before he began learning to weave, he had been involved in local gangs and in a very different kind of life. He now shares his story, experiences, and art with other young Tohono O'odham boys and men to help them understand who they are and the importance of their stories.

Sarah is also in her mid-20s and a leader in her Akwesasne Mohawk community. In directing the local cultural center, she works with a small staff, including fellow festival participant Crystal. They serve simultaneously as curators, educators, program developers, and learners. It is her intense curiosity that seems to drive Sarah's passion for learning and teaching. Sarah came to the festival as a part of a youth program that exposed participants to the behind-the-scenes work of the curatorial, documentation, and management aspects of the festival in the hopes of encouraging them to take on similar roles. A story she told about what happened in the Mohawk weavers' tent during one of the first days of the festival captured the connection between her learning and leadership. Sarah explained how she instructed two of her peers in the Akwesasne Mohawk style, and how in becoming a teacher herself, she gained new confidence in her own weaving abilities. This confidence enabled Sarah to see how much she had to contribute to, and simultaneously learn about herself from, the group. Over the course of the next several days, she shared more about her own vision for their local cultural center. She and Crystal began to make plans with the co-curator of the native basket weaving exhibit at the festival to develop a similar event for the five Mohawk Nations to come together to share their various weaving traditions, stories, and activism. Their vision is that such a gathering could provide much-needed relationship-building across their community, which is fragmented by an international border, tribal politics, and the oversight of multiple governmental agencies.

Aren't they amazing! Every time I think about their stories, I am newly inspired and hopeful about our emerging leaders! In each case, these young people talked about those who had taught and guided them, and how they, in turn, were doing their part to teach and guide others. They spoke about their responsibility in such a way that it was not so much about being given something and feeling obligated to give it back. Instead, it was more about having been made to feel a part of someone or of a community through a relationship with a mother, a teacher, or a peer. These young people are gaining confidence through relationship. They are learning more about themselves, desiring more of that type of connection, and wanting others to share in these experiences.

Through this experience and the festival participants' stories, I have come to understand that leadership comes about through a reciprocal cycle of relationships. Sustaining and inspirational leadership comes about when we enter into right relationships with our youths, encourage them to learn in relation to those around them and their environment, and celebrate their efforts to seek out new relationships through cultural traditions, language, and shared experiences. This seems to be common sense when we think about the purpose of leadership—to support the development of healthy human beings and healthy communities. Meaningful connections and relationships are at the core of both of these things. Developing emerging leaders is essential for the health and well-being of ourselves as indigenous people and our communities. To do so, we must help youths understand the importance of being in relationships by modeling healthy relationships ourselves. There is no limit to what they can create when they know they are a part of us and have a meaningful place in the world.

Chapter 11

Gustango Gold: Lessons in Leadership from Corn

Lawrence E. Wheeler

Throughout the generations of Ögwëhöweh (real people), and in particular the *Haudenosaunee* (people of the longhouse, also known as Iroquois), *onëö'* (corn) has served a principal role in people's lives. Some of my fondest boyhood memories involve preparing white corn in August at my Uncle Hank and Aunt Jean's and butchering pigs in November and December at my Uncle Russell's. Uncle Hank's *onë'da:gi'* (roasted corn soup) and Aunt Jean's *agö:nsä'* (corn mush) stand out above the other communal-familial activities of my youth. Both corn dishes, along with another variety of corn soup, hold paramount significance in the community relations in which my family participated. *Onëö'* is celebrated as one of our spiritual Three Sisters, *Johëhgöh. Johëhgöh,* literally "they sustain us," is the partnership of corn, beans, and squash. *Onëö'* provides many lessons. The processes of preparing *onëö'* provide specific lessons, which are as old as the processes themselves; they continue to evoke the same power. Everything has a purpose, and the preparation of *onëö'* serves many functions.

On the hottest days in August, the Huffs, my Uncle Hank and Aunt Jean, would start the work. On those days, we would go and help; as a boy, I looked forward to the treats that Hank would provide, but as I look back, the lessons learned on those days are what I really hold tight. We would help with the physical work of scraping or roasting the *onëö'*, and

Hank and Jean would teach us how to prepare and use the *onëö'*. My dad, my cousins, my sister, and other community members all gathered at the Huffs' home to carry out the tasks at hand. Gustango Gold (Hank's Corn) was renowned. Hank shipped Gustango Gold as far as Hawai'i. Even after his passing, when I say, "I make *onë'da:gi'* like Hank," people who knew Hank raise their eyebrows. Along with the stories that surrounded and were infused in the processing of the corn, the stories spoken by *onëö'* herself burn deep.

The mentoring of youths is mimicked in the process of *agö:nsä'*. *Agö:nsä'* is created by baking the ground innards of corn kernels while they are considered *onö'gwa:d* (in the milky stage). *Onö'gwa:d* is immature white corn. *Onëö'* is *onö'gwa:d* for only about three to five days. During this time, the family works at a steady pace to scrape the corn kernels; the pulp of the mashed innards is collected in a pan for baking. The resultant product emerges from the oven as a heavy, rich bread. It was and still is a special treat to eat the bread directly after it emerges from the oven—a treat reserved for the workers on those hot August days. When the bread is produced, the preparation process is in its early stages and is far from complete. Next, the bread is dried and crumbled into small chunks, which are then completely dried and stored. When it is time to partake of *agö:nsä'*, a portion of the dehydrated mixture is reconstituted by boiling it in water. The final touch to the preparation might include the addition of salt pork (my personal favorite).

The process of making *agö:nsä'* can be likened to youth mentorship because of the timing of the process and the actual procedure required. We are given just days to perform the initial stages of the process. The corn must be collected while it is in an immature state. All traditional corn-preparation processes are labor intensive, but the types of labor involved in preparing each corn dish are vastly different. Scraping the kernels to get to the immature innards is a painstaking process and is done with the utmost patience and care. Too much scraping or scraping too deeply introduces bitterness from the corncob, whereas too little scraping yields very little of the matter needed to make the bread. In youth leadership development, too much direction serves to strip youths of self-motivated initiative and independence, whereas too little direction serves to deter youths from accepting leadership roles.

Furthermore, similar to the process of making *agö:nsä'*, youth leadership does not in itself produce future leaders. Rather, a second stage must occur to bring out the rich flavor of the leaders that had been fostered many years before. I am happy and fortunate to attest to the fact that youth leadership development initiatives do, indeed, produce future leaders. With a father and a brother who were my first football coaches, with a mother and sisters who led by example, with aunts and uncles who gently pushed me into leadership roles as a young man, and with grandparents who held fast to their language, I have been mentored by a community of leaders composed of family members. Those family members have been coaches, school counselors, school board members, professors, and national education foundation mainstays, as well as community volunteers and local experts. Through their examples and mentoring, I am blessed to have had the renaissance man's experience as a youth. Because of my experiences as a youth, I can now, as an adult, say with pride that I can lay bricks and blocks, frame a house, or build a deck. I can read a blueprint or lay out a design and follow the plan. I can now throw a lasso and rope a calf or steer. I can shell and eat piñon nuts. I can operate a class A fire engine and drive a tractor. I know how to make Uncle Hank's corn soup and Aunt Jean's *agö:nsä'*. I have become a leader in my home community of Gustango as treasurer and chaplain of my home fire company, in my local American Indian community as the K–12 program coordinator and a member of the Seneca Nation Library Board of Trustees, and on the national level, as vice-president of the National Johnson O'Malley Association.

Another aspect of leadership development can be likened to the preparation of *onëda:gi'* and hull corn soup. *Onë'da:gi'* is prepared in the days after the *onëö'* is no longer *onö'gwa:d*. The kernels no longer produce milk, and once the *onëö* is collected, it needs to be prepared; *onë'da:gi'* is prepared by roasting the cobs that are no longer *onö'gwa:d*. I liken this process to leadership development of young adults. The *onëö'* is no longer considered immature, and the process is not gentle, but rather like trial by fire. Although most of the kernels survive the process, some of them explode during roasting and are no longer good for producing corn soup of any kind. Once the corn is roasted on the cob, the cobs are set aside to cool. Once they are cooled, the shelling process begins. In the process of *agö:nsä*, the baking, drying, crumbling, and drying can take place over several days. The shelled kernels are laid out to dry on a flat surface in the sun. The dried kernels are then collected and stored until it is time to make the soup. Similarly, young adults often receive leadership training that is trial-by-fire in nature. They are often placed in leadership roles, and although some prove to be unfit to lead, most rise to the occasion. This on-the-job training usually is provided on an as-needed basis, and young adults being groomed for leadership often prove themselves worthy. I have found that the impact of leadership development that occurs at the young adult age (18 to 23 years), while the experience is valuable, does not have as rich or lasting an impact as our youth leadership development opportunities. *Agö:nsä* is very flavorful and far richer than *onë'da:gi*. *Onë'da:gi* is more flavorful than hull corn soup, which I liken to adult leadership development.

Hull corn soup is prepared by allowing the *onëö'* to dry in the field. Because the corn is mature and hardened, the process includes steps to

"Gustango Gold," a Sketch by Larry Wheeler

soften the kernels. This process is harsh and usually entails some sort of lye-water mixture. Hardwood ash and water produce such a lye. Hull corn is soaked in the lye mixture to remove the hardened skin of the *oneo'*. After the skin peels from the harsh treatment, the *oneo'* is rinsed repeatedly to remove the corrosive agent, leaving a bland, colorless kernel of corn. Likewise, leadership development that is deferred until people reach a mature, hardened stage in life produces bland leadership.

All three forms of traditionally prepared corn dishes are important to Haudenosaunee life ways. All three are present at various gatherings, and all three have very different characters. All three forms are *onëö'* herself, but the process involved occurs at different stages in the development of the *onëö'* and the products are vastly different in taste, in texture, and in nature.

Leadership development that occurs at the middle school and early high school ages is best represented by the preparation of *ago:nsä'* (corn mush); the result is rich and flavorful. Leadership development that is initiated with young adults is like *onë'da:gi'*; it tastes good, but many kernels can be lost. Adult leadership development is likened to the preparation of hull corn soup; you need a lot of seasoning to match the flavor of the other two processes. Each can be flavorful, but in the absence of *ojihke:da:'* (salt) there is very little comparison in terms of richness of flavor. *Nya:wëh*, Hank, for those lessons in your *onëö'*.

Chapter 12

Leadership Defined by Action: "Lead by Example"

Theresa Jackson

Aanii (Hi). Theresa *nda-zhinikaaz* (my name is Theresa). Throughout my life, I have always heard the words *lead by example*. These three little words never held much meaning for me until two-and-a-half years ago. Never in my life had I imagined that some day this simple little phrase would become a realization for me and my family. This realization turned into an action, an action inspired by my son.

Stephen, my oldest son, was 16 years old and a junior in high school. During a nightly conversation, I expressed my desire for him to choose a college and a degree program. I had told him that he needed to make a decision because he had only one year left of high school. I also explained that we needed our future generations to be knowledgeable in order to maintain and build a strong tribal nation: a tribal nation that will not bow down to assimilation, a tribal nation that will prosper, rebuild, and recover its lost heritage. This is a concept not only for my grand-children, but for his grandchildren, great-grandchildren, and future heirs. When this part of the conversation was over, he told me that he understood. However, this was not the end of our discussion.

Because I had expressed my thoughts and feelings, it was his time to speak. Stephen's two questions that touched my heart and changed my life were: "Where did you go to college? What degree do you have?" To my dismay, I had to tell him that I had not attended college nor did I have a degree. At that moment, I thought, "Who am I to tell this child to do something that I have not yet done myself?" This question weighed heavily on my mind. It was then that I realized the need to go back to school. It was then that I realized the need to become the leader I wanted my son and his generation to be. It was then that I put my words into action. This conversation and these realizations became my inspiration, my motivation, and my commitment to lead by example.

Although my son is now a high school graduate and I am full-time student at our tribal college, I know my role as a leader is not finished. I need to show my children how important education is by making a commitment and finishing my degree program. Not only is my son going to attend college, my husband is returning to finish his degree program. Coinciding with our goals for the future are the accomplishments of my oldest daughter, Joelle, and my youngest son, Robert. Joelle has one class to complete before she graduates with an associate degree in General Studies, and Robert will be graduating from high school in the spring. Needless to say, I am very proud of and happy about the goals and achievements of my family. What an amazing motivator the simple three-word phrase *lead by example* has been!

Upon sharing my story with other family members and friends, it became apparent that all of us share the same ideal regarding leadership. We all agreed that actual physical involvement has more of an impact on our children than any words we speak. A majority of us, who have chosen to return to college, also concluded that we feel the need to demonstrate the importance of education. Through our education we can become more efficient leaders. One example a mother shared with me was that when her children observed the effort she put into homework, it sparked them to work harder. Higher grades were the result. Equally important is that the woman's older daughter, who never graduated from high school, is now considering a return to school, a decision that would fill any parent's heart with joy.

Another comment made during our conversation was that community activities also play a major role in preparing community leaders and creating pathways for emerging leaders to participate. Within the last year, some of the students joined an organization named American Indian Business Leaders (AIBL). Two of the requirements of AIBL are fundraising and volunteer work. So far our chapter has helped the local Tribal Academy with their school carnival and book fair, donated a decorated Christmas tree for their auction, collected donations for a tribal boarding school in South Dakota, and sponsored children from an Angel Tree Program. We have also signed up to cook breakfast for our tribal elders in the near future. Eventually, the members would like to help the younger generation form an AIBL chapter. This is truly community stewardship in action!

Along with participating in AIBL, I am currently the student council vice-president. One goal we strive to achieve is raising money for student activities. To do so, we plan gatherings that include not only the students, but also their family members. For instance, we have organized family movie nights, a spring-break picnic and game day, and a Christmas party at which Santa played games with the children. With all the time classes consume, and even perhaps the stress that academics creates, the student council likes to encourage "fun time." In many American Indian communities, when one member goes to college the whole family becomes a part of the experience. Hence, creating time for families to enjoy fellowship is essential to our success in higher education.

I know that at times in our lives it is tough to lead. Sometimes we do not want to sacrifice our personal comforts for the larger common good. However, we need to remember that not stepping-up to serve would be selfish; it does not exemplify the importance of family, of community, or of supporting all our relations. This lack of care and responsibility is not the example that I would want to show my children. We still look to our elders for advice and leadership to guide us along our life ways. We need to remember that these elders, grandparents, mothers, and fathers have made sacrifices for us in the past, and they will continue to do so to ensure that we all thrive. So, leadership is an ongoing journey in which we all have the opportunity, and privilege, to engage.

Many different words can be used to define leaders and their leadership skills; however, the one characteristic I see as important is *actions*. A person's actions tell others a lot about what leadership means. I have seen good leaders guide others with graciousness. They work hard to listen and to act in a manner that doesn't harm, but instead builds relations. Another important element of leadership that we should never forget is to be respectful not only to ourselves, but to the person or people who choose to follow our lead. Good leaders should not only listen to their followers, they should also hear what the followers have to say. Good leaders have a responsibility to take into account the beliefs, the culture, and the morals of their constituents. One of the best qualities of a leader is the ability to sacrifice one's own needs for the good of the whole group. The work of leadership never stops because we must always remember to inspire, guide, and act upon our words. As a mother and as a leader in my community, I know that I must always show the younger people that we can be self-determined, we can be lifelong learners, and, if we are interconnected, we can become stronger.

In closing, I would like to say: be true, respectful, and committed to the action(s) that you have chosen. Anyone can listen, but it takes a great leader to hear the needs and wants of their followers and to lead by example. May *gitchimanido* (the Creator) be with all of you every day.

Chapter 13

A Journey Home: Did We Ever Leave?

Jeremy Garcia

> *"I am so glad you decided to go to school."*
> *"We need you to get that education."*
> *"We need more of our children to leave to attain an education*
> *so they can come back and work among our people."*

These statements echo across our indigenous communities. I have heard them, and I'm sure that you, my peers, have heard them as well. It is empowering to hear such words and reassuring that we have great support to begin our journeys beyond our homelands—journeys that will embrace and challenge our minds, hearts, and endurance. The support, however, can be a double-edged sword. Along with the support comes the question of whether or not we'll return to our homeland, and if we do return, who will we have become?

There are *resting points* in our journeys that encourage us to rethink the footprints that we have left along the way. It is at these times that we, indigenous colleagues, sit together and talk about where we have been, what we have done, what we have seen, and where we hope to go. On occasion, the resting points entail dialogues about the time spent on our regular trips home; the vibrant laughter at new jokes our uncles share and the latest politics involving our tribal government; the sighs of relief that new schools are being built; the joy of new life welcomed into our families, the visits to spiritual places of prayer, and our appreciation that our communities continue to practice our traditions. Then, there are the times when we share our fears and sense of loss. We talk about the questions we were asked the last time we were home, questions like: "So how much longer will you be?" "When will you come home?" "You are coming home?" "Why do you choose to work there?" "Don't forget who you are, and don't become one of them." Well, my friends, this is just that time for us to sit and *talk story* (as they say in Hawai'i).

I graduated from high school in 1993. I was thrilled at the thought of leaving the Hopi community to live among those in the "outside" world. However, I have to admit that my initial thought was not centered on studying; it was centered on the basketball gym that was open until midnight. Although Hopis are teased about their height, I still boasted that I could take advantage of the courts. I was in paradise until I had my midterm report from Psychology 101. Let's just say I wasn't doing too well.

It was at that moment during my first year of undergraduate study that I realized the significance of taking responsibility for my own education. I had to make quick adjustments, as I knew how my parents would react to their son's asking to move back into his room (which was already filled with sewing materials and a new freezer). However, something greater happened as I began to think more deeply about attaining my degree so that I could return to my home community. I had no idea what to major in. I was drifting among the prerequisite courses all beginning students take.

It was my parents and sister (who are all teachers) who encouraged me to at least consider the option of becoming a teacher. Of course, they would entice me to think of the luxury of having the summers off, with pay. They really meant that such time off is valuable, as the responsibilities of our ranch and summer ceremonies are equally important. With family as my guiding force, I made the decision to enter the field of elementary education.

So, as time continued into my senior year, my hours spent at the gym decreased drastically, and time devoted to my studies increased considerably. Not only did the time I spent on my studies change, so also did my analysis of what it meant to be a teacher, a leader for Hopi children and indigenous youths. Eventually, I found myself developing a passion for indigenous education. I knew I would always be committed to my home community and the broader indigenous communities. I completed the teacher education program and planned on returning to Hopi. However, things changed.

I came upon an opportunity that encouraged me to rethink my return. My ambition to become an elementary teacher would need to be postponed because I had a chance to pursue an advanced degree at Michigan State University. This was something I had never anticipated. I struggled with the idea of traveling to a midwestern university. My wife and I were expecting a child, and my family and community were encouraging me to return home. How was I to decide between returning home and continuing my education? How could I resume my commitment to the cultural expectations of my family from such a great distance? Yet hadn't they said, "We need you to get that education"?

So there I was swirling among the questions, "So how much longer will you be?" "When will you come home? You are coming home?" Having thought long and hard, I made the decision to pursue my advanced degree. It was not an easy decision, and I vowed that this absence would be temporary. And so it was. I completed my Master's degree in 2000 and returned to Arizona to begin my career as an elementary teacher. But the return to Hopi would not be realized. While I was searching for a position, the perfect career opportunity for my wife presented itself near Phoenix, Arizona, and once again, I was faced with postponing my return to Hopi. At least, now I was within driving distance!

I found a teaching position with an indigenous community located near Phoenix. Life was great, as I had the chance to work with elementary children. As a first-grade teacher, I was ambitious about what I was going to teach. In addition to teaching, however, I found myself having a strong focus on increasing the level and types of parent involvement. I took the lead in facilitating the development of a parent and community involvement program for the elementary school. This was a great experience, so great that I was asked to continue this commitment full time. This school gained recognition among other indigenous schools for its progress in creating partnerships among the home, school, and community. I was privileged to represent this indigenous community at various conferences to share how we united on behalf of the children.

Here emerges the question, "Why do you choose to work *there?*" At educational conferences, I often met colleagues and tribal leaders from Hopi who teasingly remarked, "Why do you choose to work there? You should come back home. We need you to do the same thing for our Hopi schools." Even my family made such comments. I knew they made these comments, not to quarrel with the tribe I was serving, but to remind me that there were schools in Hopi I should not forget. In an odd way, it actually felt good that my home community had not forgotten me. They recognized what I had to offer, and they wanted to garner the same benefits. I saw this as a window of opportunity to give back to my home community by presenting on ways to address parent and community involvement among various Hopi schools.

So what happened next? Well, another opportunity crossed my path. As I *talk story* with you at this *resting point*, I accepted the offer to return to school to pursue my doctoral degree, once again in the Midwest. Oh, how I had to relive the questions from when I first left for Michigan State University. Only this time, there was an added comment by my *taaha* (uncle) Farron when I was back home for a ceremony. He commented, "Don't forget who you are, and don't become one of them." I thought, "Don't become one of them?" With a chuckle, he added, "Those white researchers ask too many questions." Often times our elders will make comments and leave it up to us to figure out their meaning. Well, knowing my *taaha*, and knowing where his support rests, he was not implying that I shouldn't go to school. Rather, he was telling me to always know where I come from and, most important, to be aware of how I had been taught to live in harmony with the Hopi ways. This is crucial as I begin to think about how research should be carried out in honor of our indigenous communities.

As an emerging leader in my community, I am away from home attending university to earn a doctoral degree, but my heart, my spirit, is at home. My effort to create more pathways for the future of Hopi and other indigenous students continues with my involvement in developing a program to support and honor future indigenous students at Purdue University.

I am striving to maintain a strong sense of self that remains committed to my cultural epistemologies and to stay connected to my family back home. I know that many of my peers who are living away from home are trying to do the same thing. This requires us to take care that we do not become strangers to our home communities, but instead, to work hard to sustain a constant, unwavering relationship with our families and extended families in those communities. Remaining connected to our physical homeland and to the ways of our people ensures that we will lead with the spirit of our ancestors.

I know I am not alone, because a Hopi colleague and emerging community leader, Darold Joseph, emphasized the importance of living and leading with our cultural foundations:

> I always faced questions. People always asked me "When are you coming home? We need people like you to lead our programs. But for me, it wasn't the time yet. I wanted to experience other things before I returned home. This didn't mean I didn't support my culture or my people. In my last position as a director, I found I was always thinking of the culture and language, even though we were servicing children or people who were not Hopi. I found that we still have to represent the importance of indigenous cultures and languages, no matter what indigenous community they are from. For instance, I had to advocate that we include the language and culture in our policy for our Native American students. Without that, they would have had greater challenges. So we always have to rely on our traditional teachings to help guide our thinking.
>
> (Personal communication, November 11, 2006)

Our journeys away from home begin with much enthusiasm and ambition. We are strangers on new horizons; our movements across multiple worlds are delicate and fragile as we walk lightly between boundaries, over borders, and through the fringes in order to join multiple worlds and thoughts. Over time, we find ourselves being transformed in these new cultural and academic spaces. I have crafted a letter to my community members to help them realize that I have never left home and that I (and perhaps you too) hold deeply and respectfully our culture and commitment to the future of our children.

> Dear Community Members,
>
> You asked me, "When are you coming home? Our Tribe needs people like you who have their degrees to return. Why are you choosing to work outside of the community?" In response to your questions, I am honored to know that you acknowledge my accomplishments and have expressed your interest in my return to contribute to tribal goals and initiatives. Although I left, I assure you that my time and energy are consistently revolving around the tribal goals from my position. For instance, my role at the university is to contribute to the development of a stronger foundation for current and future indigenous students. Increasing the number of indigenous scholars with their respective degrees will certainly offer best practice and leadership across our communities.
>
> Such questions encourage me to consider whether or not I have really

left. Your questions come to me at a pivotal time when fellow indigenous colleagues, living outside our physical "home," have acknowledged their reliance on their cultural ways of knowing to guide their thinking and actions. We are finding our spiritual home.

Please know that this is not to indicate that I do not want to return home. There is always going to be a need for leaders to collectively advocate for the survival and prosperity of indigenous peoples from wherever we stand in this world. Although I am still on my journey, eventually I will physically return home; but please know that culturally and spiritually I have never left.

In the end, at this resting point, I know that I am part of a delicate partnership of survival for our indigenous communities. My grandparents, parents, aunts, uncles, brothers, sisters, the land, water, and animals have nourished my spirit to always keep our cultural ways of knowing and acting at the heart of reasoning. The reciprocity is depicted in serving as an advocate for our people from where I stand in place and time. I assure you I will return home, but it should be known that my heart and spirit have never left.

Chapter 14

From Indian to Odawa: A Journey Toward Understanding Identity

Matthew VanAlstine

The contemporary world poses many challenges and opportunities for indigenous youths as they struggle to find cultural identity. The phrase *walking in two worlds* is often used to describe indigenous people who function within contemporary society, while at the same time embracing indigenous culture, language, and values. The challenge for indigenous youths is to retain their culture and resist full acculturation to the values and culture held by contemporary society. When indigenous youths begin to lose sight of their culture, they lose their balance, they lose their spirit, and as a result they lose their self-esteem about their cultural identity.

I would like to share a story about an Indian youth's journey toward becoming an Odawa adult. This journey was filled with mistakes, determination, love, hate, ignorance, and wisdom. The focus of this story is not on negativity, stereotypes, and racism, but rather it is about overcoming circumstances to find comfort, purpose, and peace within one's cultural identity. I would like to share a part of my story.

As a youth I remember driving to weekend powwows in my grandmother's Indian car, a red station wagon, with a speedometer that never worked. Of course, she was constantly being pulled over for speeding, but somehow she always seemed to escape getting a ticket. I spent my summers on the powwow trail, attending various Indian summer camps, and during the school year attending various events at the local Indian center. My grandmother had 12 children, which meant that I had numerous cousins to interact with at our many family gatherings. I learned about what it meant to be a family from a cultural perspective (I had eight moms) and that I was Indian. Although I was being exposed to Indian people and culture, at the time I didn't fully understand my cultural identity other than that I was different from the other students at my school.

As a youth, I attended more schools than I can remember, and at every school my younger brother and I were the only Indians. During the week, I was the Indian kid and different, but at weekends I was with people who looked like me, and I felt normal. At my predominantly white high school, my nickname was the very unoriginal "chief." I always said it didn't bother me and that I thought it was an honor because chiefs were the leaders of their people. In reality, though, I didn't have a choice about the nickname; I didn't know how to articulate the negative effects of stereotyping and how it made me feel. All I knew was that I was very good at football, was even named team captain, and that was how I was accepted. When I was a senior, during football practice one day, a freshman told me I didn't know what I was talking about because I was a (bleeping) Indian. So even though I excelled at this sport and classmates liked me for it, to some people I was still just an Indian.

Many indigenous youths learn very quickly what it means to walk in two worlds. In the indigenous world, you feel at home and normal, but in the contemporary world there are many moments to remind you that you are "just an Indian." Indigenous youths quickly learn that it is easier to succeed and fit into the contemporary society when they adopt its value system. Indigenous youths often face a choice of hiding or turning their backs on their culture, or being outcasts in contemporary society. Either way, an unfortunate possibility and frequent result of either decision is a dramatic decline in self-esteem and self-worth. As a result, indigenous youths need leadership and inspiration; they need to see examples of indigenous people walking confidently in two worlds.

My grades in high school were average, and in fact my post-high school plan was to enter the military, rather than to apply to college. Yet I graduated from high school and even managed to be accepted by two universities of my choice. I remember the look of surprise on the faces of some of my teachers when they found out what university I would be attending. I decided to apply to college for two reasons: all of my friends were going, and my mother had received her bachelor's degree (at the time, she was the only one in my large extended family to have done so). If it had not been for my mom's believing in me, I would not have applied to college because I'm not sure I had enough belief in myself. Indigenous youths need support, encouragement, and every now and then a reminder that they are smart, talented, and valuable.

It was during my undergraduate education that I began to realize the value and importance of my culture. My involvement with the native student group brought to my attention how other native students were struggling with and working through the stress and demands of walking in two worlds. I graduated with a bachelor's degree in psychology and a few years later entered graduate school. In my graduate assistantship, I was fortunate to be a part of the Native American Higher Education Initiative (NAHEI) and had the opportunity to work with and learn from some incredible established and emerging indigenous scholars. It was during this process that I was able to see how my elders and contemporaries managed the difficult task of walking in two worlds while maintaining and upholding their cultural traditions, beliefs, and values. Through my interactions in higher education with other indigenous scholars and leaders, I was able to reflect on and understand the role and purpose of indigenous mentors and leaders. It was during this time in my life that I began to develop my own personal mission and commitment to helping indigenous youths regain their promise, confidence, and identity through education. Indigenous youths and young adults need the support, advice, and stories of adults to help guide them through their struggles and concerns.

My professional career led me into teaching at a tribal community college and directing a Native American Programs office at a mainstream university. Through my work as an instructor, I was able to hear the voices, concerns, and struggles of other native students as they endeavored to find their place in both worlds. Using what I had learned from my elders and mentors, I did my best to share with them what knowledge I had and assure them that there is a place for culturally centered individuals in higher education. As a director of a Native American Programs office, my personal charge was to engage native students in higher education and expose them to the rich and meaningful histories and culture of indigenous peoples. I framed the programs, presentations, and my advising around the core idea of service to native communities, self-confidence as indigenous individuals, and creation of an environment that will be beneficial to successive generations.

Through my programs and interaction with indigenous youths, I often have heard about how students felt incapable of attending college. I have also seen how learning their language and history sparked excitement and confidence in them. It is a challenge for indigenous youths to walk proudly in two worlds; however, there is also an opportunity for growth, self-actualization, and finding meaning and purpose in one's life. It is the responsibility of indigenous people who walk comfortably in both worlds to share their stories, hope, and encouragement with our youths so that they, too, can find their way. As adults we must remain patient with our youths and fill them with our stories, so that when they are ready to learn they will have already been exposed to our cultural teachings.

Currently, I am pursuing a doctorate degree in Higher and Adult Learning and Education. I know who I am, where I came from, and, most important, where I am going. I've learned to understand the idea that I am not an Indian at all, but I am Anishinaabe, I am Odawa. Leadership can begin only when individuals know who they are, where they came from, and who helped them along the way. Leadership is about accepting your past, being humble enough to learn from all living things in life, and taking responsibility for your future and generations yet to come. I will acknowledge my ancestors, my elders, and my culture by taking what I have learned and sharing it with indigenous youths. I will listen to them along the way, I will challenge them to pursue their dreams, and I will do my part in making it acceptable and rightful to be Anishinaabe, Odawa, indigenous in any world.

Chapter 15

Passing the Torch: Preserving the Flame

Teresa Magnuson

A Mentor's Oath
I am answering the call to leadership, I will challenge the process, inspire
vision, enable others to act, model the way, and encourage the heart.
(*Passing the Torch: Preserving the Flame* brochure, no author)

This fall I was invited to attend a women's leadership-recognition ceremony entitled *Passing the Torch: Preserving the Flame*. The ceremony was a multicultural event that identified past, present, and future female community leaders. The individuals selected for the ceremony were those who have demonstrated a commitment to cultural preservation, community development, and the pursuit of social justice. These established leaders were asked to select emerging female leaders of their ethnic group to recognize and symbolically "pass the torch." The seasoned leaders were honored for their achievements and challenged to continue their good work with a focus on preparing and mentoring the next generation of leaders. The ceremony was a reflection of achievement and a source of inspiration.

During the ceremony I listened to women from cultures around the world speak on their interpretation of leadership. The undertones of their words contained love and altruism. The speakers alluded to love for their people and culture and to the importance of the act of giving to support their community. Several Anishinabek women were present for the ceremony, myself included. For the Anishinabek, love is one of our seven fundamental teachings. The gift of giving is a cornerstone of our values system. Love for and from our creator, our ancestors, our people, and for the future generations guides our values. Through the seven grandfather teachings—love, wisdom, respect, bravery, honesty, humility, and truth—we encourage acts of giving such as mentorship, demonstrate leadership, and ensure the strength of future generations.

The closing ceremony of the "Passing the Torch" experience ended in a shared chant: "My spirit soars and takes me higher. Here is where I keep my fire." This chant resounded with me because I believe that mentors have the power (and perhaps the responsibility) to recognize and light the fire in others by showing interest, igniting passion, and providing guidance and support. For example, as a student of indigenous education and graduate assistant for Dr. Maenette Benham, I am honored to have been given opportunities to advance my learning and understanding of indigenous education and leadership by traveling to tribal/native communities, meeting and speaking with renowned native scholars, and developing an indigenous-scholar network. Working with and learning from Dr. Benham has provided me with learning opportunities that I would not have had otherwise; it has given me a new voice. I have broadened my understanding and developed my thinking in the area of indigenous education, specifically language revitalization, to become an advocate for my community.

Indeed, Maenette's guidance, support, and encouragement exemplify the positive influence a mentoring relationship can have. Recently, a new teacher, Janis Fairbanks, has entered my life. Janis has helped me realize my spiritual obligation to my own spirit, *gzheminido* (the creator), and the world around me. Through her kind nature, I am reminded to treat people with love and honesty, all the while being courageous and bold in my beliefs. Janis has shown me that, in times of adversity, I must rely on my spiritual strength and know that continuing to treat people with righteousness is paramount. Another prominent figure in my professional development is Dr. Susan Applegate-Krouse. During my undergraduate career and as a participant in the McNair/SROP Scholar's Program, Susan guided me through my first individual research project, supported my pursuit of graduate studies, and encouraged me to develop relationships with native faculty nationally. Each of these women has given me a gift of herself. Each has given me a gift of her energy, her knowledge, and her spirit.

Maenette, Janis, Susan, and other scholars have given me strength and motivation to continue my higher education studies as well as learn my mother tongue language. Mentors often give of themselves, their time, and materials to help prepare learners. Mentoring is essential to developing leadership that is culturally sound, generous, and enlightened; however, we need to understand that mentoring is also a reciprocal process. That is, whereas the mentor's role is to give volume and shape to our voice(s) as well as to help us ignite the fires of our passion, the mentee must commit to being open to learn, to take action, and to pass this along. A mentee must be ready to step up.

A Mentee's Promise to "Step up!"
I will search for opportunities to change the status quo. I will experiment and take risks. I believe that I can make a difference. I will breathe life into visions because I see the exciting future possibilities. I will listen candidly to your wisdom and insight, lessons you have learned, as I prepare to receive the torch from you.
(*Passing the Torch: Preserving the Flame* brochure, no author)

This is an exciting time, as many of our native leaders are beginning to pass the torch to the next generation of community/tribal leaders. Young adults and youths are being recognized for their work and offered new opportunities to practice what they have learned. Within my tribal community, our elders are watching emerging scholars develop new skills and traits, and are asking us to take on important responsibilities and roles. Last spring, my older sister, Michaelina, was elected as our tribe's youngest councilwoman. And people recognize that, like my sister, I am ambitious, learned, and committed to advancing opportunities for our Nation. We are being encouraged to take on many new leadership roles within the community. It is our responsibility to be true to ourselves, to know our calling, and to perform honorably in those roles.

These new opportunities and challenges are exhilarating! I feel a strong sense of self- and cultural esteem as well as purpose, but at the same time, my excitement is tempered with self-doubt and fear. This is the moment when the lessons of my mentors help me the most. They have told me that our elders would not ask me to do something I was not prepared to do and that, in the end, whether or not I meet the challenge is my choice.

Let me repeat this: whether or not we step up and meet the challenge is our choice! Here is the lesson, the reciprocal action: are you willing to be uncomfortable, to be brave, to step up?

Last spring, I joined our university's immersion Ojibwe Language House committee. During the initial meetings I began to explore and discover my role as a leading contributor to the group. At first, I didn't know if I had anything of worth to offer to a group of Ph.D.s and former instructors. I didn't know if my opinions would receive the same validity as those of some of the group's more experienced members. I was also concerned about the possibility of having to disagree with committee members whom I considered my teachers and elders. I was the lone voice of the students for whom we were developing a language program. These self-doubts occupied my thoughts until I heard the voice of my mentors: "You are the only person on this committee traveling globally to study indigenous immersion programs. You are not being asked to do something you cannot do. It is your choice to engage." My initial trepidation dissipated when I realized I was prepared and that my commitment was important. Indeed, my international study of the subject has brought unique insights to the work of this committee. I am a valuable member; I belong.

When we, emerging leaders and scholars, are asked to step up to leadership roles, we need to remember that we were chosen for a reason. Our perspective and energy, our passion and commitment, our talent and promise are recognized by our community leaders and elders. Stepping up signals that we acknowledge and are respectful of the lessons from our mentors and elders, the diverse educational pathways we have walked, and our many opportunities and accomplishments. As mentees, emerging leaders and scholars, we will have to maneuver the shifting seas of new expectations as we locate our own voices in and across both local and global roles.

I know that I/we are all members of multiple interconnecting communities; therefore, we are responsible for each other. I am responsible for helping my family, my clan, and my Nation. That responsibility begins with opening my heart and mind to the seasoned leaders (my mentors) who guide my footsteps and support me in gracious ways. In turn, I have a responsibility to learn, to step up, and to continue the cycle of reciprocity by doing the same thing for a new generation of emerging leaders and scholars. Mentorship is an important component of leadership. We all have the ability to affect the lives of others—each of us has the capacity to act as a catalyst for positive change in others. I urge readers to learn and to love with abandon, to give and to receive selflessly. Strive to ignite passion in others. Be brave for your sake and for the sake of your community. Pass the torch, preserve the flame.

Chapter 16

Awakening the Power Within

Lai-Lani Ovalles

We are born with two instinctual fears: the fear of falling and the fear of loud noises. Everything else is a learned response. As an elementary school student, I was terrified of speaking in front of my classmates. This fear intensified in middle school, when my family moved from Hawai'i to the mainland United States; there I was teased for being the new kid with the funny accent, exotic features, and dark skin. In high school we returned to Hawai'i, and my fear of speaking in front of my classmates grew so intense that my eyes would water every time a teacher called on me in class. At home and with friends, I was vocal and energetic, but in class I became silent and lethargic. I learned how to be fearful because of the isolation I felt in school, my lack of self-confidence, and the belief that I had nothing important to say. My voice was shackled by a covert racism instructing me to remain quiet and timid, conforming to the status quo. *Don't cause trouble, don't speak up. No one will listen to you.* I became a spectator, voiceless and ineffective in defying the forces feeding my fears.

Beneath the insecurities, I was disgruntled with my cowardice and yearned for change. As I have learned from elders, we transform ourselves when we discover our selves and our responsibility to each other. My journey of self-discovery and self-determination became the catalyst in the development of my voice, my cultural and spiritual power. This is the story of how we are able to move through personal pain and trepidation by representing something larger than our selves, our culture, our languages, and our interconnectedness. We let loose the chains of oppression when we become the voice for our people, when we speak for justice, when we inspire hope in others.

Today I work with multicultural students in middle and high schools to engage them in transforming their communities and schools. Together we learn how to confront racial injustice, violence, sexism, and consumerism by developing nonviolence leadership skills. We develop ways to build multicultural partnerships to confront these issues. Through a process of reading, writing, and speaking, students must overcome their fears and create an environment of trust and mutual respect. In every group, I encounter similar feelings of trepidation, resistance, and outright refusal to speak in front of others. It is a deep-seated pattern that we must uproot, unlearn, and replace with confidence and belief in ourselves and in others.

Many leaders of social-justice movements speak of the process of discovering themselves during the most despairing times. They speak of the interconnectedness of humanity. Each of us concurrently is a unique individual and a self that is of others. We come from a lineage, we are someone's daughter, son, grandchild, brother, sister, friend, neighbor, classmate. It is in the realization that we belong to something larger than ourselves that we find power. Throughout history, young people have been involved from the outset in social-justice movements. Youths in the United States participated in nonviolent actions and filled the jail cells during the height of the civil rights movement. The youths of South Africa marched tirelessly against apartheid, helping to release Nelson Mandela from prison and propelling him into the presidency. In indigenous struggles worldwide, many young people are actively reviving cultural traditions and languages, and fighting for sovereignty. These young people have awakened the power within to engage in social change around them.

Studying the history of social change, we find that empowerment is not restricted to the elite or the enlightened. We find that leadership comes through finding the thread that connects us to each other—across borders, cultures, religions, and beliefs. A high school assignment to research and present our family history helped me find that power. As I spoke about my *kupuna*, my ancestors, and their intricate intersection of cultures, customs, and experience, I gained confidence in myself. I am honored to belong to a family, community, and history. My teacher reminded me that when we speak, we speak for others. In sharing my family's stories, I found *mana* and the voices of my people speaking through me. At that moment, I glimpsed my connection to a legacy of struggle in Hawai'i, from mountain to sea, from the indigenous peoples to immigrants, from colonization to sovereignty. I accept my responsibility to remember the stories and pass them on with *aloha*. The thread of connection was laid bare for me to weave into my own journey and work.

Power, properly understood, is the ability to achieve purpose. Power is latent, like a seed, in all of us. It sprouts when the elements necessary to promote growth are present. Because we can't see power, that doesn't mean it ceases to exist. Indigenous knowledge teaches us that a seed struggles through dirt and rock to grow. This process does not occur without assistance from water, air, and light, nor is it painless and purposeless. The young people with whom I work blossom when they access their cultural power to speak up and represent something larger than themselves. They speak about their heritage, for racial unity, for justice, and to inspire others to participate in the work to build community. As the youths develop their voices and ability to organize for peace with justice, they are embodying the power of their ancestral roots to achieve their purpose.

My emergence into leadership roles did not come about without discomfort. Each time I find myself doubting my capabilities or qualifications, I remember the question, "If not you, then who? If not now, then when?" I teach this mantra to young scholars when they confront their fear of stepping up to leadership roles in their families, schools, and communities. We might not always have the perfect words to say or write, but it is through the humble act of moving forward in spite of obstacles and frightening situations that we gain courage. I tell my students that the most essential part of speaking is listening to their hearts in order to find truth. The fear of leading and speaking may stay with us, but we will no longer simply surrender to circumstances. As I encourage and support these young warriors to discover their voices, I continue to find my own. Our voices resonate in unison as we march, chanting messages of peace. We collectively echo the voices of our ancestors. We represent their hopes and dreams for the continuation of our culture.

To live in harmony, we must become the link to the legacy of those who struggled before us and those who will come after us. We must take the teachings of our collective cultures and prepare the next generation to undertake the work that remains undone. These powerful lessons that I've learned from elders have increased my capacity to love. We cannot expect young people to do what we are unwilling to do—to transform ourselves through confronting our fears and injustice. With all the violence and destruction occurring worldwide, we know that each of us who cares about life has something important to say. As indigenous educators, we must constantly find and create opportunities to partner with and learn from people of other cultures. We live and work in diverse environments. We must consistently and effectively train our youths for leadership roles. We must actively advocate for our youths to speak on behalf of the common good. It is up to each of us to awaken to the power within, so that we may arouse the power of all of us to emancipate ourselves from fear and for peace with justice.

I still feel nervous whenever I have to speak in front of small or large groups of people. However, I no longer let my fear deny me the opportunity to connect with others, to organize, and to learn. We must share our cultural stories with each other. I share my stories with *aloha* with students to exemplify the process that can conquer all fears—the transformative power of love. Through love, we can commit to the struggle for justice, self-determination, and peace.

Chapter 17
What's Next?

Thoughts from Maenette K.P. Ah Nee-Benham

My experiences among American Indian brothers and sisters have taught me many important lessons. Foremost among them is the importance of the medicine wheel. What most people do not know is that the Plains people have used the medicine wheel in the Big Horn Mountains in South Dakota for thousands of years as a place for prayer. It is a circle composed of large stones, shaped like a wheel, which symbolizes the life cycle of all native peoples. The medicine wheel teaches personal balance, wholeness with family and interconnectedness with community, and responsibility for nature. It values personal volition, reflection on one's own hidden gifts, and living up to the vision of one's native beliefs and values. The medicine wheel has been telling the truth about life for centuries. That is to say, to meet the challenge of the leadership promise, one must reflect upon and act in the sacred ways of the medicine wheel, for leadership is never random nor accidental. It is always necessary and interconnected, and can lead to a time of promised wholeness.

Using the lessons of the medicine wheel, educational scholars, teachers, leaders, and policymakers can think and act more boldly, more inclusively, and more proactively to build healthy communities and healthy schools. The articulation of this model must begin with the oral-narrative truth that comes from the elders, embraces the family unit, and moves forward to include the whole community. The first step is to think deeply and thoroughly about the philosophical and spiritual constructs of one's culture and language, and then clearly articulate the guiding principles for learning that are grounded in the community's unique native language, history, and culture. This first step shapes the soul of an organization. The next section of this statement expands on the structure (the business) of an engaged educational organization.

To do the work that we each do in a culturally relevant way means to come from the spirit and commitment to do good works in the real places of our communities. Our elder for the *In Our Mother's Voice* project, Dr. Henrietta Mann, Endowed Chair of American Indian Studies at Montana State University, shared with us the story of the frog:

> *The frog is born and matures in the water. In this place, the frog learns to breathe, to survive, to navigate between both the pleasures of water life and its dangers. Then the frog moves to the land. There too frogs must be cognizant of things around them. The wise frog moves comfortably between these two places.*

So, the frog teaches us that in order for our indigenous children and youths to be proudly "indigenous in a global world," our schools must engage families and community members in culturally appropriate ways to define pathways of learning. It is clear from our work that healthy indigenous school systems and communities are linked together with a special form of leadership, leadership that each of you possesses, which comprises:

- compassion and spiritual knowing that embraces the cultural and historical contexts of indigenous knowledge, leading, and learning and teaching;
- goodness of spirit and mind, which locates action in relationships between self and the other;
- belief and vision that expands ideas of usefulness with collectivity and connectivity;
- good words that link language, thought, and action, and inspire self-determination and sovereignty;
- respect for place and time that *mālama i ka honua* cares for the land and traditional ways of knowing.

Thus, it is our challenge to build indigenous educational systems that embody the following elements:

- an organizational mission that leads to sovereignty, engagement, and empowerment beginning with an individual's spiritual and cultural, emotional, physical, and cognitive strength and self-esteem;
- organizational policies and practices that embrace interrelated disciplines, including the humanities, professions, social sciences, and natural sciences, so that learning is balanced and equitable, and develops high ethical standards;
- organizational structures that support and challenge the learner/teacher to design solutions and actions that address social, political, cultural, and economic issues that affect community wellness, the family and tribe/clans, and the land, water, and natural resources that sustain life.

Recommended Resources

Allen, P.G. (1992) *The Sacred Hoop: Recovering the Feminine in American Indian Traditions*. Boston, MA: Beacon Press.

Barth, R.S. (2001) *Learning by Heart*. San Francisco, CA: Jossey-Bass.

Basic Call to Consciousness, edited by Akwesasne Notes (limited printing). Contact Kahniakehaka Nation, Akwesasne Mohawk Territory Mohawk Nation, P.O.Box 366 via Roseveltown, NY, 13683–0196.

Bateson, M.C. (1994). *Peripheral Visions: Learning Along the Way*. New York: HarperCollins Publisher.

Benham, M. & Stein, W. (eds) (2003) *The Renaissance of American Indian Higher Education: Capturing the Dream*. Mahwah, NJ: Lawrence Erlbaum Associates, Inc.

Benham, M., with Cooper, J. (eds) (2000) *Indigenous Educational Models for Contemporary Practice: In Our Mother's Voice*. Mahwah, NJ: Lawrence Erlbaum Associates, Inc.

Brayboy, Bryan (2004) "Hiding in the ivy: American Indian students and visibility in elite educational settings." *Harvard Educational Review*, 7(2), 125–152.

Cajete, G. (1994) *Look to the Mountain: An Ecology of Indigenous education*. Durango, CO: Kivaki Press.

Coelho, Paolo (2003) *Warriors of the Light: A Manual*. New York, Harper Collins.

Farber, Joseph M. (1997) *Ancient Hawaiian Fishponds: Can Restoration Succeed on Molokai?* Encinitas, California, Neptune House Publication. Published for Pacific Islands Development Program, Honolulu, Hawai'i.

Friere, P. (1993) *Pedagogy of the Oppressed*. New York: Continuum.

Harjo, J. (2002) *How We Became Human: New and Selected Poems 1975–2001*. New York: W.W. Horton.

Harjo, J. & Bird, G. (edited 1997) *Reinventing the Enemy's Language: Contemporary Native Women's Writing of North America*. New York: W.W. Norton.

Iroquois Woodland Favorites, Phyllis Eileen Williams Bardeau. Contact the Seneca Nation Education Department (limited printing) www.sni.org.

King, M.L. Jr. (1967) *Where Do We Go From Here: Chaos or Community?* New York: Harper & Row.

LaDuke, W. (1999) *All Our Relations: Native Struggles for Land and Life*. Cambridge, MA: South End Press.

LeBeau, P.R. (2005) *Re-Thinking Michigan Indian History*. East Lansing, MI: Michigan State University Press.

Mankiller, W. and Wallis, M. (1994) *Mankiller: A Chief and Her People*. New York: St. Martin's Press.

Mankiller, Wilma (2004) *Everyday Is a Good Day: Reflections of Contemporary Indigenous Women*. Golden, Colorado: Fulcrum Publishing.

McCarty, T. (2002) *A Place to be Navajo: Rough Rock and the Struggle for Self-determination in Indigenous Schooling*. Mahwah, NJ: Lawrence Erlbaum.

Mihesuah, D. A. & Wilson, A. C. (eds) (2004) *Indigenizing the Academy: Transforming Scholarship and Empowering Communities*. Lincoln: University of Nebraska Press

Tippeconnic, J., Fox, M. J., Lowe, S.C., & McClellan, G.S. (eds) (2005) "Serving Native American Students [Special issue]." *New Directions for Student Services*, 109.

Wilson, W. A. & Yellow Bird, M. (2005). *For Indigenous Eyes Only: A Decolonization Handbook*. Sante Fe: School of American Research Press.

Websites to Visit

KQED The Digital Storytelling Initiative. http://dsi.kqed.org/

Llano Grande Center for Research and Development. www.llanogrande.org

The Center for Digital Storytelling. www.storycenter.org

University of Hawai'i at Hilo, Ka Haka 'Ula O Ke'elikōlani College of Hawaiian Language. http://www.uhh.hawai'i.edu/academics/hawn/

PRISM (Portal Resources for Indiana Science and Mathematics). http://www.rose-prism.org/moodle/

Project Kahea Loko: Teacher's Guide to Hawaiian Fishponds. http://ulukau.org/cgi-bin/cbook?l=haw

PART III

INDIGENIZING ACCOUNTABILITY AND ASSESSMENT

Basket as Metaphor: *Weaving the Basket*

Samuel Suina

We pray to thank our ancestors for their guidance. In weaving a basket, when we come to a place where we are having difficulty, we call upon our grandmother and grandfather spirits to help us to get through that challenge. We acknowledge that we are never alone but that those who taught us the art of basket making are with us.

We ask ourselves, "How strong is our basket?" As we build and sustain our indigenous communities on the foundation of our culture and language, we need to continually ask ourselves, "How true are we to what we're teaching?" Interlacing the extending leadership branches with the weave of our lattice brings form to our basket and requires us to check and recheck our work so that we maintain the harmony and integrity of the plaiting.

> *Weave four together then two at a time without tying with string*
> *Weave always in a circle, coming back to where you began*
> *Take care not to pull quickly or sharply*
> *The weaving branch gives support to others*
> *As you weave the base gets tighter, stronger.*

Repeated reexamination of our work is a metaphor for the important tasks of accountability and assessment. This is essential work that will sustain us. Like the baskets that are used to carry our food into our ceremonies, assessments that are skillfully and thoughtfully constructed can bring our work into the twenty-first century. And remember, it is important to have good thoughts while you are weaving.

Weaving the Basket

Chapter 18

A Story Shared

Katherine Tibbetts, Susan Faircloth and Maenette K.P. Ah Nee-Benham, with Tamarah Pfeiffer

In November 2006 at the *Kuʻi Ka Lono* conference in Honolulu, Hawaiʻi, a group of middle school students stood tremulously in front of a room packed with unfamiliar adults, perhaps 80 to 100 people. The children were there to share the story of their efforts to perpetuate the knowledge and history of a place with special significance to Native Hawaiians. This was to be a demonstration of their learning.

The place the children described was soon to be the location of a handful of million-dollar homes meant for people from backgrounds much different from those of these *keiki ʻo ka ʻāina* (children of the land). The children told the story of their research into the history of this place, their time spent experiencing it, their heartbreak that it would be transformed for another use, and their fear that the knowledge of the historical and cultural significance of this place would be lost. The children gained confidence and their poise increased as the story was told.

When the storytelling was completed, a woman raised her hand and asked the children whether they had lobbied against the change in land use. This was something they obviously had not done and that would not be successful at this late stage in the development process. Some of us gasped, stunned by her action. What was she doing? Why was she "making the children wrong" in such a public way? The adults accompanying the children intervened, providing more background about the sale and development of the land, the struggles within the community over the development, and the purpose of the activities in which the children had been engaged. Then, another woman rephrased the original question inquiring again what role the children played in the protest against the proposed land use. The children were again bewildered and outwardly embarrassed. The teachers again responded emphasizing the cultural as well as political and economic lessons the children learned, and that the students did not participate in any lobbying activity.

Soon after the teachers explained the work of the students (for the second time) a Native Hawaiian *kupuna* (elder) stood. He spoke directly to the children at some length. He described the importance of what they had done for their ancestors, themselves, their community, and future generations. He thanked them for all they had done. The children smiled and one could see their pride and love quickly diminish the shame and fear created by the two audience members. The *kupuna* had made it right for them.

The next day, I had an opportunity to speak with the *kupuna*. I thanked him for what he had done for the children. He said that all he had done was to fulfill his responsibility as a *kupuna* to protect and nurture the growth of our *keiki*. In short, he fulfilled his accountability to the present and the future by offering the *keiki* a strengths-based assessment of their performance. But he went beyond an assessment of their immediate efforts and products. By situating these in a larger social and historical context (including the future), he reinforced for them the meaning of their work.

Still Strong, Still Here! Making Visible Indigenous Accountability and Assessment

As previous sections of this book have clearly demonstrated, our peoples are still strong, still here despite a campaign of more than 200 years to force the assimilation of the indigenous peoples living within the boundaries of the United States through public education and other policies (National Indian Education Association, 2003). Many, if not all, of us have been educated in a system focused on the production of cogs for industrial America and influenced by the old New England discipline of "I don't need to tell you when you've done something right, you already know that. I need to tell you when you do something wrong."

This is different from what the *kupuna* in Katherine's story was teaching. Indeed, our children and youth must engage in dynamic, critical studies that are rigorous as well as teach life-long skills, but they also must be taught that they are good people and that they each have a responsibility to their ancestors, to their communities, and to the generations yet to come. Being held accountable for the spirit of our Native peoples requires that we make our educative systems and practices our own.

The sections leading up to this one have addressed strategies for indigenizing our educational system: making our educational philosophy, pedagogy, and system our own. Just as indigenous education is based on a holistic view of the world and deep appreciation of interconnectedness, so our perspectives on an indigenized educational system must consider the connections among all its elements. One of these elements comprises the outcomes, methods, and tools by which our schools, educational programs, and students are judged to be successful. These aspects are not inert and culture-free, so, we must assume accountability, responsibility for the ways in which our schools, educational programs, and students are assessed to ensure that these reflect the value systems, goals, and traditional practices and knowledge of our unique Native communities.

Why is this so important? Tamarah Pfeiffer shared her story of getting to truth at Rough Rock Community School:

A recent teacher in-service of about 200 professionals at Rough Rock Community School (RRCS) focused on the topic of "TRUTH" and [asked the question,] "What is the Rough Rock Community School mission?" As the day opened, we were asked to think about our school mission, which is based on the Diné Philosophy of *Saah Naaghai Bikei Hoozho*. To facilitate this process, a Navajo wedding basket containing a feather, corn pollen, a pencil, a book, and an iPod was presented to the group. We were asked, "What is the purpose of these items?"

As people moved into groups we heard beautiful stories about how each part of the basket is a living representation of our students and ourselves. The feather story was the most profound and illustrated just what kind of place Rough Rock is. "It is a symbol of protection," said an elder. "It represents and guards everything in the universe." The feather helps guide people into their own safety and understanding of the world around them. The corn pollen (*Taa'da'diin*) is a symbol of the protection that then gives one the path to follow, all based on Beauty Way thought and actions.

We were all spellbound. The stories went on for almost 30 minutes, and by the end there was not a dry eye in the room. We are a community that takes adequate yearly progress (AYP) seriously, but we also know that we have our own roots placed in Diné thought and practice of language, culture, and traditions. I believe the strength and courage of the school come from our staff's commitment to language and culture. Every day we have students participating in traditional sweats, traditional prayers, and traditional counseling. This daily foundation helps our students stay focused on who they are and why they are here at RRCS.

At the same time, we are highly proactive in creating authentic assessments that help define what students can do, rather than what deficiencies they have been told they have. This is a long and detail-oriented process that both outside evaluators and Navajo Nation-related assessment individuals realize is needed and desired by all. In this respect, RRHS is doing something different. We are starting to see that our students need to have many measures that show what they know. What better tool is there than one that is founded in Navajo language and culture?

This section is about what educators at Rough Rock and other Native schools are doing, that is, indigenizing accountability and assessment to support the well-being of indigenous communities through education. What do we mean by the terms *accountability* and *assessment?* The Miriam-Webster online dictionary defines accountability as the obligation or willingness to accept responsibility for one's actions. Assessment, with roots in the Latin *assessus* (to sit beside, assist in the office of a judge), is the process of determining the importance, size, or value of something. But these concepts have older and deeper meanings in our Native traditions.

Paul Boyer (2003), in his work to describe accountability and assessment in and for Tribal Colleges and Universities, situated both ideas within the local, historic community context of a Native peoples, and not in the context of external accreditors, state legislatures, and federal agencies. He describes a multi-layered, highly reciprocal model of accountability, which "begins with a sense of personal responsibility, an awareness that the strength of an institution is built on the thoughts and actions of the individuals who participate in the work [of the college]" (p. 139). He explains that accountability extends beyond the institution:

From here, like ripples in a pond, accountability reaches out to embrace others—family, friends, relatives, a clan, the tribe the surrounding non-Indian community, the state, accreditors, foundations, and the nation as a whole. It is important also to recognize that responsibility exists not only to people, but also to the natural world. Nor is accountability only for the living; there is also accountability to ancestors and to generations yet to come.

(pp. 139–140)

Although there are sufficient commonalities in worldviews, values, and goals across indigenous communities to speak of an indigenous perspective on accountability and assessment, it is important to keep in mind that there may be differences in how these worldviews are practiced in local contexts.

Accountability, therefore, within the framing of an indigenous lens requires attending to both internal as well as external accountability (e.g. standardized testing, meeting national rubrics, and so on). To be clear, *internal accountability* is the focus in this section because we believe it to be more relevant to Native communities. It is essential to self-determination, as we have learned from the *kupuna* in Katherine's story, the stories shared at Rough Rock, and Paul's description of accountability at tribal colleges. Internal accountability is also more relevant because it values knowledge and learning that are relational, historical and place-based, and culturally appropriate. Because it is culturally astute and grounded in local values and goals, internal accountability cuts across people rather than institutions (e.g. schools).

Valued outcomes, therefore, go far beyond the degree to which academic skills or content knowledge has been learned. For the purposes of indigenous learning and teaching, the outcomes must include (at minimum) how the learned skill or knowledge base connects the learner to her/his community, builds a deep commitment of responsibility for the community, and prepares the person for future action and knowledge generation. As the *kupuna* in Katherine's story reminds us, our responsibility is to ensure that our young people understand, "the importance of what they had done for their ancestors, themselves, their community, and future generations."

An Indigenous Framing of Accountability and Assessment: Rigor, Respectful Relations, Relevance, and Reciprocity

Few, if any, of us can find a word in our native languages that translates directly as some form of "accountability." This may be because accountability is so implicit in indigenous worldviews, that there has been no need to speak of it directly; accountability was so pervasive in the values of the community that it became invisible except in its violation. From an indigenous perspective, the primary purpose of accountability is to improve the well-being of our communities and ensure their perpetuation. The goals of indigenous education include cultural identity and perpetuation: the strengthening/support of positive cultural identity and the capability to practice and perpetuate cultural ways of being and, perhaps most important, coming to understand who we are and what our responsibilities are to family, clan, and community.

It follows that indigenized accountability will include cultural identity, cultural perpetuation, and character as valued outcomes. It also follows that indigenous assessment will evaluate these outcomes using methods that reflect culturally grounded and valued ways of knowing, such as observation, authentic performance, and expert judgment. Furthermore, these assessments will be strengths-based, emphasizing what the learners can do rather than what they cannot do. Where appropriate, these assessments will be conducted in the language of the community.

From a contemporary indigenous perspective, accountability is crucial for reasons that are both proactive and reactive. From a proactive perspective, we use the tools and methods of accountability to ensure that what we do is the best we can do in all of our relationships. This entails being watchful and reflective, as well as seeking and building upon strengths. It also means taking responsibility for the values that are represented in accountability and assessment systems and activities. We must ensure that accountability and assessment in indigenous education represent the goals and ways of knowing valued by our communities.

From a reactive perspective, we are concerned about mitigating the effects of past and present practices that may be harmful to the well-being of our youths and communities. In our current context, there is a prevalent belief that we cannot assume educators are willing to be accountable for the results of what they do. For example, the No Child Left Behind (NCLB) Act can be characterized as a statement that local school systems have failed to be accountable for the education of the youths entrusted to them. As a result of this perceived lack of accountability, the federal government has stepped in to ensure that high-quality educational opportunities are provided to all children and that all children achieve proficiency in reading and mathematics. In doing this, the focus of accountability has been shifted to the federal government, and the object of accountability has been narrowed to a focus on student performance as measured by their performance on tests of reading and mathematics (typically with variations on mass-market, multiple-choice achievement tests). Castellano, Davis, and Lahache (2000) observed that "aggressive gatekeeping of 'standards' has repeatedly challenged the legitimacy of Aboriginal knowledge and values, imposing an assimilative cultural agenda that is both pervasive and coercive" (p. 251).

We do not argue that all children (particularly low-income indigenous and minority children) have been well served by the public education system. There is an abundance of literature documenting the use of education to eradicate indigenous and minority-group identities, gross inequities in access to high-quality education, and other systematic discrimination (Adams, 1995; Ah Nee-Benham & Heck, 1998). However, we do not believe that moving the focus of accountability to distant governmental agencies and narrowing what we are accountable for to competence in reading and mathematics aids us in fulfilling our responsibilities within our relationships.

Deloria and Wildcat (2001) speak of the primacy of relationships for our Indian ancestors among individuals, tribes, and the natural environment. They also write of our ancestors' deep understanding of the interconnectedness of all things. From this traditional perspective, all relationships have a moral content; therefore, our forbearers "were concerned about the products of what they did, and they sought to anticipate and consider all possible effects of their actions" (Deloria & Wildcat, 2001, p. 23). Thus, they passed to us this legacy: an understanding of accountability that is always present, always personal.

Our most important relationships are with our communities. Thus, the focus of accountability is the well-being of our communities. Because we strive to live in harmony with a deep understanding of interconnectedness, we understand that we have accountability to the past, present, and future. We honor the past and the heritage passed to us by our ancestors when we tell their stories, live their values and customs in the present, and work to ensure their perpetuation in the future. We are accountable to the present as we strive to increase the well-being of our communities, in part by strengthening and sustaining a positive cultural identity. We are accountable to the future when we seek to anticipate the consequences of our decisions and actions.

As we collect knowledge about the achievement of our schools, educational programs, and students, we recognize that the practice of assessment is inextricable from our beliefs about accountability. We suggest that indigenous assessment is characterized by the following four principles: (a) rigor, (b) respectful relations, (c) relevance, and (d) reciprocity.

Rigor

Indigenous assessment must demonstrate the value of *rigor*: We begin with a mindset, followed by who does the assessment, and then the approach. The pursuit and achievement of excellence is just as important in indigenous groups as it is in other ethnic communities. However, in societies that are based on interdependence and respect, excellence reflects individual achievement and collective benefit and is not a result of or supportive of competition or one person besting someone else. Also consistent with this attribute is an emphasis on growth and the continuous improvement that results from diligent effort.

Given that humility and collective responsibility is a valued outcome it is essential to consider "who" does the work of assessment. Because work in Native contexts requires knowledge and expertise in local history, deeply held cultural values, protocols, and etiquette, people who develop, administer, analyze and disseminate what is being learned must have the ability to appropriately and effectively translate the information to meet the needs of a variety of audiences. At the same time, they must respect and care for the sacred; that knowledge which is protected. The "who," we would suggest is an inclusive collective of both local, cultural, and professional/educational experts who bring a mix of fluency in cultural and disciplinary texts as well as mother-tongue language.

To be sure, educative tasks are complicated and varied as our Native schools and serve multiple purposes. At the same time, because resources are limited we have to be vigilant to use them wisely to meet and exceed our educational goals. Making key resource decisions requires that our assessment processes provide dependable and appropriate data, otherwise our efforts will be scattered and we will fail our children and their families. The element of rigor requires a clear line of thinking from problem to intellectual and cultural context to design and to conclusion. In addition, assessment processes must explicitly show how results will contribute to practice and/or continued study. This transparency of design and impact of results should also take into account that indigenous people are not a homogeneous group; in fact, there are both intra and inter-ethnic differences. So, the reporting of assessment results must avoid the pitfalls of pan-indigenous depictions.

Respectful Relations

Indigenous assessment must also demonstrate the value of *respectful relations*. A key principle of indigenous ontologies is the recognition that people are sacred and their bonds with one another, with their ancestors and cultural stories, and with their place fortifies their spirit and well-being. Respectful relationships generate, nurture, and sustain essential links and networks that ensure the lifeblood of a community. A grounding belief of respectful relations is that the individual and collective are inextricably linked and that both contribute to the will of the community to self-determine. Because of this, and because people connect on a personal level, assessment strategies must understand the learner "in context." Assessment processes, therefore, must build and nurture respectful relations with local people.

Historically, assessment processes have left the Native poked, prodded, and empty-handed as reported findings and outcomes have rarely served their best interest. Building trust, an integral part of developing respectful relations, will work to resolve differences, make visible unforeseen problems before they surface and destroy the process, build ethical approaches to the mechanics of defining legitimacy and intellectual property rights, and provide meaningful opportunities for community members to engage in defining and deepening strong educational contexts.

In developing these relationships, it is imperative that we be cognizant and respectful of "the funds of knowledge" (Moll & Gonzalez, 2003) that are held by the students and communities with which we work. Gaining access to and making the best use of this knowledge requires the establishment of a reciprocal relationship in which all partners, students, communities, educators, and assessors benefit. By being granted access to the cultural knowledge and wisdom of the students and communities with which we work, we are better able to meaningfully link assessment to the larger process of culturally relevant teaching and learning. None of this can successfully occur without the establishment and maintenance of mutually respectful relationships, which set the stage for relevant teaching, learning and assessment.

Relevance

Indigenous assessment demonstrates the value of *relevance*. As the two proceeding elements suggest, assessment approaches should provide indigenous educators and the communities they serve with a more robust understanding of the implications of policies, made at every level of decision making (e.g. local, tribal, state, national, and so on) on learning and teaching. In addition, because it is inextricably linked to account- ability, the specialists who develop and conduct assessments must acknowledge the profound impact of their findings on families, and con- sequently on the educational outcomes of students. For these reasons, relevancy is defined by epistemological standards as well as principles of utility. That is, the relevancy and validity of an assessment approach is explicitly linked to the potential use of findings for tangible improve- ments in teaching and learning.

Embedded in this work are tensions of differing epistemologies, cogni- tive theories, and political and historical assumptions. Because account- ability and assessment procedures are situated in local social, cultural, and philosophical contexts, they should acknowledge the human points of view from which they derive. What we do not propose in this writing are specific approaches to establishing relevancy. Instead, our case to define relevancy presents a set of considerations that should underlie the selection and use of assessment processes. These include (but may not be exclusive) to the following: (a) congruence with local context includ- ing both the intra and inter-ethnic and tribal dynamic; (b) collective ownership of the process (authentic partnerships and participation); (c) recognition of the roles of family and extended family in learning and teaching, and student outcomes; (d) deep understanding of the import- ance of the individual as well as the relationship between the individual and the collective; (e) relationship with and to time; (f) sound understanding of and valuing of cultural protocols and use of mother-tongue language in daily life; and (g) ability to see how differing ways of knowing and doing collide and the ability to translate these tensions in ways that empower by creating understanding across contexts.

Reciprocity

Indigenous assessment demonstrates the value of *reciprocity*. Just as the teacher is always learning and the learner is always teaching, learning requires assessment, and assessment of learning always entails more learning. From this we draw two inferences. First, it is important to be cognizant of what our assessment tools and methods teach or communicate. What do they say about what we value? Second, it is important for the "teacher" to be open and receptive to the lessons from the "student." The principle of reciprocity encourages us to utilize assessment to build capacity. This is a tangible outcome of reciprocity as it demonstrates commitment to self-determination.

Additionally, assessment findings must be accessible to a broad community of stakeholders; from the youngest member to the elder. Participation in the development, administration, analysis, and dissemination of assessment results is again a key element. This shared experience can lead to shared resources and knowledge, which can serve to create valid instruments (understanding that cultural norms and protocols will have an impact on how and what is measured), increase the value of assessment findings, ensure validity and legitimacy of the findings, and, in the end, present recommendations that are useful and beneficial to the community.

Summary

It is important to note that the absence of a truly indigenous model of education in most mainstream public schools sets the stage for continued dissonance between the values and goals of indigenous students and their families and schools. To be truly accountable to all stakeholders we must strive to educate in such a way that all students are held to rigorous standards that reflect and respect the cultural knowledge and values of the students' families, tribes, and communities rather than forcing students to choose between educational attainment and preservation of their culture. The value inherent in this framing is that it views indigenous cultures as capital rather than deficit.

While the basic constructs of accountability and assessment are manifest in many cultures, each group will view these from their own perspectives (e.g. current, historical, and future; political, social, and economic, and so on). This requires that we collectively set goals for our children and our educative systems, develop tools and strategies that are culturally appropriate and meet standards of rigor, provide ample opportunities for capacity building, and build useful networks that support a healthy, vibrant learning environment for the development of our children and youth. At the same time, we would impress upon the reader the need to continue to reflect on what it means to ensure that indigenous assessment and accountability systems are relevant not only to indigenous students and communities, but to the larger field of education.

Chapter 19

Our Stories: Turning Our Gaze Inward

Overview of the Stories in this Section

We offer a series of stories based on our own experiences. Through these stories we hope to share with you our always growing, always improving understanding of accountability and assessments that are consistent with indigenous worldviews and the framing principles of rigor, respectful relations, relevance, and reciprocity. While each of the stories highlights a particular principle, they make visible all four, in that the principles are dynamic and interconnected.

We know that the lessons that emerge from the stories will vary depending on the perspective from which the reader approaches them. For those who already see the importance of indigenous models of assessment and accountability, our work reaffirms their beliefs and provides them with a few examples of ways in which this work may be moved forward. For those struggling to define the role of language and culture in the process of assessment and accountability, we hope that our work will "inspire" them to think even more critically about this issue.

MAKING ASSESSMENT PERSONAL: THE RELEVANCE OF LOCAL KNOWLEDGE AND HOLDING ONESELF ACCOUNTABLE

Told by Susan Faircloth

"Let us put our minds together, and see what life we will make for our children."
Tatanka-Iyotanka (Sitting Bull)

Teaching, learning, and assessment are inextricably linked in the world of education. However, for educators working in indigenous schools and communities, these terms often fail to recognize and demonstrate a meaningful and useful connection between the home and school communities in which Native children live and learn. Current state and national systems of assessment and accountability might, in fact, intensify this disconnect by focusing on school- and group-level measures of performance and achievement rather than the individual needs and abilities of students. However, rigorous standards and the development and use of culturally/linguistically appropriate methods of teaching, learning, and assessment can peacefully and meaningfully coexist (Yazzie, 1999). To redefine and operationalize these terms in ways that are more culturally and linguistically relevant for indigenous education, we must first go back to the fundamental question of what is the purpose of education—asked from both a global and a more local, tribally-based perspective. We must be concerned with not only the purpose of education, but how this purpose is being carried out and the effects of these instructional methods on students and their communities. Thus, larger questions loom. For example, we must ask ourselves: to whom and for what are we accountable?

One statement that speaks eloquently to this need to redefine educational assessment and accountability was delivered in 1774 by a member of the Iroquois nation, Canasatego, as he declined an offer from the commissioners of the states of Maryland and Virginia to educate young Iroquois men at William and Mary College:

> We know that you highly esteem the kind of learning taught in those colleges and that the Maintenance of our young Men while with you would be very expensive to you. We are convinced, therefore, that you mean to do us Good by your Proposal; and we thank you heartily. But you who are so wise must know that different Nations have different Conceptions of things and you will, therefore, not take it amiss if our Ideas of this kind of Education happen not to be the same as yours. We have had some Experience of it. . . .
>
> We are however not the less oblig'd by your kind Offer tho' we decline accepting it; and, to show our grateful Sense of it, if the Gentleman from Virginia will send us a Dozen of their Sons, we will take great care of their Education, teach them all we know and make Men of them.
>
> (Clark, 2000, paragraphs 4–5)

In his speech to the state commissioners, Canasatego was clear that we, as Native people, know and always have known how to educate our children. The problem is that much of the responsibility for determining the direction of education has been stripped away by external forces.

Just as Canasatego did in his speech to the state commissioners, each of the stories in this book reflects the educational experiences of Native students and educators. Although many of our experiences recount failures of the educational system to acknowledge and respond to our unique cultural and linguistic characteristics as well as our academic potential, all of us have been successful in our own right in navigating the educational system and becoming productive members of our communities and of the larger society.

Breaking Down Negative Stereotypes

Like so many indigenous students, I was educated in an environment that was not always a comfortable place for me; yet I knew that not going to school or doing poorly in school was not an option. So I plugged along, graduated from high school, and entered college, all without ever having truly learned how to study or be a student. In spite of this lack of preparation, I went on to graduate from college and eventually found myself teaching and conducting research at a university.

While I was teaching a class during my first year at the university, one of my graduate students indicated that if you told her the address of any student in her class, she could predict, with some degree of certainty, what his or her future would look like. Taken aback by her comment, I began to recite my childhood address and to ask whether this address was predictive of someone's not only graduating from high school but going on to teach at a university.

The point here is that many Native and non-Native educators are guilty of judging the potential of students on the basis of immutable character-istics or factors beyond either the students' or teachers' control. As a result, the students might be destined for low-level academic tracking and other educational placements that generally limit their options for further education and employment. Herein lies a fundamental discon-nect between teaching and learning, and ultimately assessment and accountability.

Respecting Indigenous and Local Knowledge

In spite of my own experiences in the educational system, I, too, at times have failed to respond to students in ways that are respectful of their cultural backgrounds and experiences. In my first semester of college teaching, one of the topics was collaboration and communication among parents, families, and schools. When I administered one of the course tests, I asked students to list and briefly describe principles of effective communication. As I graded the test, I deducted points if students did not list the principles outlined in the text and discussed in class.

When the grades were distributed, a Native graduate student asked to discuss her grade with me after class. She was concerned about my grading of her answers on the effective-communication question. I explained that her answers did not match what was presented in the book or in class. She explained to me that although the literature identified these as effective principles, her many years as an educator and as a Native person had taught her that not all of these principles would, in fact, be effective with Native parents and families. Although I listened to her argument, I was reluctant to change the grade. I had presented a list of research-based principles, and these were the answers I expected.

Now, three years later, I reflect on this experience as one in which I allowed my position as scholar and teacher to outweigh the lived experiences of an educator and Native person. All of my years of education had not prepared me to individualize or indigenize my approach to teaching, learning, assessment, and ultimately accountability to my students. In effect, I had failed to do the very thing that I was teaching my students as future special educators to do.[1]

MAKING ASSESSMENT DATA MEANINGFUL: RIGOR THAT IS PURPOSEFUL AND CULTURALLY GROUNDED

Told by Malia Villegas

In the summer of 2005, the First Alaskans Institute (FAI) brought together thirty Alaska Native undergraduate and graduate students as

---

[1] According to Yazzie (1999), "Discussion on appropriate curriculum development should examine the ideologies teachers have internalized during their own schooling and will take with them into schools serving American Indian children" (p. 95).

part of its Summer Internship Program. Each intern was placed with an organization in the field of health care, business and community development, education, research, public policy, or energy to work for the summer. Every Friday we would come together at the FAI for leadership development training. In the following pages, I will describe what I learned that summer from these leadership sessions and through my ongoing internship with the Alaska Native Policy Center (the Policy Center) at the FAI. Specifically, I took to heart three particular lessons I learned during my time with the FAI:

1. Alaska Native leaders and communities need data on demographic, health, education, and other policy trends in order to determine our own futures;
2. Intergenerational and intragenerational connections are essential to our development as a people; and,
3. Cross-community networks will help us meet our own goals and enable us to support others facing similar challenges.

These lessons reflect how a group of current Alaska Native leaders administering the internship program understand accountability and assessment and the efforts they are making to bear out their responsibility to the next generation of Alaska Native leaders.

The FAI was founded by the Alaska Federation of Natives (AFN) in 1989 as the AFN Foundation. According to the FAI website, "The Foundation received a sizeable payment from Alyeska Pipeline Service Company and its owners as part of a negotiated agreement over Native hire requirements in constructing the trans-Alaska pipeline. In 2000, the Foundation became independent of AFN and received a $20 million endowment pledge from the owner companies of the trans-Alaska pipeline." One of the first and primary initiatives of FAI has been to establish the Alaska Native Policy Center.

The leaders and staff of the Policy Center have developed several research reports providing demographic and other data on the status of Alaska Native people and communities. Two such reports are *Our Choices, Our Future: Analysis of the Status of Alaska Natives Report* (2004) and the *Alaska Native K–12 Indicators Report* (2005). The purpose of these reports is to provide data and trend information to Alaska Native leaders and community members to support ongoing community development. In fact, the first report is an analysis of other data on the status of Alaska Natives. So these reports not only provide access to data, but present ideas about how the data are being used in Alaska Native communities and guidance on how to make better use of these data. One example of how access to data has influenced what we know about ourselves as Alaska Natives is research on K–12 student attrition. As part of the Policy Center's research initiatives, it became clear that student attrition is of major concern to Alaska Natives and that dropout statistics indicate a crisis situation in many Alaska Native communities.

The Fairbanks North Star Borough School District decided to try to determine why Alaska Native students were dropping out of school at a much higher rate than other students, so they developed a project to track down Alaska Native students who had left school and ask why they had left. This initiative resulted in two important outcomes. First, just by virtue of the fact that district staff made an effort to find these former students and talk with them, 95 students, or a full 16 percent of the 591 who had been recorded as having dropped out in 2004–05 re-enrolled in school (FNSBSD, 2005). Second, several of the students who were interviewed over the phone because they had left school indicated they did so because of a lack of challenge. Many of these were high-achieving students who became bored by the curriculum. This information refutes the assumption that it is students who are struggling to keep up academically who are always at greater risk of dropping out (FNSBSD, 2005). We believe that data on the experiences of Alaska Native people are essential for making decisions about how to grow our communities and support our children. But the Policy Center also recognizes that it is not important merely to have access to data, but to use those data to understand Native students' experiences and to find new solutions to the challenges Alaska Natives face each day.

The Policy Center has three specific mechanisms in place to assist Alaska Native people in using these data. One effort, as noted above, one way to use the data is to publish information on community-specific trends to guide leaders in making decisions about their own local contexts. Second, the Policy Center is working to train Alaska Native students and other researchers to work with these and new data. Having skilled Alaska Native researchers and scholars is essential for our self-determination because Alaska Native people have knowledge about our communities that others do not and thus can ask questions and seek answers using data in different and important ways. A final effort is to take the data and findings from analyses they perform back to Alaska Native communities. Staff present the data and findings, as well as solicit feedback about whether the findings make sense and are presented in an appropriate and respectful manner. This is a crucial step in ensuring that Alaska Native people have direct access to data about their communities and in affirming that research addresses their needs

Data on the experiences of Alaska Native people largely constitute the "what" of the work at the Policy Center and FAI, but the "who" is just as important, if not more so. As noted above, putting data in direct conversation with Alaska Native people and their lives is a prime goal. In addition, the FAI has prioritized efforts to bring elders and youths together, as well as to develop peer cohorts among emerging and established leaders for support. Specifically, the FAI has taken on the role of coordinating the Alaska Federation of Natives/First Alaskans Elders and Youth Conference each year. Each Alaska Native community sponsors Elders and youth to attend in order to share experiences and coordinate efforts across the state. This is the only large-scale effort to bring elders and youths together across Alaska Native communities, while also preserving smaller meetings of regional elders and youths. Issues that emerge are brought to the Alaska Federation of Natives gathering where delegates are making decisions about community issues for the coming year. In the past few years, the conference planners have been young Alaska Natives who gain important leadership experience working to convene communities of Elders and youth and to articulate a program that reflects priority areas of discussion and celebration. These intergenerational gatherings are essential to self-determination because they provide opportunities for youths to learn their history and stories and for elders to pass these along.

The FAI was instrumental in creating space at the 2006 Elders and Youth Conference for a group of Alaska Natives who had been sent to boarding schools as children to share their stories with each other and with youth conference participants. The stories they told and emotions they expressed were a powerful reminder of the dangers of boarding schools when established without the support of local communities and without respect for children. Along with other young Alaska Natives present at this conversation, I was moved to tears and anger upon hearing some of these stories. Yet, the boarding school era is an important part of our history and one that we cannot forget, especially in light of recent efforts to establish regional boarding schools in Alaska—an effort recently sanctioned by the Alaska State Board of Education and Early Development (Resolution 01–2005). Without these gatherings, we cannot come to know about ourselves as Alaska Natives with a rich and varied educational history, nor can we develop the relationships that can help sustain one another and our communities over time.

The FAI focused its initial efforts on building a foundation in local Alaska Native communities by providing access to and use of data and by fostering leadership development through inter- and intragenerational gatherings. The next phase of work involves developing networks with other indigenous communities and organizations. Leaders and staff of the Alaska Native Policy Center also have begun identifying other indigenous policy organizations to learn from and potentially partner with. Some of these include: the National Congress of American Indians (NCAI) Policy Research Center, the Diné Policy Institute (Navajo), and Ngā Pae o te Māramatanga or the National Institute of Research Excellence for Māori Development. Organizations like the Alaska Native Policy Center work in the service of both local communities and policy leaders, but they often end up working to translate for these constituencies. In order to move their policy and research work forward, these organizations need to find ways to develop relationships with similar entities so that they can move beyond translating, but work to move forward their efforts to leverage resources in support of community needs. These kinds of relationships are essential for the long-term sustainability of indigenous policy organizations because they can facilitate the sharing of information, resources, best practices, and support through challenging times.

On the surface, this might not seem to be a story of accountability and assessment in the ways that we commonly think of these terms. For me, however, this is the ultimate story of accountability and assessment because it is about a community's taking control or making use of the knowledge, leadership, and relational resources already in place to determine its future course. The FAI has recognized the wealth of resources we have in our Alaska Native communities and people and has worked to bring these forth in order to build even stronger bases of culture. In this way, the goals and the means are inseparable: in order to build knowledge, leadership, and relationships, we need to make use of our existing knowledge, leadership, and relationship resources. We have what we need to improve our experiences and opportunities; yet, we need to recognize the resources and take action together to make use of them.

Interestingly, the measures of assessing our progress toward achieving these goals are the same as the goals and means themselves—having more and better knowledge, leadership, and relationships in place. One powerful example of this comes out of Aotearoa, or New Zealand. Community and educational leaders there recognized that the healthy future of their communities required Māori scholars to conduct research for Māori people. They set a goal of graduating 500 Māori doctorates by 2020. Their means to achieve this goal were to leverage traditional knowledge about Māori education and ways of knowing to develop effective doctoral programs, to affirm and support leaders like Linda Tuhiwai Smith and Graham Hingangaroa Smith to teach and create new opportunities for these students, and to build and strengthen domestic and international relationships in support of this cohort. Their assessment criterion is whether they will graduate 500 Māori doctorates by 2020. They are well on their way to exceeding that goal at this time—graduating more than 500 Māori doctorates in every imaginable field of study!

In Alaska, our goals are to preserve and grow our knowledge about what it means to be Alaska Native and Alutiiq or Inupiaq, for example, to develop and support a new group of leaders to guide us into the next generation, and to build healthy relationships in and across communities. So rigor is determined by the extent to which these goals reflect the needs of Alaska Native people and whether or not our communities' well-being is strengthened in this pursuit. Thus our systems of accountability and assessment must include indicators, logic models, methodologies, and all the other tools of the trade that will help us to attain these goals. Yet, these tools should not drive our systems. It is our goals that determine our systems of accountability and assessment. Through these goals, we recognize an important balance between the local and the "global" in that we see ourselves and our futures as members of local communities, as Alaska Native people, and as part of a global community of indigenous peoples. These are all the places we are "from," and as such we must recognize the bounty of resources available to us, as well as our responsibility to work together to ensure our healthy future as indigenous peoples.

MAKING ASSESSMENT MATTER: ALL OUR RELATIONS

Told by Lawrence E. Wheeler

When I was growing up, I did not know the purpose of the tests we were taking; yet I was a good test-taker, so I did well in school without doing homework. I never really had to work hard until I entered college. Even when I knew the purpose of a test or quiz, the assessments failed to fulfill their purpose; to me it seemed like, "What is the point of taking this?" I was able to succeed in school without really reading anything longer than a page; when we took quizzes to "prove" that we had read an assignment, I would ask a number of my friends, "What happened in the story?" Because everyone took something slightly different from the reading assignment, I had a good, albeit superficial, picture of the reading assignment and did well on those quizzes.

In math, if I paid attention to the lesson, I could nail down the concept (more or less). I was forced to complete lab assignments in science, so there was no real "homework" for those types of classes. I exerted little effort throughout the majority of my primary and secondary education. My lack of work ethic proved to be detrimental when I needed to get academic work done (particularly reading) and when there was no one left to ask, "What happened in the story?" The use of testing as the sole form of assessment failed me because it rewarded me in the short term for being a good test-taker. In the end, because I exerted no meaningful effort to learn the material, I was unprepared to take on more challenging scholarly work.

There was no evidence of authentic assessment in the core subjects at my school. Testing was the sole means of assessment in mathematics, English, social studies, and science. Although this type of assessment worked for me, it did not work for many of my friends. Homework seemed to be used solely to generate a grade, not to serve as practice; it was graded for accuracy, which seemed to defeat the purpose of practice. How did the educators at our school know whether students knew a subject or whether they were merely good test-takers? Conversely, I did well in wood shop, art, and technical drawing as these were hands-on courses. I was able to demonstrate that I knew what I was doing by producing operable products.

In many ways, my high school French class helped me to become a better learner and gave me the confidence I needed to succeed later in life. The instructional format of the class was highly interactive, concrete and hands-on. My teacher, a fluent speaker of French, German, and English, had a remarkable grasp of the languages she taught. As part of her curriculum, our teacher encouraged conversation in French. We also read aloud, in French, while the teacher tolerated our mispronunciations. More importantly she shared the cultural aspects of the language so that we could live the language. Needless to mention, I enjoyed the class and I missed few assignments, and because of her influence I continued to dabble in French in my postsecondary studies. In school, the shop-type electives and French were the only classes in which I experienced any type of authentic assessment.

Outside of school, throughout my upbringing, my father was the professor in my *Université Du Père*. The lessons I learned from him were the result of hands-on exercises in masonry, carpentry, football, baseball, and what I have referred to at times as becoming a modern-day renaissance man. He was formally trained as a brick mason and offset printer at Haskell in the 1950s. What he learned about carpentry, he passed on to his sons. We had "tests" during our upbringing, which consisted of (for me) building a dog house (complete with rafters, floor joists, framed walls, and shingle roof) and assisting my father and his brothers in constructing a first-level addition on my grandfather's house when he was ailing and no longer able to ascend the stairs leading to his bedroom. My father was my first coach. Through his guidance, I gained an appreciation for football that few young men have the opportunity to enjoy. He taught me how to hit hard (without getting hurt) and how to hold my ground against larger boys. I became the center and long-snapper (a role that I was called into during a crucial point in one of my high school games). I received no accolades on the gridiron, but just did my part when the coaches called on me.

Some of my fondest memories involve hunting with my father. He showed me the woods. He showed me how to read a compass and look for landmarks. He shared the Seneca names for some of the animals and was always willing to share the little Seneca language he knew. Both of his parents were fluent Seneca speakers, but due to the nature of the boarding school experience, my father was discouraged from speaking his mother tongue. He carried a single-shot 20-gauge shotgun, but I do not recall his ever raising the gun to his shoulder or killing anything. The point of his hunting trip was to spend time with his youngest son (me), not to demonstrate his skills with a firearm; rather, he seemed to be saying, "The time I spend with my son will form his fondest memories." During our walks, I occasionally would raise up an animal in my sights. My father would whisper, "Do you think you can kill it?" "Yeah," I would answer. "Then take the shot," he would reply. More often than not, my father was probably just as surprised that I took the shot as he was that I dropped the animal clean. Now when I am hunting, I often ask myself, "Can I kill this animal?" If I don't think so, I don't take the shot. I have to thank my father for the lessons in patience, persistence, and open-mindedness.

When I made the transition from attending graduate school to teaching high school, I was alienated in a number of different ways. First, I was a Native American in a school district with only two Native American families, and I was the only brown face on the faculty and one of just two staff members of color in the school district. Second, I was coming from a research institute into a field of practice; most of my colleagues in the department had earned tenure. Third, in my graduate studies, I had been conditioned to question mainstream teaching methods; however, my teacher colleagues were fixed in their day-to-day teaching that there was no room for change or innovation. The unspoken motto was, "If it ain't broke, don't fix it!" Last, I respected my students as responsible young people and not as children. I gave them choices and held them to the consequences of their decisions.

The fundamental difference between my life and those of my colleagues was that I had lived a life outside of their familiar town, thereby experiencing life in a vastly different way. A majority of my colleagues had grown up in or around the school district. All of the teachers in my department had obtained degrees from the same local college two miles down the road. I, on the other hand, had moved around, traveled the "Powwow highway," living in completely different cultures (e.g. academic, diverse ethnic communities, and so on), and, I believe, understood things from a completely different point of view.

During graduate school, I became an advocate for a constructivist framework for lesson development and teaching. I believed that students constructed meaning from their experiences and that it was my job to provide meaningful experiences in mathematics. I still provided the worksheets and "drilled and killed," but I wanted to provide a safe learning environment in which students would feel free to interact with and learn from each other. I wanted my students to write more (yes, even in math) and have more opportunities to share what they were learning with the other students in the classroom. I was leaning toward more authentic assessments, but the rigid quiz-test-quiz regiment was impossible to break. My efforts were not supported by the department because the model that had been established was not failing, and students were still getting good grades on the state tests. Without the support of my department, teaching became like marching in an ant line. It was time to move on.

A short time passed, and the position of Education Research/K–12 Program Coordinator opened in my home community. I was excited because this was work with my indigenous people. The first week of my employment as an administrator proved to be challenging. The department had already started the summer kindergarten readiness program, and I felt like I was treading water just to learn the job and keep the programs running smoothly. The idea of the summer program was to offer students a six-week school experience. Youngsters participated in everyday school activities to help them make a smooth transition from home to school. They participated in calendar and circle times; writing, pre-reading, and numeracy activities; and Seneca language and culture. The day was structured much like the average school day.

A major function of my position is to engender good working relationships with area schools that contract services for Native American students (of whom there are three). In developing good relationships, I am invited to attend and participate in school administrative meetings and school board meetings. But most important, I am asked questions about how to shape the programming for Native American students. These last questions involve an understanding of not only what the students are supposed to be learning, but also their family and cultural backgrounds, and what experiences they have in common. In my position, I have been able to look at the state assessment results for our students, examine where they are succeeding, and develop incentive programs based on the data presented. The idea of accountability comes in strongly here. It then becomes my responsibility to inform school personnel that they are accountable for the students' learning. Educators have taken notice and have attempted to become more culturally sensitive (understanding that the students' cultural traditions are to be maintained). A number of students could have been denied credit because they had numerous absences due to attendance at cultural ceremonies, and the schools have made an effort to allow students to make up work they missed.

The challenges of helping parents regain their sense of accountability still remains. With the prevalence of television and longer work days for parents, the electronic babysitter has done more than anything else to disrupt the natural order of families. As an administrator in a tribal education department, I find it a challenge to help parents assume the role of advocate for their own children, in part because the educational system was vastly different when they were students and because they do not want to relive their perceived failures in schools that didn't want them in the first place.

Now, as a parent of two school-aged students in one of the New York State Native American Tuition contracting schools, I have been enlightened about the need for increased involvement by Native American parents. When I attend school functions, the number of non-Native American families in attendance disproportionately outweighs that of Native American families. I have taken on the role of advocate for my own children with teachers and school administrators, and I see that although the school, as a whole, has taken steps to assist our children, prejudice still exists among some teachers and administrators. Parents of the students who are now entering school attended schools that were not so accepting and understanding. Despite efforts and some success in renegotiating attitudes toward cultural differences on an administrative level, the history and belief systems of some parents, teachers, and administrators make the change process slow at the school level. For me as a parent, this situation can be disheartening at times. Yet as a parent, my level of accountability is immeasurable.

I see accountability and assessment from so many different lenses because of my life experiences: as a primary, secondary, post-secondary and graduate student, as a new teacher, as a new administrator, and as a young parent. The theme that continues to come up for me is the fact that in each stage of my life, I have felt responsible for both my own and others' level of learning. The methods in which my level of learning (and teaching) were measured have changed, but I tend to prefer being assessed and assessing the understanding of others through monitoring experiences and behavior over time rather than measuring student achievement by one test. We are all accountable for providing learning experiences for the people that surround us (it makes our life's experiences more meaningful). In the end, students (either child or adult) need to know the value and relevance of the assessments being used and they need to know what the purpose of those assessments are.

MAKING ASSESSMENT INDIGENOUS: REFLECTING THE RECIPROCAL NATURE OF LEARNING

Told by Kū Kahakalau and Katherine Tibbetts

In 1999, a handful of Hawaiian communities joined a small group of educational reformers to successfully lobby for a revision of State of Hawai'i statutes to create the opportunity to form "start-up" charter schools. By 2000, a dozen Hawaiian communities joined together to form *Nā Lei Na'auao*—Native Hawaiian Charter School Alliance (NLN) to provide a quality choice in education. In the past seven years, these schools, which currently serve over 2000 Hawaiian K–12 students on three islands, have unleashed the potential of Hawaiian-focused education to initiate systemic change.

As Hawaiian-focused public charter schools, NLN schools are committed to provide their youth with a quality education rooted in traditional Hawaiian culture, values, and pedagogy. This education is at once ancient and modern and aligns with both traditional practices as well as the new three R's in education: relations, relevance, and rigor. All NLN schools are unique as a result of their place, their resources, and their specific circumstances. Yet, all have collectively, over the past seven years, incubated a vibrant approach called *Education with Aloha*. This approach focuses first and foremost on creating and maintaining positive relations among all stakeholders, through the establishment of a dynamic learning 'ohana. Like a traditional Hawaiian family, this learning 'ohana practices aloha, aligning with the Hawaiian proverb: *Aloha kekahi i kekahi, pēlā ihola ka nohona 'ohana.* (Love one another, such is family life.)

Education with Aloha builds on a strengths-based approach, a positive attitude towards youth and learning, and an ongoing commitment to improvement and growth. This includes participating in longitudinal action research to create, implement and evaluate relevant culturally-grounded curriculum, instruction and assessment, that assist stakeholders to meet and exceed rigorous academic standards and achieve personal excellence.

A significant body of research and experience supports the proposition that cultural and individual assets can exert a significant influence on students' engagement and success in school (for example, Lee, 2005; Scales *et al.*, 2000). Furthermore, literature on developmental assets asserts that understanding and promoting the strengths of youth requires affective approaches (Wasler, 2006)—such as those promoted through *Education with Aloha*. To date the most well-researched and established perspective on understanding and measuring assets is called "the assets framework." For this study, we utilized the most comprehensive of the surveys developed by Search Institute (2005) to better understand the strengths of the youths attending NLN schools.

Despite a high prevalence of risk factors among the NLN students (for example, low incomes as evidenced by eligibility for the free/reduced price lunch program) our students evidence nearly as many assets as Search Institute's national benchmark group. However, the prevalence of individual assets is different from that of the benchmark group and may be unique to our population and context.

While the results reported here are descriptive at this point and do not establish causality, we note that the assets in which the NLN students scored highest relative to the benchmark group were consistent with the *Education with Aloha* approach. For example, the external assets on which NLN students scored highest relative to the benchmark group were: *Caring School Climate*, *Parent Involvement in School*, *High Expectations*, and *Time at Home*. All but the last of these assets are directly influenced by school contexts. And, the internal assets on which NLN students scored highest relative to the benchmark group areas are also the ones that are directly influenced by the schools: *Bonding to School* is consistent with student-centeredness; and internalization of values as demonstrated by *Caring*, *Honesty*, and *Responsibility* is consistent with the emphasis on traditional Hawaiian values.

Internal assets that were less well represented among the NLN students include *Interpersonal Competence*, *Peaceful Conflict Resolution*, *Personal Power*, *Self-Esteem*, *Sense of Purpose*, and *Positive View of Personal Future*. We believe that these results are, in part, a function of cultural differences in how students present themselves and also reflect the environmental factors that place many of these students at risk. Initially, it seems incongruent that these students, who report that caring relationships among their peers at school are a source of strength, thought that others would rate them low on their own interpersonal skills. However, when one reflects on the high value and esteem that many Native Hawaiians place on relationships as well as the premium placed on humility (ha'aha'a in the Hawaiian language and value system), the data become more congruent. *E noho ma ka 'ōpū weuweu, mai ho'oki'iki'e*, remain among the clumps of grass, don't elevate yourself, is an important Hawaiian proverb, which promotes public humility. We believe that this cultural value is likely to depress scores on scales on which respondents are asked to evaluate themselves in favorable terms. This interpretation is consistent with our personal experiences and those of others and is supported by cross-cultural work on the construct of self-enhancement or self-promotion (Brown, 2003, p. 604).

However, culturally biased outcomes are not the only reason for the lower prevalence of some Internal Assets. We believe that the data are also reflective of the environmental factors that place many of these students at risk. For instance, NLN schools are located in areas with high concentrations of Native Hawaiians. These communities are in some of Hawai'i's most destitute areas, with high crime rates, and other socioeconomic ills, such as high unemployment, homelessness created by exuberant rents, and a never-ending influx of change as a consequence of disintegrating family units. These environmental factors create disempowering situations that leave students feeling a lack of personal power and purpose.

Overall we feel strongly that our findings are encouraging. At the same time, we need to go beyond the limits of mainstream assessments to develop and validate a strengths-based survey of student assets that reflects a Hawaiian perspective on well-being (Kana'iaupuni *et al.*, 2005). We are currently engaged in such work. Our definition of assets includes cultural practices, language and traditions; access to traditional knowledge; and a sense of place that includes the land as a resource and ancestral foundation. It also includes spirituality and spiritual connections to the natural environment, the ancestors, and all living beings.

In summary, we believe that although factors that contribute to the educational failure of too many low-income, minority and indigenous youths are complex, we must count among these the lack of readiness and unwillingness of mainstream schools to begin where these children are. By recognizing the strengths these students bring to the process and by validating and building on these strengths, significant changes could occur. The *Nā Lei Na'auao* schools, grounded in the *Education with Aloha* approach, are designed to do just that. We found a high prevalence of assets that may be directly influenced by the schools and that are consistent with the *Education with Aloha* approach. Although we cannot establish causality with the data that are currently available, we believe the findings suggest that the NLN schools contribute to the healthy development of our 'ōpio. We also believe that the strengths-based approach implicit in the study of student assets will continue to provide insights into the positive effects of these schools and enhance our capacity to generate actionable knowledge to support their continuous improvement.

Chapter 20
Looking Forward

Katherine Tibbetts and Susan Faircloth

If we are to have an effective system of indigenous education founded in sovereignty, self-determination, and empowerment, our accountability and assessment practices must reflect these central values. We must envision pathways and practices that clearly articulate indigenous views grounded in local cultural ontologies, which then define the community we want for our youth, and in particular, the educational systems that teach our children and youth. This requires assessments that are owned, undertaken, and used by the communities for and within which they are conducted. Findings and recommendations, therefore, would contribute in meaningful ways to practice and policy, that is, to how and what we teach as well as to the generation of indigenous frameworks that can better build the capacities of indigenous people.

As we reflect on our experiences, we suggest that this movement to indigenize educational accountability and assessment requires that we respond to Sitting Bull's challenge to "put our minds together, and see what life we will make for our children," hence, using this opportunity for internal and cross community dialogue and collaboration to build healthy schools. This process requires that we "uncover the underlying philosophies and ideologies embedded in the educational goals set by curriculum planners for Native communities" (Yazzie, 1999, p. 85). This is not a formulaic process that can be described in five or ten easy steps. It is much more complex and is rooted in Native principles of sovereignty and self-determination—the belief in the right to determine locally the direction and method of delivery of education to native students and communities, whether these students attend mainstream public or tribally controlled schools.

To begin this process, we offer the following questions as challenges to ourselves and to our readers:

- To whom and for what are we most accountable? Are our actions consistent with this?
- How well do the outcomes, methods, and tools by which our schools, educational programs, and students are judged to be successful reflect the value-systems, goals, and traditional practices and knowledge of indigenous communities?
- How do our assessments communicate and strengthen the values of rigor, respectful relationships, relevance, and reciprocity?

As we bring this part of the book to a close, we are reminded that the lessons our mothers have taught us about accountability and assessment are to be found in their actions. To honor their legacies and the lessons that they have taught us we must continually ask ourselves the following questions: if our mothers were to voice their beliefs, to guide us explicitly in these practices, what might their words be? If our mothers looked at our actions, would they know that we have understood their lessons? Would they take pride in the legacy we are creating for future generations?

Recommended Resources

Adams, D. W. (1995) *Education for Extinction: American Indians and the Boarding School Experience 1875–1928*. Lawrence, KS: University Press of Kansas.

Ah Nee-Benham, M. K. P. & Heck, R. H. (1998) *Culture and Educational Policy in Hawai'i: The Silencing of Native Voices*. Mahwah, NJ: Lawrence Erlbaum Associates.

Alaska State Board of Education and Early Development (December 6, 2004) *Supporting Boarding Schools in Alaska and Calling For a Plan of Action: Resolution 01–2005*. Juneau, AK: Author.

Boyer, P. (2003) "Building tribal communities: defining the mission and measuring the outcomes of tribal colleges." In M. Benham & W. Stein (eds), *The Renaissance of American Indian Higher Education: Capturing the Dream*. Mahwah, NJ: Lawrence Erlbaum Associates, Publishers, pp. 137–146.

Brown, J. D. (2003) "The self-enhancement motive in collectivist cultures: the rumors of my death have been greatly exaggerated." *Journal of Cross-Cultural Psychology*, 34(5), 603–605.

Cajete, G. (2000) *Native Science: Natural Laws and Interdependence*. Santa Fe, NM: Clear Light Publishers.

Castellano, M. B., Davis, L., & Lahache, L. (2000) "Conclusion: fulfilling the promise." In M. B. Castellano, L. Davis, & L. Lahache (eds), *Aboriginal Education: Fulfilling the Promise*. Vancouver, BC, Canada: UBC Press.

Clark, R. J. (2000, 2001) *Advocating for Culturally Congruent School Reform: A Call to Action for Title IX Indian Education Programs & Parent Committees*. Retrieved January 6, 2006, from http://www.nwrac.org/congruent/.

Davidson, J. (June 6, 2003) Personal communication. Honolulu.

Deloria Jr., V., & Wildcat, D. R. (2001) *Power and Place: Indian Education in America*. Golden, CO: Fulcrum Resources.

Else, I. (May 24, 2006). Personal communication. Honolulu.

Fairbanks North Star Borough School District (FNSBSD). (2005). *Dropout Prevention Steering Committee Report and Recommendations*. Fairbanks, AK: Author.

Kana'iaupuni, S. M., Malone, N., & Ishibashi, K. (2005) *Ka Huaka'i: 2005 Native Hawaiian Educational Assessment*. Honolulu, HI: Kamehameha Schools, Pauahi Publications.

Lee, C. D. (2005) "Intervention research based on current views of cognition and learning." In J. E. King (ed.), *Black Education: A Transformative Research and Action Agenda for the New Century*. Mahwah, NJ: Lawrence Erlbaum Associates for the American Educational Research Association, pp. 73–116.

Moll, L. C., & Gonzalez, N. (2003) "Engaging life: a funds of knowledge approach to multicultural education." In J. Banks & C. McGee Banks (eds), *Handbook of Research on Multicultural Education* (2nd edn) San Francisco: Jossey-Bass, pp. 699–715.

National Indian Education Association. (2003) *History of Indian Education*. Retrieved January 7, 2007, from http://niea.org/history/educationhistory.php.

Scales, P. C., Benson, P. L., & Leffert, N. (2000) "Contribution of developmental assets to the prediction of thriving among adolescents." *Applied Developmental Science*, 4(1), 27–46.

Search Institute (2005) *Introduction to Assets*. Retrieved April 17, 2006, from http://www.search-institute.org/assets/.

Wasler, N. (2006). " 'R' is for resilience: schools turn to 'asset development' to build on students' strengths." *Harvard Educational Letter*, 22(5), 1–3.

Yazzie, T. (1999). "Culturally appropriate curriculum: a research-based rationale." In K. G. Swisher & I. J. W. Tippeconnic (eds), *Next Steps: Research and Practice to Advance Indian Education*. Charleston, WV: ERIC Clearinghouse on Rural Education and Small Schools, pp. 83–106.

PART IV

THE PROMISE AND JOY OF PARTNERSHIPS

Basket as Metaphor:
The Braid Links all Parts of the Basket

Samuel Suina

Basket making can be very tiring. So we do the work collectively, men and women, children and elders, every member of our families. Braiding is the final step of our work. It is like braiding your mother's or grandmother's hair, so you do this with a lot of care and love. This activity intertwines our lives, connecting us to all the gifts of life. This *In Our Mother's Voice* basket reminds us that we must be unified in our efforts to regenerate our indigenous cultures and languages. Our leaders must keep the willow branches together, interlacing them carefully. Educational leaders, too, must have a full understanding of where we have come from, what we have done, and where we will go in order to weave together the talents of many stakeholders.

Pray first.
You need to prepare branches before beginning to weave.
Ask them not to break.
As you work with another to weave, know that together you have a better view.
So reach across to weave and take turns.

To make a basket, you don't need money, only a knife. To succeed on our journey, we need partnerships; we need to be interconnected with others. Working with only one willow makes for a weak basket—but when working with a bunch of willows, together, they become a sturdy basket. Indigenous communities face similar challenges, but we can overcome them if we learn to work together.

> *The braiding at the bottom brings the basket together.*
> *Bring the branches down, out, and upwards.*
> *Because it's braided, it will not come apart.*

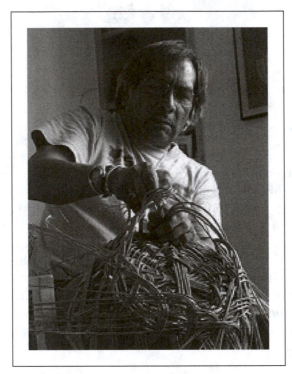

The Braiding

A Poem of Partnership

Lai-Lani Ovalles and Partners

Each moment of expansion creates new life
Land
Cordage to our ancestors
Older life reaching out to the newer life
To remember where we're going Newer life reaching back to the older life
To remember where we came from
You are awake. I feel you. You are real.
The baby will be born on its birthday
Of the mother's voice
Of the child's countenance
Her knowing eyes, my first gaze
Into our deep essence
Tightly she weaves my braid, gently our family
Unites, intertwines, strength in numbers
Partnerships may not always last
We should learn from the past
I remember her voice in mine
Stories given to us, a fire in your belly they live
waiting for you to tell them
to caress, chant, dance, share them
as the ocean stretches its waves across generations
I transfer to you wisdom, purity, good health, happiness
Our roots do not grow in one direction
Mindful of animals, trees, water, wind

Life sustained by love for others and self
The Spirits are with us, always guiding us
Never let go of each other. She will know. They will know.
The core of what we are, of what we will be
Remember your responsibility.

Chapter 21

The Foundational Partnership: Learning from the Voices of Our Elders

Maenette K.P. Ah Nee-Benham and Francisco Guajardo

Introduction

At the core of native storytelling forms is the connection between the elder and child/learner, where the passing of legacy that comes from mentoring and apprenticeship is given. This essential partnership, between elder and learner, is also at the heart of the "Go to the Source" vision (Benham with Cooper, 2000) as successful "educational endeavors must be interdisciplinary, intercultural, and involve generations from the community. Furthermore, the survival of an educational initiative would also require the involvement of elders, diverse internal and external Native and non-Native agencies, the support of sustained research and development of Native epistemology and pedagogy, and linkages with other Native educational projects" (p. 18). Partnerships, therefore, are an integral element of rejuvenating, leading, and assessing our indigenous educational programs. But partnerships are slippery and often messy, so they must be approached both graciously and strategically.

The authors of this section begin with a story shared by Francisco Guajardo that captures the essence of the meaning of partnership. That is, we visualize partnerships as a *koru*, the spiral-scroll shape of a fern shoot that slowly unfolds to a fern leaf. Cherrington (2000) described it in this way:

The shape symbolizes the *whenua* (womb). The child is at the bottom and the mother is at the top. This shape could also be viewed as the *tuakaa–teina* (older–younger sibling) or the *mokopuna–tupuna* (grandchild–grandparent). All related to the concept of *kaiako–akonga* (student–teacher). . . . It is from this center that the meaning and reasoning for education originates.

(p. 31)

Successful partnerships, whether it is between organizations or people, require a commitment to these essential relationships.

To explore how partnerships work, five short teaching case studies that recount real-life partnering experiences are presented. Each of the case authors worked with mentors (senior scholars) or mentees (emerging scholars) who provided guidance and feedback on drafts of their case stories. This relationship provided an opportunity for both author and mentor/mentee to understand more deeply the complexities and tensions presented in the case. These cases are followed by commentaries written by invited scholars. These are short essays that present, from the perspective of the scholar, a point of view that at minimum serves to push readers to think more about (a) alternative pathways to view the challenges presented in the case, (b) what lessons were learned, and (c) what we might do next. An epilogue that takes the form of questions and answers follows the commentaries, presenting critical perspectives from both the case author and the mentor/mentee. This section provides readers with an opportunity critically to examine robust stories that illustrate the intricacies of forming and maintaining partnerships. It is our hope that the written text gives way to candid debate and meaningful dialogue.

References

Benham, M. with Cooper, J. (2000) *Indigenous Educational Models for Contemporary Practice: In Our Mother's Voice*. Mahwah, NJ: Lawrence Erlbaum Associates.

Cherrington, K. (2000) "Building a child-centered model: 'An indigenous model must look to the future.'" In M. Benham & J. Cooper (eds) *Indigenous Educational Models for Contemporary Practice: In Our Mother's Voice*. Mahwah, NJ: Lawrence Erlbaum Associates, pp. 29–34.

Chapter 22

The Heart of the Story:
Framing Partnerships

Francisco Guajardo

I experienced a déjà vu moment when I entered the Ziibiwing Center of Anishinabe Culture and Folkways during the fall of 2006 and saw the central image of the *Diba Jimooyung*, which is the exhibit that tells the story of the original people of the Great Lakes region. The image includes two characters, an elder and a youth, juxtaposed in a manner in which the elder appears to be conveying wisdom, or a set of instructions, to the youth. It is a noble image of an honorable practice, and I felt spiritually uplifted as I witnessed the image. I also felt a heightened sense of comfort, mostly because the conversation and teacher–learner relationship between the elder and the youth are at the core of how I was raised—it is how I have learned the most important lessons in my life. But it was a déjà vu moment because several years ago, as I participated in the design of a museum in a community close to my rural south-Texas home, I suggested to the design committee that the first image a visitor to the museum sees should be an image showing an elder and a youth engaged in conversation. It is the most genuine and enduring image that captures the mode through which I learned life's important lessons as a Mexican boy growing up on both sides of the Texas–Mexico border; it conveys the essence of my culture. In the end, the south Texas museum design committee opted to use the space for other purposes, but as I entered the Ziibiwing Center, I was nostalgically struck by the image, as if it were a dream from the past.

Two voices most filled my mind, soul, and spirit with lessons as I grew up; they were the lessons of my mother and father—two committed storytellers. Parents who loved to tell stories raised my brothers and me, and they had a purpose for the stories. We learned values through strategically related anecdotes, developed a sense of humor through the unrelenting *chistes* (jokes) told by our father, and learned how to care for one another through narratives my mother recalled from her own childhood. The process of learning from stories is such an integral and salient part of my life that even my professional work as an educator is conspicuously characterized by the importance of the narratives. Looking at titles of my recent publications "Narratives of Hope and Courage," "Narratives of Transformation," and "Teaching Leadership Through Story Formation" indicates that my scholarship is guided by stories. Indeed, I am inseparable from stories, and from the voices of those who share them.

My Mother's Voice

The Ziibiwing elder may as well be my mother. I recall my mother's voice as most formative in shaping my identity, my values, and the way I deal with my children and others. Beyond the nurturing influence she exerted on my siblings and me, my mother also taught us how to build relationships, how to be well humored as we developed trust with others, and how to do human networking. The electronic networking that is so commonplace in modern-day culture is profoundly limited in comparison to the quality and depth of the networking my mother and other elderly women in my family modeled. Through the stories these women shared, we also learned how to plan, implement, and assess events.

I remember the moment some ten years ago when I began to record my mother's oral history. She told a story of when she was 26 and had recently given birth to my oldest brother. As she pulled out a tattered black-and-white photo from the family album, she pointed to the dress she wore, as she held her three-month-old baby in her arms. In her native Spanish language, she shared the story of how she wore her favorite dress that day because she feared she would die and wanted to be buried in that pretty dress. The photo, she said, was her attempt to leave her only child with a reminder of how she looked. My mother suffered through post-partum depression, but she hadn't shared the story with anyone, until more than 35 years later. My mother taught us how to be resilient and how to find hope, even in the most adverse situations. Although as a child she never spent a day in a formal school, she was as wise and as skilled as any teacher I have known. Her voice guides me every day.

My Father's Voice

The Ziibiwing elder may as well be my father. As in the image, my siblings and I found ourselves listening upward to our father, as he narrated lofty ideas such as the great virtues of humanity, or as he taught us how to plant crops or how to skin a goat. My father taught us about power, about how to negotiate spaces, and about how to do it all with a sense of humor. He taught through stories and frequently recalled his four years of schooling in rural Mexico, where his teachers played a pivotal role in disciplining and shaping young people. He especially valued the role of the teacher in a community; "the teacher," he said on numerous occasions, "is the most important person in the community." My father was the quintessential teacher.

I recall one particular night during my undergraduate years when I called my father to express my frustration with my studies as an English major. Although he didn't understand much about the college experience, having attended school only to the fourth grade in rural Mexico, he understood my concern when I told him that I simply could not find the kind of literature I most longed to study—the literature of Mexican people in this country. As he listened carefully on his end of the phone, I then asked if he had ever written down any of the thousands of stories he had shared with his children through the years. I suggested to him that those stories constituted an important part of the "life curriculum" he and my mother had used to raise us. As he listened intently, he first responded by saying he had not written the stories. Then he dedicated the ensuing six months to writing his autobiography. When I wrote my doctoral dissertation many years later, one of the most frequently cited sources was my father's autobiography. His stories have been essential to my development, and they have been formative at every stage of my life.

The Elder and the Youth

As I reflect on the most effective teaching and learning models, whether they are for indigenous or nonindigenous people, I cannot imagine a more effective model than the one represented by the Anishinabe elder and child. Through the elder's voice, the child learns to listen, to understand, and to find the ways of the world. My mother's stories and voice have nurtured me as a learner and as a human being who has learned how to respect others, the earth, and that which is greater than we are. Similarly, my father's voice and stories have sustained and helped me understand other dimensions in life. We are limited as learners, as teachers, and as important people in our communities if we do not respect and obey those voices.

Chapter 23

Teaching Cases, Reflections, and Commentaries

CULTURAL PARTNERSHIPS CONFRONT SCHOOL CULTURE

Jeremy Garcia (Mentor: Michael Pavel)

Honoring Our Children: In the Ways of Our Ancestors

Tipos'asna *(Hopi naming ceremony)*

On the morning of December 12, 1998, our family united for the purpose of claiming, honoring, and welcoming our new daughter, Nawinmana, into this world. As part of the Hopi culture, newborns are not to be exposed to the sun until they have been given the proper passage and must be guarded until this ceremony is complete. The ceremony, which followed a certain cultural protocol, took weeks of preparation before the baby was born. My wife's (the birth mother's) family prepared the food to feed family and community members who came to honor our daughter. Her *so'ohs* (grandmothers) would be up all night monitoring the *noq'kwivi* (Hopi stew) and *pikami* (Hopi pudding). I provided the meat for the *noq'kwivi*, and my mother and sister made regular visits throughout the week to complete specific cultural practices.

At 5:00 a.m. our families and clan family arrived to honor our daughter. My (the birth father's) family arrived to wash Nawinmana's hair and provide her with a Hopi/Tewa name, a clan name. This signified that my family honored and claimed her as their responsibility, committing to support, guide, and teach her. One by one, my grandmother, my mother, my sister, and my aunts approached Nawinmana and caressed her hair

169

four times with the *soots-me-wa* (white ear of corn representing mother of life). *Kwa-kwi* (male thank-you) and *askwali* (female thank-you) were expressed throughout. Nawinmana was wrapped in a blanket with her mother as each member of my family approached her with *homa* (corn-meal used for prayer) and a blanket for comfort as they presented her with Hopi and Tewa names.

In the end, my mother walked with Nawinmana and her birth mother to greet the sun. They announced Nawinmana's presence and offered prayers for her to have a good life, happiness, prosperity, perseverance, and humility. To name a few appellations, she is: *Sonewmana* (Pretty Girl), *Hospoamana* (Female Roadrunner), *Himbe kambi aa yang* (Tewa-Heoto Girl), *Halayvimana* (Fast Female Roadrunner), *Taatawmana* (Heoto Girl Who Is Singing), *Hohokyawman* (Girl Who Has Legs Like a Roadrunner), and *Nawinmana* (Beautiful Girl).

Kwa-kwi! Askwali!

Story

Cultural ceremonies attract unquestioned offerings of energy and sacrifice made for the well-being of children. It is through our ceremonies that we collectively make conscious efforts to advocate for a prosperous life. As evidenced by this Hopi naming ceremony, every child has an extended family of support comprising grandparents, uncles, aunts, and clan relatives. These are lifetime partnerships; indeed, they are cross-generational partnerships as many generations of family and clan-family members share responsibility for the children. So, when we hear that our indigenous children are not doing well in school, we need to reflect on our family and clan-family involvement in schools.

Unfortunately, we do not encounter much indigenous pedagogy or calls to involve indigenous community members in the schooling of their children. Too often, too silently, our schools purchase widely marketed curriculum programs. This case will focus on the potential pitfalls when schools serving indigenous students partner with established educational-product firms. The case provides a background of a school, reasons for purchasing adopted programs, background of the community, curriculum concerns, approach to confronting the curriculum, and an interaction with the visiting monitor about one of the adopted programs. Toward the end of this story you will see why indigenous cultural sensitivity is what grounded my response to a representative of a widely marketed curriculum program.

Background of the School

Like many indigenous schools, this school was constructed in the mid-1900s by the federal government. Despite the history of circumstances surrounding its development, the school did all it possibly could to keep up with maintenance, as well as adding modular classrooms to accommodate increases in enrollment. The school averages an enrollment of about 300 students, 30 teachers, and 20 paraprofessionals. In accordance with the Office of Indian Education Program school report cards, the school has averaged a 35 percent to 40 percent proficiency rate on state assessments in reading and math for the past four years. The school has done an excellent job of working to establish a cohesive partnership that has a shared vision with their pre-K schools, high school, and organizations and departments within the community. In addition, the partnership has extended their efforts to include higher education institutions for professional development and degree advancement for faculty.

Background of the Indigenous Community

The community has about 7,000 members and is located near a large town. Many of the students' parents and grandparents also attended this school. The community has given great attention to revitalization of the Native language and culture, although this has presented a challenge. One community member noted, "It is very hard to convince our younger generation of the importance of learning this, because all they see is the life of the dominant culture." Despite many competing factors, the community continues to endorse the ways of their ancestors.

Although the community has been innovative in generating community-based economic revenue, they continue to struggle with socioeconomic adversities such as low income, alcoholism, and low higher education completion rates. Nonetheless, the leaders are to be commended for their efforts to establish a strong economic foundation for the community. The community continues to become more self-sufficient through tribal revenue sources. As a result, the community is experiencing a growth in quality facilities and services. The zeal for socioeconomic development can either be the catalyst to preserve traditional language and culture or the focal point that serves as a distraction. Community members have begun to think about how they can better preserve their traditional language and culture by considering the school's curriculum.

Purchasing an Adopted Curriculum

The adopted school curriculum consisted of reading, math, science, behavior (military-like), early childhood, and family enrichment programs developed by external sources. Each claims to be a "scientifically research-based" curriculum program. The parents and community had advocated for the inclusion of culture and language in the curriculum, and school administrators seemed to be receptive to these recommendations. That was one of the main reasons parents elected to have their children attend this school rather than public schools. So why did the school decide to adopt such programs? It appeared that decisions were related to reliance on and acceptance of programs that administrators were told would improve student achievement, the administration's concern with continuing trends in low achievement scores, and pressure from policies within the No Child Left Behind Act, indicating that adopted programs should be scientifically research based. I recall attending meetings focused on consideration of new programs where the recurring question was, "Is it scientifically researched?"

Curriculum Concerns

Just as people come together for a traditional ceremony, some parents in this indigenous community came together to question certain adopted academic programs because they did not understand why their children were failing and not improving academically. The parents questioned the effectiveness of the academic programs being implemented in the school. When referring to teachers who advocated for more community input, one parent asked, "Why do we have to pay all that money for a program that is failing our kids? What is wrong with trusting our teachers?" Another parent stated, "A major reason I don't care for it is because I just don't understand the expectations of the homework. It just seems redundant, bland, and it sometimes offends our culture." Another parent asserted, "My child is becoming frustrated that he cannot move up with his class, and that he can't until he passes this level. He has had the same material for a long time now. It got to a point that my son and I are frustrated with each other."

Because of community members' critical inquiries about the program, administrators and the school board began to question whether they should continue to invest thousands of dollars to pay for certain curriculum programs. During one meeting, a school board member asked pivotal questions of the school administrators: "In your opinion, are these programs effective? What are the strengths and weaknesses of the programs? Should we continue using them? How do the teachers feel about these particular programs?" Another school board member pointed out, "We have had these programs for several years now; why are the scores and results still showing similar trends?"

After in-depth reflection and dialogue among the stakeholders, the school board decided to have the school review both the reading and math programs. This action reflected consensus among the teachers, parents, and administrators to consider another program. Opportunities were provided for parents, students, teachers, administrators, and the community to consider and select new reading and math programs. So, in a way, they did omit certain programs, only to adopt other ones.

Confronting the Curriculum

As an elementary school teacher, I joined the parents and community members in analyzing adopted academic programs, namely, the reading and math programs. My role as an indigenous educator was not only to teach the children, but to counter the numerous inequities that indigenous children face in education and society. What was the risk to me? In the beginning, I was given the keys to my classroom, the faculty handbook, and a list of materials to check out from the curriculum resource room. My initial reaction was that it was great to have a ready-to-use curriculum.

As a novice teacher, I didn't have much time or money to spend on materials. Unfortunately, I soon recognized the materials to check out were several prepackaged curriculum programs. Not long after gathering the materials, I was sitting among several days' worth of instruction on how to implement the programs. I could not believe how limited and confining the programs were. This ranged from the specific words to say and when to say them, to the materials to use, to extreme cases of adhering to the details of the curriculum schedule. On several occasions, I expressed my concern to administrators and colleagues during professional development meetings and at grade-level meetings, and asked them to take a critical look at how this curriculum ignored the diversity of student learners. I often would ask how, if at all, fellow teachers modified this curriculum to meet their students' learning abilities. A response I was often given was, "In my experience with the program, we simply have to stick to it because that is what they will be looking for." When I did not receive any resourceful responses, I realized that my colleagues accepted the programs despite their own concerns and did not question the limitations.

I implemented the reading and math programs by following the detailed instructional and curricular scripts in my class. However, my tension and frustration grew as I found myself limited to the guidelines of reading from a manuscript and keeping to the schedule, when students clearly were either ready to move on or did not understand the core concepts and were getting left behind. The tension became evident when I had to choose between perpetuating this stipulated structure to satisfy the program or countering that to address student disinterest, complaints, misbehavior, and disconnects in learning styles and abilities. I recall students commenting, "I know what we have to do next. We do that every day" and "I have heard this story already" and "How come I can't read different books?" and "Mr. Garcia, I know I can't sit still, but I will try my best during reading." The lack of student progress was evidenced by low test scores, incomplete assignments, absences, classroom disruptions, and a decline in students' self-confidence.

Then one day, I decided to modify the program to meet the needs of my students. The onsite curriculum specialist strongly advised me to return to the structure of the prescribed curriculum because external program monitors would be arriving to observe whether the program was being successfully implemented. I resisted and continued to teach how I thought the students learned best and in a way in which they responded to my instruction.

The External Monitors Arrive

"Good afternoon, Mr. Garcia," the monitor began. What I have here is your evaluation of the implementation of our program. I noticed that you have taken down some of the posters from the last evaluation. Please remember that these posters are an important part of the program so the students can refer to them as needed. Secondly, I also noticed you have changed the structure of the daily routines of our program. Can you tell me why?"

I responded, "To be quite honest, my students were given the opportunity to experience the daily structure of the program. Unfortunately, there was a mismatch after reassessing their learning styles, curiosities, and abilities in relation to program expectations. Changes to the program were made in the best interest of the students: socially, academically and culturally. I realize that some of the materials are not a part of the program, but it is essential for the group of students I have."

The monitor replied, "Mr. Garcia, I have to stress that the success of this research-based program relies on the accuracy of its implementation. That means the posters, selected materials, schedule, and assessments of the students must be upheld. You may not see the results now, but in time, if everyone complies with the program, the results will be reflected in the scores of the school."

Believing that my indigenous ancestry guides my pedagogy and encourages me to trust the parents and community members of this indigenous community, I responded, "I understand, and I respect your position; however, I hope you will respect my position to continue teaching my students in a manner that promotes learning and engagement among my students. The results from my modifications, largely derived from the indigenous community, show that my students are engaged, aware, excited, and learning. The program does have some good concepts to it, but overall, it doesn't fit the learners in my classroom."

The monitor chided me by saying, "Well, Mr. Garcia, I am sorry to hear that you have a strong opposition to the program and hope that, by our next visit, you will have reconsidered. I hope you know that we share our evaluations with the curriculum specialist and the administration of your school."

Lessons We Learn: Commentaries From Scholar-Practitioners

Cultural Partnerships Confront School Culture

Iris PrettyPaint

Indigenous educators are reclaiming the ability to educate by choosing to work in schools serving indigenous children. Although we differ in our history, world view philosophy, languages, and customs, as indigenous educators we hold a common desire to preserve, protect, and promote our cultural values, teachings, and traditional educational pedagogies. In doing so, we hope to reverse the history of devastating educational practices that removed us from our culture and language and failed to effectively teach indigenous children (AIHEC, 2007). Today, the critical challenge facing schools serving indigenous students is to implement curriculum that makes learning more meaningful to tribal context and culture.

Critical Challenge #1: Cultural Context

Indigenous people always have ways of assessing merit or worth based on traditional values and cultural expressions (AIHEC, 2007). This knowledge should inform how our children are educated. The truth of what we "come to know" is found in understanding the story within its context. We know that context is critical and that schools are understood only in relation to place, setting, and community. Indigenous educators are at the beginning of a journey to articulate cultural context in teaching while maintaining the integrity of indigenous knowledge and ways of learning. In undertaking a new reading or math curriculum, the focus should be to understand its relevance to the community and place. The social, political, and economic currents surrounding a school can, and usually will, affect the teachers. We can only appreciate whether and how a school is responding to a community concern when we explore the school's cultural context.

Cultural context also influences the way teachers communicate, make decisions, negotiate, and build relationships. Some teachers leave schools because they feel they do not "fit" or do not "belong" socially or culturally. They believe the school is "not right" for them. In the jargon of researchers, there is a lack of congruence between the teacher and the school. Likewise, in order for students to learn and develop in an educational setting, the school's environment must have a "cultural fit" with its students, meaning the school should meet the "cultural needs" of students and encourage learning from the beginning. The "cultural fit" between teacher and principal is fundamental in creating a healthy learning community.

Critical challenge #2: Indigenous Pedagogy

Lorna Williams, assistant professor in Aboriginal Education at the University of Victoria, designed a course for teachers that integrates the essential indigenous elements of inclusivity, community building, and recognition and celebration of individual uniqueness. It is through mentorship and apprenticeship that teachers experience the principles of traditional indigenous ways of teaching and learning: learning by doing; learning by closely observing; learning through listening, telling stories, and singing songs; learning in a community; learning by sharing; and learning by being in service to the community (Williams & Tanaka, 2007). The challenge for schools is to create a place for teacher educators to incorporate their indigenous knowledge along with research-based instructional programs and documented evidence of student achievement. It is imperative that we do not confuse these two forms of knowledge or exchange the roles they play in our lives (Deloria and Wildcat, 2001).

A first step in developing an indigenous pedagogy is to understand our own epistemologies—our own Indigenous ways of knowing. Indigenous educators should consider the question of what core common values influence their perspective and take time to sort out which values should inform their praxis. What does this mean to the educator's community and school? What are these values? In defining our own indigenous pedagogy, its meaning, practice, and usefulness in our own terms, we have ownership and do not merely respond to the requirements imposed by outsiders (AIHEC, 2007).

It is important to view cultural values and beliefs of the community within a historical, cultural, and spiritual context. This story, *Cultural Partnerships Confront School Culture*, identifies the cultural values and beliefs of this community and school: (a) being a people of a place (7,000 community members, 300 students, 30 teachers, and 20 paraprofessionals), (b) centrality of family and community (parents, students, school board, administration), and (c) the recognition that students bring their own gifts to the classroom (creativity, self-expression, uniqueness). Cultural values have a profound influence on how we learn to navigate the principles and methods of instruction.

The current climate of reform provides all of us an opportunity to reexamine old assumptions and develop new bases of knowledge from which to re-create instruction and assessment (Trumbull Estrin & Nelson-Barber, 1995). Instead of asking, "How can we make the curriculum better?" we need to ask, "What kinds of indigenous teaching strategies will meet our needs in reading and math now and in the future?" We do not need to write a new curriculum, we need to add new strategies of instruction that expand the potential we can derive from the science or theory of educating indigenous children. What we have learned is that indigenous pedagogy emerges from a collective effort to make traditional values the core of what drives an approach to teaching in our communities.

References

American Indian Higher Education Consortium (AIHEC) (2007) *Indigenous Evaluation Framework*. Washington, DC: Author.

Deloria, V. & Wildcat, D. (2001) *Power and Place: Indian Education in America*. Golden, CO: Fulcrum Resources.

Trumbull Estrin, E. & Nelson-Barber, S. (1995) "Issues in cross-cultural assessment: American Indian and Alaska Native students" [Electronic version]. *Knowledge Brief*, 12, 1–8. San Francisco: Far West Laboratory.

Williams, L., & Tanaka, M. (2007) "Schalay'nung Sxwey'ga: emerging cross-cultural pedagogy in the academy" [Electronic version]. *Canadian Journal of Education*, 1–4.

Lessons Learned: Connecting Stories

Shelly Valdez

How one connects "story" to one's home environment, from which the essence of story emerges, is important to our lives as Native peoples. In this particular case, Native students embrace a deep sense of relationship to their family, to their community, and to their home environment. The natural elements of their physical environment are intertwined with their daily lives, thereby creating a positive balance for every child. In a traditional environment, it is the family and community that share this responsibility to create educational pathways for children. However, the concepts of Western education have become infused into their natural systems of education, creating a separation of once-held holistic perspectives of community-based education. Native students have been placed in compartmentalized systems, where they become alienated from their natural environment. The story shared in Garcia's case is an example of how these systems have created a dysfunctional environment for Native students as they cannot find "place" in school, and hence will find it difficult to succeed in the school environment as well as feel a sense of personal balance.

I find it interesting when reading educational research that describes and targets Native students' limited progress, poor test scores, and low self-esteem. I often ask, by whose definition, by whose assessment, and by whose research criteria? Educational institutions and researchers have voiced the same concerns since the introduction of Western educational systems to Native communities, and the same old systems of educational rhetoric and research are being conducted, using the same methodologies, pedagogies, and tools. On another level, the monopoly on prescribed curricula by textbook companies that tribal educational communities and programs buy into is outrageous. Again, we must ask who is actually in charge of educating Native children, who is directing and assessing the curriculum that is federally mandated, and who is making the purchases of such curriculum mandatory? The preceding story is a critical reminder that it is time to begin listening to the Native voices that have been echoing the importance of systems change.

There are two things that resonate in this story. The first concerns cultural relevance in curriculum and instruction. In the preceding story, one teacher is attempting to make a difference because he is grounded in the community and understands Native children's inherit learning styles. Through observation and alternative assessment strategies, this teacher was aware that the prescribed or packaged curriculum was not having the appropriate effects. Thus, on the basis of his understanding of Native ways of knowing, he created more innovative and culturally appropriate teaching activities that resulted in more positive student learning. This teacher did not recreate the entire curriculum; he merely abstracted concepts and elements and created activities that were more natural and appropriate to the environments of the students. However, the system scorned his innovation and direct understanding of how Native students learn. Perhaps this is why staff members did not want to engage in curriculum modification; they feared reprimand if they moved outside the status quo. Had they, too, been subjected to the threats of administrative mandates, and to the forced theories of Western research-based programs? Where is the community voice that was accepted by the administrators and the educational system as indicated in the first part of this story? Perhaps that voice was misunderstood, not taken into account, or lost. Native communities must recognize dysfunctional environments in their school systems and work to rectify that situation for all the obvious reasons that benefit their Native children.

The second topic concerns relevant assessment and evaluation. Native communities have continued to be exploited by research institutions that focus on paradigms of viewing progress in academia through one lens. In most cases, scientifically based educational research has been defined through prescribed systems that do not take into account indigenous epistemologies, philosophies, values, and the natural environments that are vital to the learning of Native children. Although scientifically researched evaluation programs that are driven primarily by one set of assumptions may work for general populations, they are not necessarily valid for Native communities. In considering the historical context of Native Americans, educational institutions, researchers and evaluators must be aware that there are 562 federally recognized tribes in the United States, and each of those tribes has its own distinctive cultural norms, traditions, philosophies, and understandings. For evaluation and assessment models and tools to be balanced holistically, educational institutions, researchers, and evaluators must be willing to step beyond their comfort level to learn about and understand the background of those Native communities with which they are working, and to provide a mechanism for acquiring community input into the evaluation and assessment processes. This begins with respect of the people and their unique Native ways of knowing.

It is when we consciously make efforts to include community voices and leaders in organizing educational pedagogies and systems that we will begin to understand that there is real potential for Native students to succeed in the worlds of Western and, for that matter, global thought. This would also serve to support Native communities in their efforts to maintain their cultural ways and sustainable systems that are a part of their natural environment. It is with their own voices, within their own stories, that Native communities will endure.

Reflections on the Case: An Edited Interview with Jeremy Garcia and Michael Pavel

Michael Pavel

As readers, we might ask ourselves whether it is important to ground teaching and learning within a cultural context. For me there is only one answer. Tribal communities across the nation seek to control their own destiny and commit to addressing the needs of their people. Native communities are poised to address their own needs and even the federal and state government with respect to their much larger constituencies. Tribes are developing or want to develop culturally context-based teaching and learning practices to address the failure of America's educational system to consider the unique perspective, needs, and talents of Native people. Clearly, a viable option is that tribal communities move ahead and continue to expand upon dynamic educational and responsive culturally-based offerings. By embracing a central place for culture in our schools serving Native students, we offer a genuine representation of the unique needs of our tribal communities.

There should be no debate about the importance of grounding teaching and learning in a cultural context. Schools partnering with Native communities must embrace a dual mission: (a) bring in the culture of Native peoples into the teaching and learning process, and (b) overcome the historical barriers that Native people experience on a daily basis. Little argument exists about the societal and personal value of education. The more complicated issue is attending to who benefits from education. Unless we reverse the cycle of failure which Native children experience in the school system, our society will contribute to the growing inequality of economic and social opportunity in the land of the free, not reduce it.

Personal benefits from education are clear, and Native students and their parents believe this. Increasingly, education is associated with lower disability rates, longer job tenure, more on-the-job training opportunities, and more opportunities for promotion. The value of these non-monetary benefits adds to the economic returns from education. Human capital theory holds that effective educational systems contribute to community development by creating new knowledge and increasing the skills and abilities of citizens who are able to creatively address the systemic issues confronting their communities and society. More education means less criminal activity, less reliance on welfare and public assistance, and less drug and alcohol abuse. We all benefit from the nonmarket public effects of education. Society gets a better citizen—one more likely to vote, raise healthier children, and volunteer in the community.

Jeremy Garcia

I am fortunate to have collaborated with several indigenous schools working to develop partnerships, which has provided me with new understandings of what a partnership means. Through this interaction, I realized many points of promise and tension that determined how receptive, proactive, and unwilling stakeholders would be in joining such notions of partnerships. While improving partnerships around the development of curriculum, pedagogy, and policy is certainly important in contributing to the learning experiences of indigenous children and youths, minimal movement to strengthen this partnership will occur if there is no concerted effort to build trust, respect, ownership, communication, and integrity among all the partners. Some consider this a "romanticized" or "utopian" view of the character of partnerships. In my experience, however, these principles are critical to establishing healthy and constructive partnerships.

Through conversations with indigenous stakeholders, I observed disconnects between teaching and learning and the resources that might be tapped to support curriculum due to lack of trust and communication, thereby leading to fragmented efforts. This is not to imply that good work is not occurring in our schools and that partnerships do not exist, but rather to note that potential community partners may not be aware of how they can collectively work with schools. The first step is to develop trust, which is a fragile process that requires patience and consistency. It is vital to offer opportunities for stakeholders to have a voice in the development of and decision-making about what their partnership will look like. This builds value and meaning.

Our school leaders must provide avenues that allow community stakeholders to find their place at the education table. This means inviting local support services, departments, universities, and other organizations to share their visions and expectations to sustain the community. A challenge to this partnership might be organizational policies that can limit participation due to budgets, personnel, protection of family records, and conflicting missions (to name a few). Our school, Tribal, and community business leaders need to work together in ways that allow meaningful partnerships with schools to cross organizational boundaries.

Michael Pavel

It is true that before we take action it is important to reflect on our indigenous cultural partnerships to help guide our actions. We, as a collective in various positions within the schools and communities, are the foundation. As a foundation, there should be a seamless and transparent partnership in which it becomes difficult if not impossible to see the separation between schools and our communities. Our schools are our community and vice versa. The bond that holds us all together should be tempered by trust, respect, and reciprocity while being grounded in integrity. To cultivate such a domain of existence, communication becomes key to sharing and owning the process in order to keep the focus on what is best for our children. I cannot imagine that such a worthy and sacred responsibility could be carried out otherwise.

The time and energy we have already put forth show that the spirit of our ancestors is guiding our actions; the positive results are obvious. Tribal communities are inspired by the timeless wisdom of their culture(s), and this inspiration provides the motivation to keep on trying to do what is best for our children. The social forces that have undermined tribal community efforts to be a significant player in the educational arena were centuries in the making, thus leaving us with the challenge of staying the course for generations to come. Our leaders need to be prepared to make lifelong commitments to transform the educational system to include more of our cultural knowledge, in order to promote teaching and learning that is conducive to honoring the stories of our ancestors.

Our stories are important because how we refer to human knowledge and how we preserve it has changed significantly since the development of written languages. Conveying shared knowledge of cultural concepts through stories is a tool for survival and prosperity, by developing belief in a common origin and history, a moral and ethical system, a story symbology, and a spiritual belief system. These beliefs can inform character development and a formal educational system because we live in a time when we can still draw upon our stories and the stories of other American Indian and Alaska Native people for inspiration, advice, and motivation.

We honor the very act of being human any time we broaden our intellectual horizons while gaining a deeper understanding of some area of interest. Many traditional elders convey that to be human is to accept the responsibility to carry forth a love of learning. It is this love of learning that encompasses remembering traditional teachings and preparing to live into tomorrow. It is a sacred responsibility to gain knowledge throughout one's life about how to care for other entities, to maintain a sense of harmony, to enjoy life, to nurture new life, to carry on the positive cycle of existence, and to deal with hardship.

THREATS TO OUR ANCIENT PARTNERSHIP WITH THE LAND: *MOLOKAI NUI A HINA*

Noelani Lee (Mentor: Julie Kaomea)

The *'Āina*: The Land

Molokai nui a Hina, Molokai no ka heke, 'Āina Momona

These are ancient Hawaiian names: *Molokai nui a Hina*, Molokai, the child of Hina; *Molokai no ka heke*, Molokai, greater than the best; *'Āina Momona*, the fat land. Molokai is an island full of seductive promises, full of secrets, and full of *mana* (a spiritual power). The first time I came to Molokai, I felt as if I'd been here before. Since that time, I've learned that my ancestors were here before me, and that the "déjà vu feeling" that arises when I drive over a hill and into a lush valley for the first time or when I walk across a pristine beach for the first time or when I meditate in a cool mountain stream is really the loving spirit of my *kūpuna* welcoming me back again for the first time.

As residents of this land, which many consider to be one of the most (or the last) truly "Hawaiian" islands, we pride ourselves on the things that we don't have, as well as the things that we do have. After all, with an understood building code (i.e. no buildings taller than a coconut tree), unheard-of traffic patterns (e.g. three cars in a row is prime time), and a population just under McDonald's radar at 8,000, what *isn't* here makes Molokai as much of a paradise as what *is* here. The red-painted sign facing you as you leave the airport is one of the few traffic signals you'll encounter on the island; Molokai does not have street lights. This sign reminds visitors and locals to "SLOW DOWN—This is Molokai!"

All of these aspects make Molokai what it is today, but there are two features that visitors to this island remember most. The first, although some may consider it trivial, is that this charming island is known for its famous late-night hot bread: warm pieces of heaven stuffed with jam, cream cheese, and cinnamon served only from 10 p.m. to 3 a.m. The

185

adventure of walking down the back alley, knocking on the green door lit only by a single light, handing your money over to a woman who mysteriously closes the door in your face and then returns moments later with the awaited loaves and your change is an experience that is not easy to forget.

Although the hot bread is delicious, it is the people's bond with the 'āina, the land, that is most visible. We see and experience this daily as it is rooted in the lifeblood of the island, passed down from generation to generation. Molokai is known for its subsistence farmers, hunters, and fishermen. If you cannot farm, hunt, or fish, and don't have a family member who can, you most likely are not from Molokai. Because the people are attached to their land, they are very protective of who is permitted to fish in their waters, hunt in their mountains, and plant in their fields. Without a doubt, power is connected to the land.

Previous Land Tensions

Molokai is known for its celebrated history of activism. Over the past two years alone (2005 and 2006), there have been major battles—all over land—that have threatened the sacred cordage of land, ancestry, and quality of life on Molokai. The first battle I remember, after having moved to the island, was a protest against John McAfee (of the famed McAfee anti-virus computer software). McAfee had taken out a full-page advertisement in *The New York Times* to auction off his Molokai residence to the highest bidder. However, after the success of the auction, McAfee was nicknamed "the virus" and driven from the island. (The county tax structure on Molokai bases assessments on the highest-priced property sold in the area.)

The next fight was launched against the Molokai branch of the Missouri-based agricultural company Monsanto Corporation and, ultimately, the University of Hawai'i. Molokai residents and land activists first protested heavily against the corporation's experimentation and growth of genetically-modified-organism (GMO) corn. The conflict then moved on to the patents that the University of Hawai'i claimed to own on Hawaiian *kalo* (taro). Protesters invoked the revered Hāloa, who, according to Hawaiian creation stories, was *kalo*, one of the eponymous ancestors of Native Hawaiians today. In the end, Molokai protesters won their battle with the University of Hawai'i, which eventually relinquished its patents. But the fight goes on today, as a bill prohibiting genetic experimentation with taro was recently defeated in the Hawai'i State Legislature.

A Case of Appropriation: Stealing the Soul

Molokai's latest struggle is over a point of land on the west end of the island called *Kalae o Kala'au*, or *Lā'au* Point. It has been called the biggest battle of our (Hawaiian) generation. As Molokai activist Hanohano Naehu said, "This war is not over hate; it's over love of the land." In brief, the battle is over 200 proposed million-dollar two-acre lots to be developed along the coastline of some of the most pristine waters in the state of Hawai'i. But the long story is about a people's connection to their ancestors through land, and that is the story I will tell here.

The war has been perpetuated in my memory as a sign war. Lovingly hand-painted signs protesting the proposed development of *Lā'au* Point are posted at almost every residence on the island—hundreds of them. One community member described the signs as colorful new flowers blossoming on every corner. Supporters of the *Lā'au* development plan reacted to these hand-painted signs by erecting signs of their own that are twice as large; however, there are only a handful of them, and they all are posted at Molokai Ranch employees' homes. Most of these development supporters' signs broadcast messages about aspects of the proposed plan that would benefit absentee owners and tourists, whereas the anti-development signs are about listening to the land as it speaks the truth of connection.

To better understand the *Lā'au* controversy, it is important to know that for many months the idea of a sacrificial tradeoff that allowed *Lā'au* Point to be developed in exchange for thousands of Molokai Ranch-owned acres has been the central theme of the conflict surrounding the Ranch's Master Land Use Plan (Yamashita, 2006). The owner of Molokai Ranch, Molokai Properties, Ltd. (MPL), had applied to the State Land Use Commission to have 613 acres near *Lā'au* reclassified from agricultural to rural land use to allow for development of 200 two-acre residential lots, along with related infrastructure (Perry, 2006). At the same time, the Molokai Ranch, which bought the Kaluakoi Hotel in 2001, was seeking support for a community-based land trust, which would fund a $30-million-plus renovation and reopening of the property (Schaefers, 2007).

The Ranch spokesperson has said it cannot pay for the $30-million-plus renovation of the Kaluakoi Hotel without revenue from the sale of land near *Lā'au* Point. John Sabas, general manager of community affairs for Molokai Ranch, estimated that it will cost about $80 million to develop a community near *Lā'au* Point, but he expects a return of more than $1 million for each of the 200 lots that surround the federally protected land (Schaefers, 2007). A percentage of the *Lā'au* sales will go to the Molokai Land Trust to pay the costs for managing 24,950 acres of land that are being donated to the Land Trust by Molokai Ranch (MPL Press Release, February 23, 2007).

Of crucial significance is that the Molokai Land Trust is a private nonprofit corporation started by the Molokai Enterprise Community (EC), which has touted itself as the community's representative and dealmaker in bartering an approval of the *Lā'au* development in trade for thousands of acres of MPL's unused land (Yamashita, 2007). In addition, the EC board members, in support of the development of *Lā'au*, have appointed themselves trustees of the Molokai Land Trust (the nonprofit receiving land from MPL), and under their bylaws, only they may vote to add new members to the board.

In January 2007, the EC announced that a public vote would decide who in the community would become the organization's two new board members (Yamashita, 2007). EC election results on January 31 showed that the only two candidates who ran on anti-development platforms won the two open seats, with an overwhelming 68 percent majority. It is notable that the EC community election drew 1,284 voters, which surpassed the number of Molokai residents who had turned out to vote at the 2006 general election.

One hundred forty-five comments were submitted concerning MPL's Draft Environmental Impact Statement (EIS). This is more than the State Land Use Commission has ever received on any EIS in the state of Hawai'i. Of the comments that were submitted by elected officials, private organizations, and individuals, only one was in outright support of the development.

This battle is far from over. At the present time, the State Land Use Commission is considering the MPL's rezoning request. The majority of Molokai people want the island to remain undeveloped. One of my *kūpuna* used to give tours on the island. He told me he would share many of the beautiful stories of Molokai along his drive with the tourists, but as soon as they began to talk about real estate and buying property he would ask them, "What is it that you like about Molokai?" He told me they invariably would answer that Molokai was so Hawaiian—so peaceful, so quiet, so private—and had so much beautiful land. And then he would gently caution them, "Then don't buy property here. Molokai is not for sale. We are happy to have you visit us, and you may visit us again. But don't buy land here or you will take away what it is you like most about our island."

"Keep Molokai, Molokai" is a favorite modern motto reminiscent of the island's ancient names. It exemplifies the fact that the people of Molokai are just as happy with what isn't here, as what is. The community does not want more development; instead, we celebrate our connection to the *'āina*.

> *Molokai nui a Hina*—Molokai is the child of Hina.
> *Molokai no ka heke*—Molokai is greater than the best.
> *'Āina Momona*—Molokai, the fat land.

The Importance of Land to Our Learning

If all the secrets of sustaining the lifeblood of a race could be held in one thing, that thing would be the land. The Hawaiian diaspora will be safe as long as there is still some place that is rooted and steeped in culture and tradition. But if all of our Hawaiian islands sell out to development and tourism, then we have lost the core of our spiritual beings; we will have succumbed to genocide.

Molokai is a place where Hawaiians thrive, where Hawaiians are still the majority on their own land, and where culture and traditions are still daily practice. Here is a place where our children are being taught how to earn a sustainable living in an environment that values the cordage that links them to the *po* (the land hereafter) of our ancestors. Connection to and hence protection of the land are of great importance to Hawaiians. We look to Molokai to fight. We look to Molokai, to the *keiki* and the *kūpuna*, for leadership.

References

Perry, B. (2006, September 21) "Dozens in Molokai group protesting *Lā'au Point development plans.*" *Maui News.* Retrieved from www.mauinews.com.

Schaefers, A. (2007, January 7) "Restoring Molokai jewel . . . but at what price?" *Star Bulletin.* Retrieved from www.starbulletin.com.

Yamashita, T. (2006, December, 15) "Molokai land trust in detail." *Molokai Dispatch.* Retrieved from www.themolokaidispatch.com.

Yamashita, T. (2007, February 23) "Dispatch editor submits comment on Molokai Ranch's proposed development of *Lā'au Point.*" *Molokai Dispatch.* Retrieved from www.themolokaidispatch.com.

Lessons We Learn: Commentaries From Scholar-Practitioners

Indigenous Philosophy, Maintaining Integrity and the Problems of Development

Troy Richardson

I want to suggest that we hear the central concerns raised in Noelani's essay—"development" of indigenous lands, traditional knowledge (TK), and cultural integrity—as having significant philosophical underpinnings. Although it is not her purpose here to cast these issues in the mold of indigenous philosophy or to employ an explicitly philosophical language, I nonetheless recognize much of her emphasis as the right to maintain a Native Hawaiian philosophical tradition specific to the place of Molokai. "Molokai is a place where Hawaiians thrive," she writes, "where Hawaiians are still the majority on their own land and where culture and traditions are still daily practices. Here is a place where our children are being taught how to create a sustainable living in an environment which values cordage." Noelani articulates an indigenous philosophical perspective, which is not separate from the place from which such philosophies emerge, but instead is wholly dependent for its vitality on maintaining these lands in specific ways. "It is the people's bond with the 'āina, the land," she writes, "that is most visibly apparent." This bond with the land cannot be understood as a romantic, pastoral aesthetic but instead as a process of continued learning. Moreover, such learning is dependent on the actions and interactions in a specific geography, not an isolated intellectual activity.

According to Noelani, native Molokai philosophies are sustained—taught and learned—in a set of daily practices and uses. She writes elsewhere that "Molokai is known for its subsistence farmers, hunters, and fishermen. If you cannot farm, hunt, or fish and don't have a family member who can, you are most likely not from here." In this way, there is an understood dimension of physical labor, not aesthetic musing, in maintaining indigenous philosophies; traditional knowledge and philosophical systems are based on the lessons learned through the work of understanding how a particular geography can sustain not only a people, but all the forms of life within it. Accordingly, in placing themselves in the position of being learners, reliant on the integrity of the biotic system for their existence, Native peoples like those on Molokai assume roles of stewards. Noelani writes in this regard, "Because the people are attached to their land they are very protective of who is permitted to fish in their waters, hunt in their mountains, and plant in their fields." Here she alludes to an implicit indigenous philosophy of stewardship, which highlights the tension of maintaining the integrity of the complex interdependence of cultural and biotic systems in the context of a demand for development.

These statements by Noelani remind me of the comment by Vine Deloria, Jr. (1999) that, "Adherence to traditions means that the fundamental sets of the historic relationships—with the land, with the animals and birds and with the larger cosmos—become the defining boundaries within which the people find their being" (pp. 269–270).

Read through and with Deloria, Noelani and the Native Hawaiians of Molokai are struggling over boundary definitions, of a line or set of parameters, which should not be compromised as they move into the future. But again, it is important to resist reading Noelani and the Molokai community as anti-modernist, naïvely romanticizing a set of traditions. Instead, how might we read her as a woman committed to maintaining intellectual, philosophical, and cultural diversity through active participation in and application of traditional ecological knowledge systems to sustain a complex biotic culture? The physical and intellectual work to maintain the integrity of traditional ecological knowledge and its related philosophical and cosmological systems is imperative not only for the communities of Molokai, but likewise for their allies who understand Native Hawaiian knowledge as highly relevant to the continual refinement of human knowledge. Simply put, educators, scientists, resource managers, and developers have a lot to learn from the people of Molokai.

Differing Philosophical Systems and the Need for Indigenous Based Standards for Development: Moving into a Future

Given the philosophical framing I have brought to the issues and my subsequent interpretations of Noelani's essay as a struggle for integrity, a variety of challenging questions and opportunities are presented. One challenge I have already alluded to is that of competing perceptions of the natural world. I have highlighted how Noelani speaks from an indigenous philosophical perspective, which is inclusive of and drawn from a specific topography and seeks to sustain that. It is difficult to speak of the philosophical worldview of those seeking to develop *Kalae o ka Lā'au* or its own form of integrity based on this single essay. Of course it, too, has its own sense of wholeness, with its own unique configuration. Yet two things seem clear: it is a world view that would appear to give less regard to the disruption of traditional Native Hawaiian intellectual, physical, and cosmological integrity, and, relatedly, it does not seem to give utmost priority to the biotic integrity of *Kalae o ka Lā'au*.

Of course, the issue is more complicated than this, and Noelani outlines some of it with regard to the establishment of a land trust and land "swap" by the same multi-national corporation that seeks to develop *Kalae o ka Lā'au*. Political maneuverings of these various Land Trust and Enterprise Community board members aside, these are hints of some concern for maintaining biotic integrity for at least parts of Molokai. But the question that arises here and the potentially stark difference between these worldviews pertains to where and how compromises are made and for what reason. Why are the intrusions into the biotic and Native Hawaiian cultural integrity of *Kalae o ka Lā'au* acceptable to the developers, while at the same time they would claim to be invested in the biotic integrity of other lands such that they are placed in "trust"? As Noelani makes clear, overlooking the profitability of beachfront properties on Molokai would be disastrously naïve. The concern for biotic integrity, then, perhaps ends for these developers where highest profits begin. The opposite would seem to be true of Noelani: no profit is large enough to compromise the integrity of our traditions and the knowledge we recognize as integral to the survival of everything in this place.

These complications between competing philosophies and world views nonetheless provide potential opportunities for Native communities to put their holistic philosophical perspectives at work in potentially new arenas. One such area of intervention involves negotiating codes for infrastructure in or around Native lands. For those of us invested in helping indigenous communities in their struggle not only to maintain traditional ecological knowledge and cultural integrity, but also to exercise sovereignty, we can encourage and assist them in developing and monitoring a set of building codes, water-quality standards, energy-efficiency standards, impact assessments (both cultural and biotic), and so on.

There is a growing trend in this direction as many indigenous communities are employing indigenous philosophies as they deal with issues of water quality and renewable energy. The Miccosukee Nation, for example, has developed water-quality standards and the Miccosukee Water Management Plan, which is an effort to enhance water quality in the Everglades (See http://www.epa.gov/waterscience/standards/wqs library/tribes.html   and   http://www.evergladesplan.org/pm/projects/ proj_90_miccosukee.aspx for more information). With such examples in mind, Native communities and their allies in natural resource management, environmental science, and conservation might collaborate on a set of standards founded on indigenous knowledge and philosophies, affirmed by a variety of Western scientific paradigms. In cases like the one Noelani has shared, development might be halted or perhaps significantly limited, such that maintaining biotic and cultural integrity for the forseeable future remains the highest priority and obligation. Such a vision is neither idealistic nor easily achievable; it will take struggle, hard work, and lots of listening and learning. Accompanying the ecological and environmental dimensions of such work are the legal and jurisdictional questions, which attend not simply to building codes, but also to the broader areas of international law concerning the rights of indigenous peoples.

Noelani's essay brings into relief, then, the complexity of what it means for one indigenous community to maintain its integrity. Serving as a steward of the healthy, sustainable life ways of Molokai, as Noelani does, requires not only a continuing education in the sophisticated traditional knowledge systems, philosophies, and cosmologies of her community but simultaneously a mustering of the best knowledge—

legal, scientific, and academic—to provide the indigenous cultural and biotic elements of Molokai with the environment necessary to flourish.

Reference

Deloria, V., Jr. (1999) "Introduction to Vision Quest." In J. Treat (ed.), *For This Land: Writings on Religion in America* (pp. 269–270). New York: Routledge.

Reflections on Molokai Nui a Hina
By Nālani Wilson

The work of Noelani's case study serves as a reminder of our deep, ancestral, *Kānaka Maoli* connection with, and protection of, that which we love and embrace as one of our first ancestors, *Papahānaumoku, ka 'āina*. *Ka 'āina* and *nā kūpuna*, the land and ancestors, are alive and well, living and breathing. Our relationship with *nā kūpuna*, including the land, can never be severed. It is a part of our *mo'okū'auhau* (Kame'eleihiwa, 1992; Aluli Meyer, 1998; Trask, 1999). We are inseparable from *nā kūpuna* because our ancestors live within us, through us.

Aloha 'āina, our love and appreciation of the land, is perpetuated through this *mo'okū'auhau*, genealogical lineage. It is neither ancient nor contemporary. Rather it is continual, ever present. Aloha transcends time, over more than 200 years of colonization, and space, whether that is miles across the vast Pacific Ocean or the passing of our *kūpuna* and the lessons they teach us. Noelani's writing beautifully affirms this feeling of connection and aloha *nui o ka 'āina*, as she describes the heartbeat of activism on Molokai. It is vital to reiterate that it is this very activism, and the force of its *mana*, spiritual strength, that is intergenerational on the island. Activism lives and breathes in our *mo'okū'auhau*. This ongoing legacy has created the Molokai that exists today and will continue to exist tomorrow.

It is also conceptually useful to remind ourselves that colonization is a part of our contemporary *mo'okū'auhau* (genealogy), and it is just as important to recite and remember. Colonization did not end with the arrival and demise of Captain James Cook in 1778, or the signing of the *Māhele* in 1848, or the annexation of the Hawaiian Islands to the United States in 1893, or statehood in 1951; rather, it is ongoing and is not finished. As long as foreigners seek to exploit our islands economically, colonization will continue. Our genealogy of colonization is as ever present as our ancestral *mo'okū'auhau*. Thus, activism is a form of perpetual decolonization. It is a reaction to colonization and globalization, fuel to the fire, because when that which we love is threatened, passion is ignited.

In this case study of *Molokai Nui a Hina*, we are given three examples in which this passion has come forth in the form of *mālama 'āina* and *aloha 'āina*—love, care, compassion, relationship, and protection of the island of Molokai. The examples of John McAfee, genetic modification, and the development of *Lā'au* Point represent competitive economic ventures emitting values that are the extreme opposite of a *Kānaka Maoli* world view. *Kānaka Maoli* have survived and thrived for centuries without individualistic opportunism. Priorities that maintain a healthy Hawaiian economy are values of aloha—love and respect, giving and receiving. When the land is objectified and sold off to the highest bidder, or its value calculated in terms of its "natural resources," integrity is lost. Such is the history of Western colonization of the Hawaiian Islands and the difference between Western and Pacific perceptions of place (Wilson, 2005, p. 38).

Contemporarily, we see neo-colonialism in the form of blatant real estate advertisements and transactions, as exemplified in the case of John McAfee and Molokai Properties, Ltd. At the same time, globalization and neo-colonialism can be inconspicuous, silent perpetrators, in the form of genetically modified cornfields distributing their pollen in the gusty Molokai wind. In these instances we are met with rich complexity. It is important that we consider the perspectives and intentions surrounding colonial and globalizing processes because it is often in this analysis that we find the grey areas, the tensions.

The example of John McAfee is fascinating. He donated the revenue from the sale of his land to nonprofit organizations on the island, but in the process advertised "the pristine beauty of Molokai" in *The New York Times*. In my opinion, John McAfee either falsely advertised or perhaps truly believed in an imaginary, "pristine Molokai," because from the west side to *Mana'e* (East Molokai), and everywhere in between, the island is far from pristine. It has experienced vast environmental degradation: deforestation, the near demise of native species such as *'iliahi* (sandlewood), introductions of foreign species of plants and animals, ranching, farming, and erosion. We are still recovering from two centuries of colonization and environmental exploitation. Furthermore, not only are we recovering from environmental degradation, we are also in the midst of *re*-presenting ourselves after decades of tourism advertisements, which both exploit the image of our islands as "paradise" and portray a romantic, sexual view of our people.

The next issue discussed is the debate about genetic modification of, initially, corn and later *kalo*, or taro, our eldest brother. Noelani poignantly articulates that *kalo* represents our ancestor, *Hāloa*. It is difficult to comprehend putting a patent on that which is a part of yourself, feeding your family, your ancestors, and your island for generations. In all of the case-study scenarios, we are met with epistemological barriers and conflicting worldviews. The epistemological perspectives that I will now discuss surround the debate about genetically modified organisms (GMOs).

An interview conducted by Diverse Women of Diversity with Jessica Hutchings, a Māori lecturer in the Science Faculty at Victoria University in Wellington, inspired the following epistemological analytical deconstruction. The desire to dissect the DNA of an organism derives from Western science and reductionism. Historically, the Western epistemology of science has excluded the holistic knowledge and relationship of indigenous peoples worldwide to our places of origin. This epistemic exclusion undermines holism and the cultural and intellectual property rights of our peoples. We have experienced a *mo'okū'auhau* (genealogy) of discrimination that has led to a lack of equitable participation in scientific and ethical debates, such as the case of genetic modification on Molokai.

There are a couple of points that I want to raise about the genetic-modification experiments and real estate ventures on the island of Molokai. I think it is vital to mention that the examples Noelani describes in her case study are interrelated. Molokai Properties, Ltd., the same Singapore-based subsidiary of BIL International, Ltd., interested in selling off 200 million-dollar properties at *Lā'au* Point, granted Monsanto, the genetic-modification corporation based on Molokai, a 99-year lease on 1,650 acres of land for their experiments (Wu, 2007). That is nearly a century of biological experimentation. The long-term effects of GMOs have not been adequately tested, although scientists have concurred that there is a possibility of GMOs cross-pollinating with organic crops. These experiments are not being conducted in the homelands of the corporations and scientists; rather, they are being brought to our shores, without knowing what kinds of devastating environmental effects they will have on the island.

The activism that Noelani highlights in her case study is a reminder to all indigenous peoples that we cannot sit silently and allow environmental racism, such as the case of GMOs on Molokai, to continue. We need to ask questions and demand answers. When school children near the genetically modified cornfields broke out in a mysterious rash, local people began questioning Monsanto about the GMO experiments being conducted to the east and west of the school grounds. They found that Monsanto holds exclusive information about the testing that is taking place on the island. Walter Ritte, the long-time community leader, activist, and coordinator of Hui Ho'opakele 'Āina, says, "We see the corn fields, but we can't get any information about what they're doing. We don't know the impact on our health or on traditional medicines and plants" (Wu, 2007, p. 78). Ritte might not know what kinds of long-term effects genetic modification will have on Molokai, but he certainly is a living example of a *Kanaka Maoli kūpuna* who is not going to sit idly by and watch it happen.

It is this deep ancestral connection and *mo'okū'auhau* of activism that has guarded Molokai *Nui a Hina* for centuries. Molokai is the *piko*, the center or umbilical cord, of the Hawaiian Islands. Beyond being Molokai *no ka heke*, Molokai *momona*, it is Molokai *Pule O'o*, a place guided by spirit and powerful prayer. Our *kāhuna* used to chant away invaders as they approached our shores (Wilson, 2004). It is not at all surprising that their descendants would hold the same *mana*-spiritual strength. No *laila*, it is with a humble and grateful heart that I share these thoughts and pay my respects to *ka mo'okū'auhau*, the genealogy, of my *Kānaka Maoli* lineage to Molokai *Nui a Hina* through the *Kamakahukiolani 'ohana o Waialua*. *Mahalo e nā ākua, nā kūpuna, nā 'aumākua. Mahalo no ka po'e o Molokai Nui a Hina, Molokai no ka heke, 'Āina Momona, Molokai Pule O'o. Mahalo.*

References

Aluli Meyer, M. (1998) *Native Hawaiian Epistemology: Contemporary Narratives.* D.Ed. dissertation, Harvard University.

Diverse Women for Diversity (2007) *Māori point of view on genetic modification.* Retrieved May 11, 2007, from http://www.kahea.org/gmo/.

Kame'eleihiwa, L. (1992) *Native Land and Foreign Desires: Pehea La E Pono Ai?* Honolulu: Bishop Museum Press.

Trask, H. K. (1999) *From a Native Daughter: Colonialism and Sovereignty in Hawai'i*. Honolulu: University of Hawai'i Press.

Wilson, K. L. K. (2004) *Na Wahine Piko o Molokai: Pacific Women's Connections to Place*. MA, Pacific Islands Studies, University of Hawai'i, Mānoa.

Wilson, K. L. N. (2005, December) "A view from the mountain: Molokai Nui a Hina." *Junctures, The Journal for Thematic Dialogue*, 5, 31–46.

Wu, N. (2007, March 24) "Biotech firm grows on Molokai." *Star Bulletin*. Retrieved May 5, 2007, from http://starbulletin.com/2007/03/24/news/story03.html.

Reflections on the Case: An Edited Interview with Noelani Lee and Julie Kaomea

Julie Kaomea

The *Lā'au* Point controversy clearly illustrates the complications involved when economically motivated outsiders attempt to exert their power over an indigenous place. In the case of *Lā'au* Point, we have an international investment company that owns Molokai Ranch and wants to put million-dollar homes on the coastline to make a good return on its investment. In order to do so, the company needs to gain permission for rezoning from a Honolulu-based land use commission, which was established to ensure that Hawai'i's land is used to maximize the state's economic interests. For both of these groups, the power in land (or power in place) is largely economic.

In contrast, the local Hawaiians on Molokai have a very different conception of the power in land, and in *Lā'au* Point in particular. The Hawaiian word for land, *'āina*, is literally translated as "that which feeds." For the subsistence practitioners whose families have hunted and fished at *Lā'au* Point for generations, the land holds power because of its ability to feed their extended families. Subsistence fishermen speak of the south and west coasts adjoining *Lā'au* Point and the near-shore water as their "icebox." It is where they get fish, *'opihi* (limpets), and crab for their families' meals. These subsistence fishermen are justifiably concerned that the proposed development will hinder, if not entirely abolish, the traditional gathering activities currently enjoyed at *Lā'au* Point, as the multi-million-dollar community's future residents are unlikely to appreciate or tolerate these subsistence activities in what they perceive to be their front yards.

The *Lā'au* area also is regarded as a special place of *mana* or spiritual power. It is a place of burial sites, fishing *ko'a* (shrines), and *heiau* (temples), and a place where Hawaiians continue to carry out traditional cultural practices. Hawaiians on Molokai contend that the development of the area will destroy this special quality of *Lā'au* as a place of spiritual power. To exercise traditional customs in a *pono* (proper) manner, practitioners require space and privacy to carry out their ceremonies, rituals, and spiritual practices. As one community member aptly expressed, "Traditional practices lose their *mana* if millionaire residents are peeping through their windows and snapping photos" (Ritte, 2007, p. xx). Thus, local Molokai community members are using every means at their disposal to voice their concerns about the desecration of the *mana* of *Lā'au* and urge the State of Hawai'i Land Use Commission to stop the development. We are yet to see whether their voices will be heard.

Noelani Lee

The *Kumulipo*, the epic Hawaiian genealogical *oli*, chanted far before Darwin's time, told of our connection to the earth and how we are related to its deep darkness, the rocks, the birds, and fish. Herein lies the ultimate lesson of power. It reveals the truth that all Hawaiians (and most indigenous societies) intrinsically know: we come from the earth, we live by the earth, and eventually, we will return to the earth. These truths should dictate how we teach, how we learn, and how we live. And yet, at many recent conferences I have heard the awed murmurings of people who are just now learning that broccoli and human beings share DNA.

The power on Molokai comes from its people, who come from its earth. The natives of this small island in the Pacific recognize the importance of caring for their environment because they know that it is their land that takes care of them. *Kama'āina* of Molokai, unlike other societies, have not severed that sacred cordage that binds them to the fields which they farm, the ocean where they fish, or the mountains where they hunt.

Julie Kaomea

To quote the motto of the Ka'ala Farm and Cultural Learning Center in Wai'anae, O'ahu:

> If you plan for a year, plant *kalo* (taro).
> If you plan for ten years, plant *koa* (largest native forest trees).
> If you plant for the future, teach the children, *mālama 'āina* (to care for the land).

Similar to the place-based educators at Ka'ala, I believe that it is our responsibility as teachers to instill in our younger generations an appreciation of and respect for the subsistence value and spiritual *mana* of our *'āina*, so that they will one day assume the *kuleana* (responsibility) of becoming local stewards of our land and fighting for its protection.

Individuals who possess strong science backgrounds, but who have little, if any, connection to the places and the communities they are intended to serve today hold many land-management jobs in Hawai'i. Relevant place-based curricula that integrate local and cultural knowledge with rigorous scientific training will help prepare youths from our local communities to assume careers in Hawai'i's high-need areas of environmental stewardship, land-use law, coastal zone and marine resource management, and archaeology. As Hawaiian educator Mehana Blaich asserts, we should aim to produce individuals who are as well-versed in ancient place names and traditional *mo'ōlelo* (stories) as they are in cutting-edge techniques for Geographic Information System (GIS) mapping. They should be skillful in designing and conducting scientific research, as well as in facilitating local community meetings. They should be equally comfortable writing *oli* (chants) about the places they serve as they are in drafting legislation. Ultimately, these individuals should be able to stand in both worlds to serve as "culturally-based resource managers" (Blaich, 2006).

Noelani Lee

Our Molokai nonprofit, Ka Honua Momona (the fat or bountiful earth), developed a philosophy of learning and teaching based in "the place" that I think would be valuable guidance for educators just entering the field of land-based pedagogy today. We have worked hard to teach our *ōpio* (youths) that our Native Hawaiian ancestors were brilliant teachers and that their lessons are still here for us to learn. Hawaiian fishponds are an excellent example of lessons in science, mathematics, aquaculture, social studies, history, and art. Of course, we encourage our youths to seek education worldwide, but it is important for them to know that they also need look no further than their own back yards for this education. Place often defines identity. And we feel that by teaching the ōpio about "their" place, we are giving them a firm foundation from which they can draw their strength. When you are grounded with a strong sense of place, you are more powerful.

References

Blaich, M. (2006) personal communication, December 12.

Ritte, W. (2007) "Comments on the *Lā'au Point Draft Environmental Impact Statement.*" *Letter to the State of Hawai'i Land Use Commission, February 23.*

MAINTAINING YOUR MISSION WHILE PARTNERING WITH PEOPLE, EDUCATIONAL INSTITUTIONS, AND COMMUNITIES

Lynette Stein-Chandler (Mentor: Katie Cherrington)

Introduction

Indigenous language-immersion preK–12 schools are not a new concept. In fact, they have flourished in Māori communities in Aoteroa (New Zealand), and are well integrated into the fiber of the public school system in Hawaiʻi. The development of Native language-immersion programs is fairly new in American Indian and Alaskan Native communities. A handful of preK–12 Native language-immersion programs have led this important movement among American Indian communities. For example, Darrell Kipp established the Piegan Institute, which has operated successfully for more than ten years. This is at the private Blackfeet Language Immersion School, with grades K–8. As of this writing, there is only one preK-elementary program located at a tribal college, the A'ani Language Immersion School at Fort Belknap College in Harlem, Montana. This partnership between the A'aninin (White Clay) people and Fort Belknap College is unique in that the focus is to extend language and cultural learning across all generations of our people.

Fort Belknap College and the A'ani Language Immersion School have embarked on a successful, powerful, and cutting-edge model of indigenous education. The first partnership of its kind, the A'ani Language Immersion School is paving the way for students from ages 4 to 70+ to succeed. Today, the partnership between Fort Belknap College and the A'ani Language Immersion School is at the forefront of the next Indian education movement as it has added a new dimension of educational opportunity for all generations of our people.

The Path I Have Journeyed

I gave birth to my daughter Wozek in 1997 and soon began to teach her what I knew of our mother-tongue language. I wanted Wozek to grow up knowing our language, to become a strong White Clay person. A year later, in 1998, my great-grandmother Florence Skinner-Stiffarm passed away. She was one of the last fluent-speaking White Clay elders. With the birth of my daughter and my *Neewah*'s passing, I realized that I had few elders to turn to for further language guidance. I didn't want my daughter to be left with no one to turn to, so I started researching what other tribes were doing to revitalize their languages. I heard many stories from peers, friends, and family members living in Browning, Montana, on the Black-feet reservation about the Piegan Institute. So, in March of 1998, I began actively working toward establishing a White Clay Language Immersion School in Fort Belknap, Montana.

I traveled to Browning, Montana, to visit with the founder of the Blackfeet Language Immersion School, Darrell Kipp. Darrell graciously visited with me and answered my questions. During our conversation, he inspired me to "Just Do It!" Begin! He, himself, had profound dreams. For example, Darrell said, "When I meet my Maker and he asks me, 'Did you do everything you could to save your language?' I know that I can honestly answer, 'Yes!' " He told me that I needed to establish the school as a nonprofit 501c(3) organization and gave me the information to do so. He also shared with me the experiences I would encounter; the wonderful highs and the horrible lows. Darrell warned me that there would be many people, friends and strangers alike, whose pessimism and lack of vision would wear down my soul. He told me I would need to find the place in my heart that would keep me strong and help me persevere and remain true to this work. Darrell encouraged me to work diligently to overcome these obstacles because what I was about to do was worth the effort. So, this was the start of my journey into the tumultuous and inspiring work of indigenous language immersion. I began to advocate for and act on behalf of my daughter and the children of our community.

During the spring of 1998, I began working with the Montana Secretary of State office to lay the legal groundwork for a nonprofit organization. This would enable me to begin work on an immersion school program with the legal and financial benefits of tax-exempt status. After writing bylaws and articles of incorporation and paying a $500 fee (from my own pocketbook), I formed the Istahook Institute 501c(3) non-profit organization. Although the fee was a financial sacrifice at the time (my husband and I were both full-time students with an infant), I knew that the seed that had been planted would grow into a sturdy tree.

Throughout the next year, I continued to prepare myself for the path I would walk. I graduated with a bachelor of arts degree in English literature from Montana State University (MSU), in Bozeman, Montana, and began a Master of Arts program in Native American studies, also at MSU. During my school breaks and on weekends, I continued to visit Darrell Kipp (in Browning) to learn more about the day-to-day workings of an immersion school. In addition, I returned home to the Fort Belknap Reservation to record oral life and history stories told by our elders in our mother-tongue. After the passing of my great-grandmother Florence, I worked closely with Theresa Walker-Lamebull, Elmer Main, and my great-grandfather Merle Skinner (Florence's youngest brother).

Teacher/Apprenticeship Program: Speaking White Clay

During my last year in the Master of Arts program in Native American studies, my great-grandmother's sister, Madeline Colliflower, passed away. She was the head of our Speaking White Clay program. Her passing impelled me to complete my graduate studies quickly and begin the work of establishing an immersion school. I immediately applied for and got a job on the faculty at our tribal college, Fort Belknap College. Without delay, I began forming a teacher/apprenticeship program that would prepare a cadre of young-adult Native language speakers with Class 7 certification. In Montana, the Office of Public Instruction certifies Native language speakers, who can then earn elementary teacher status.

I quickly found that money was not enough of an incentive to entice young adults to enroll in the teacher/apprenticeship program. Providing this external incentive was helpful in getting interested young people through the door, but what kept them there was their own internal fire. It is not an easy task to learn and teach your Native language. This is hard work! I knew that students who would become teachers of our language must realize the importance of what it meant to learn, speak, and teach our Native language. Different from any other teacher preparation program, our course of study required students to do more than study a content area and the foundations of pedagogy and practice. The goals of our program required students to commit their hearts and spirits to learning and teaching our Native language, which had to be a priority in their lives. The students who remained to learn and to teach needed to bring love to their Native community and be committed to communicating in the language given to us by Beyhaatek.

In addition to a small but strong cohort of students, I had a good deal of support from our elders, fluent speakers of our mother tongue. The knowledge they shared and their acknowledgment of my efforts encouraged me and gave me strength. I always knew that I was walking the right path. Indeed, the elders were happy to be involved in the project, feeling a renewed sense of purpose and pride. They worked diligently with our students and often became emotional when the children would visit them in their homes and speak to them in the White Clay language. It is powerful moments like these that stay with you throughout life.

White Clay Immersion Begins

During the second year of the Speaking White Clay teacher/apprenticeship program, my daughter began kindergarten. There was a great deal of talk on the reservation about starting a White Clay Elementary Immersion School, and I was disappointed that there was none already. So I decided to create a morning immersion-school program for kindergartners (at that time, kindergarten was a half-day program). With the support of our tribal college administrators, we were given a classroom on the college campus, donated time from staff, and snacks for the children. Interested families with kindergartners would bring their children to the college for morning language classes. Considering this a great learning opportunity for our students (a laboratory school of sorts), I offered our teachers/apprentices an opportunity to work within the program during the mornings. Two came regularly.

At the time, there was no school where I could learn how to manage, design, and teach in a language-immersion teacher-training program. Hence, much of what I learned emerged from the day-to-day bumping and rolling along. For example, it became apparent that our teachers needed more than just White Clay language classes that helped build their fluency. As we all know, having fluency in any language does not automatically make one an effective teacher of that language. Future teachers need to have training in classroom management, positive reinforcement of children's learning techniques, nonstressful teaching methodologies, and learned patience. Of great importance in our language-immersion program was that students gain a deep understanding of our people's history and the powerful cultural norms of our community, as well as a zeal to be innovative and resourceful (there's not much money to support immersion curriculum development, and yet a good deal of development work needs to be done). I undertook the arduous task of developing these components of our teacher/apprenticeship program.

Six of eight students graduated after three years in the Speaking White Clay program. The graduates were placed at Hays (southern end of the reservation) and Fort Belknap (northern portion) Head Start programs and at both of the elementary schools on the northern and southern borders of our reservation. Our growing immersion program soon became an after-school program; the students who began as half-day kindergartners were now in third grade. Every day, the school bus dropped our elementary-aged students at the college, where they would study our mother-tongue for two to three hours in an immersion setting with members of the teacher apprenticeship program. In addition, the college had recently finished construction of a new cultural center on campus designed to house the Native American Studies program, our tribal archives, and a White Clay Immersion School!

Full-day White Clay Immersion School

We began a full-day White Clay Immersion School in September 2005 with classes for second and third graders. The children were kept together (similar to a looping process) over three years for multiple pedagogical reasons and, more important, to help them establish a supportive community of learning that would ensure a strong foundation for daily use of the White Clay language. We were growing our own teachers! We had begun to create culturally sound White Clay children who were rooted in a strong sense of self, family, and community. We believed that each of the children, in his or her own way, would carry forward the soul of A'aninin (White Clay) people, turning our dreams of a revived mother tongue into reality.

During that time, a Native Studies Director, who happened to be my husband, joined the teaching staff of our school. Not only did he teach the language, but he also brought more knowledge of our culture into the curriculum. In addition, we hired an elder who was teacher certified and held a teaching degree, and a recent graduate student who had excelled in our White Clay language courses. All three brought expertise that helped our curriculum and instruction to grow with stronger curricular materials and innovative teaching approaches. Our work-study program at the college allowed us to hire teaching assistants from the elementary education program. Our hope was that they would return to our community as teachers so that our school would continue to grow.

Although I believed in the value of our program, I did not know whether the college community supported our work. However, I would soon be pleasantly surprised! When one of our young lead teachers resigned early in the school year for personal reasons, we had to turn to the tribal college community for help. The tribal college faculty stepped up and filled our teaching needs without hesitation! Faculty who taught for us had either elementary education degrees or experience teaching young children. What at first appeared to be a devastating setback for us turned into a true blessing. The combination of their expertise with that of our current teaching faculty allowed the school to develop more fully its core curriculum and work more effectively to fulfill our mission.

During that school year, we also added the lower elementary grades (second, third, and fourth) to the preK, kindergarten, and after-school offerings. Older elementary students became tutors, leaders, and teachers for both new and younger students. In fact, the "veteran students," as we began to call the older students, began writing and speaking about their desire to become White Clay teachers.

Partnerships Help Support Our Work

We do have funding issues such that we have been dependent on grants from nonprofit organizations and foundations. We do have first-rate parental involvement that benefits our annual fund-raising activities. We also charge a symbolic tuition fee of $100 a month. Our partnership with parents requires them to sign a contract stating that they will remove their child(ren) from the school if they are habitually absent, tardy, or disrespectful to teachers or other students. We are unique in that Fort Belknap College, our home campus, supports the immersion school. This corresponds with their mission regarding Indian education for

American Indian people by creating a viable, optimal learning environment for all ages and generations of American Indian people. I understand that, in light of fiscal constraints, there will come a time when tribal colleges (Fort Belknap included) will have to decide whether they are willing to incur the costs of a preK–elementary/middle-grades Native language-immersion school. Therefore, we continue to seek private funding.

We have been unrelenting in our requests to the Montana State Office of Public Instruction to be granted accreditation without losing our tribal autonomy. We have developed a partnership with our tribal and public schools so that our children can interact with their peers (in social settings) and can transfer to the public school system with ease. Our students can participate in the after-school activities provided by the tribal and public schools and, in exchange, we provide instruction in Indian education and White Clay language at the public schools. Our state has a law called Indian Education for All, which mandates that every public school teach Indian education; hence, the public school complies with its mandate and our children can benefit from contact with their peers in the public school system—a win–win situation for all!

Where We Are Today: 2007

There are many daily decisions that one must make and many things that need to be in order before an immersion school can function smoothly. For example, staff members need to be ready to work hard by devoting endless hours and energy to this effort. Because people are key to the success of an immersion school, one needs to build a healthy team of dedicated administrators, teachers, and students and their families. School management is essential, which includes clear lines of communication, well-defined roles and responsibilities, and transparent deadlines regarding curriculum development, assessment, and outreach to our community.

We have implemented a strong curriculum that has at its core White Clay teachings and language. Drawing on both the teachings of our elders and the curriculum of the public school, we believe that we are preparing our students to do well in public school and be successful in college without compromising our White Clay language and culture. We have created a space in which our students have built a sturdy and robust White Clay world. Our elders regularly teach in our classes, enriching the cultural elements of our curriculum. We have a waiting list and have another class of 2 to 3 year olds waiting to begin kindergarten with us. If we can raise money to build an addition onto our school, we will enroll a new class of students. In the end, it is our dream that our students will one day be teaching and running our school.

Lessons We Learn: Commentaries From Scholar-Practitioners

Maintaining Your Mission While Partnering with People, Educational Institutions, and Communities

Mindy Morgan

Issues of loss and revitalization of indigenous language are of critical importance today. Not only do indigenous languages code complex and intricate world views, but their persistence also speaks to the courage and strength of tribal members who maintained their languages despite colonizing efforts aimed at their eradication. Lynette Stein-Chandler's teaching study is a valuable contribution to the growing literature on indigenous language revitalization in the United States as it draws attention to the real obstacles communities face in creating and maintaining language-immersion programs. In particular, Stein-Chandler's study motivates us to think about three critical issues in indigenous-language programming: the personal and familial ties that both inspire and support indigenous-language learning, the importance of providing a place for language use, and the necessity of building collaborative partnerships. Lynette's story of language revival and her attention to intergenerational learning illustrate the connections between language maintenance and the building and strengthening of family and community.

Stein-Chandler reminds us of the central role family and kinship plays in language-renewal efforts and the meaning that these connections have for indigenous communities. Recent works regarding loss of indigenous language worldwide have sought to draw attention to the crisis by equating it with the loss of biodiversity (Crystal, 2002; Nettle & Romaine, 2002; Zepeda & Hill, 1991) and by emphasizing statistics that quantify both languages and speakers (Hale, 1992; Krauss, 1992). But these abstract rhetorics and rationales, offered largely by outsiders, often fail to adequately reflect the beliefs of the speaking communities (Hill, 2002). Stein-Chandler reminds us that language revitalization is not about numbers, but about individuals and relationships between and among individuals. According to this view, language is inextricably bound up with a community's history and genealogy. Her personal relationships—with both her daughter and her great-grandmother—inspire and sustain Stein-Chandler's efforts to establish the immersion school. Hers is more than just a personal story; she sees generations as being connected through language, and that she herself must provide the link between fluent speakers and her own children.

Languages identify and position us in the world; therefore, language revitalization is about honoring our ancestors and providing inspiration for future generations as well as language learning. These intergenerational connections are not abstract; they are embodied in the people and relationships within the community. Stein-Chandler's work builds upon those that have come before (such as Madeline Colliflower), and she recognizes these previous efforts. These local and kinship connections are vital for the success of a language program, and they need to be highlighted and reinforced.

Just as local connections are important, so are local spaces because languages are intertwined with the places they occupy. Throughout the twentieth century, indigenous languages retracted as spaces for their use diminished. Forced out of schools by governing authorities, the indigenous languages were stigmatized and community members stopped using them in public (Adams, 1995). After a period of dormancy, they are now being used again. However, the gap in usage means that dedicated spaces need to be created for their use and transmission. Immersion schools, such as the A'ani Language Immersion School, provide just such places. Here, as Stein-Chandler emphasizes, the language, history, and culture are all celebrated. But language cannot be contained in these spaces if it is going to thrive. Scholars have noted that the reason the often-cited Māori and Hawaiian language programs have been so successful is that other, complementary programs in the community help to support the work of the schools (Hinton, 2001, p. 182). Similarly, Stein-Chandler describes ways in which the immersion program at Fort Belknap ensures that the language extends beyond the limits of the classroom. The after-school and teacher/apprenticeship programs are two examples of how the work of the immersion school affects a wider population. Opportunities to speak must be created, and language destinations must be expanded to make a speech community viable.

A separate issue but one that also is related to space is the placement of the immersion school on the campus of Fort Belknap College. As mentioned previously, in the nineteenth and early twentieth centuries, schools often were sites of the most overt attacks on indigenous languages; therefore, the situation of language programs in educational institutions is problematic. However, the tribally controlled college provides an alternative space in which the history of indigenous schooling can be written. Unlike other educational institutions, these places blend Western and indigenous approaches to knowledge, and are more responsive to the needs of the reservation community (Stein, 1992). Here, indigenous languages are ascribed the status they deserve, and the language programs can benefit from the resources of the larger college community. The newly constructed Cultural Learning Center at Fort Belknap College, which houses the tribal archives as well as providing meeting rooms, not only provides necessary space for the programs, but also symbolizes the central role the languages serve in the college's curriculum.

The role of the college reinforces the third issue that emerges from the teaching study, the importance of collaborative relationships for indigenous language programs. Stein-Chandler notes that the success of the school is dependent not only on the dedication of its staff, but also the support it has received from others. These support networks come in two primary configurations: intra-reservation programs, and language-immersion programs within other communities. In addition to providing space, Fort Belknap College has worked in close collaboration with the immersion school. In particular, the partnership between the immersion school and the Speaking White Clay program demonstrates the symbiotic relationship between training teachers and serving students. The new participation with Montana State University-Northern shows additional potential to develop effective collaborative networks.

These local and regional networks are further supported by the participation with other indigenous language-immersion programs. Stein-Chandler credits Darrell Kipp, the founder of the Piegan Institute, with providing her with key information and unconditional support; however, his success builds upon the successful model of the Pūnana Leo and Māori language nests and immersion schools (Kipp, 2000). In fact, over the last 15 years, productive global partnerships have been built between indigenous communities that are involved with language maintenance and revitalization (see Burnaby & Reyhner, 2002; Cantoni, 1996; Hinton & Hale, 2001).

In the mid-1990s, groups such as the American Indian Languages Development Institute (AILDI) in the Southwest and the Native American Language Issues Institute (NALI) in Oklahoma began to assemble speakers, teachers, and linguists as a means of coordinating political as well as pedagogical strategies (McCarty et al., 2001). This movement has had a number of positive benefits; it has created networks that share pedagogical innovations as well as information about funding sources, and has increased awareness and status of indigenous languages throughout the United States and abroad. There are, however, obstacles to these collaborative relationships. First of all, although many communities share a similar history in terms of the suppression and stigmatization of indigenous languages, contemporary speaking communities vary considerably in terms of numbers of speakers and available resources. This means that what works for one community will not necessarily work for another because of differing needs. However, as Stein-Chandler illustrates, these larger networks can help people discover their own paths for language renewal.

Significant challenges lie ahead for communities that are creating and maintaining immersion schools. Despite efforts to the contrary, communities are continuing to lose speakers, and training language teachers is a difficult and time-consuming endeavor. Further, as Stein-Chandler notes, funding for immersion programs often is not sufficient to cover operating costs, which are high as a result of the labor-intensive work required. These problems are daunting and call for new resources, financial and otherwise, to be dedicated to these efforts. But the inspiring message from Stein-Chandler's piece is that there is a cadre of young scholars who are personally and professionally invested in this work. Her story can be compared to the efforts of similar young language activists who have, for example, created and maintained *Waadookodaading*, an Ojibwe immersion school in Hayward, Wisconsin, and developed the *Myaamia* Project, which focuses on revitalizing language and local knowledge among the Miami community in Oklahoma. In short, there are individuals who have an affirmative answer for Kipp's powerful question, "Have you done everything you could to save your language?"

References

Adams, D. W. (1995) *Education for Extinction: American Indians and the Boarding School Experience, 1875–1928*. Lawrence: University of Kansas Press.

Burnaby, B. & Reyhner, J. (eds) (2002) *Indigenous Languages Across the Community*. Flagstaff: Northern Arizona University.

Cantoni, G. (ed.) (1996) *Stabilizing Indigenous Languages*. Flagstaff: Northern Arizona University.

Crystal, D. (2002) *Language Death*. Cambridge: Cambridge University Press.

Hale, K. (1992) "On endangered languages and the safeguarding of diversity." *Language*, 68(1), 1–3.

Hill, J. (2002) "Expert rhetorics' in advocacy for endangered languages: who is listening, and what do they hear?" *Journal of Linguistic Anthropology* 12(2), 119–133.

Hinton, L. (2001) "Teaching methods." In L. Hinton & K. Hale (eds), *The Green Book of Language Revitalization in Practice*. San Diego: Academic Press, (pp. 179–189).

Hinton, L. & Hale, K. (eds) (2001) *The Green Book of Language Revitalization in Practice*. San Diego: Academic Press.

Kipp, D. (2000) *Encouragement, Guidance, Insights, and Lessons Learned for Native Language Activists Developing Their Own Tribal Language Program*. St. Paul, MN: Grotto Foundation.

Krauss, M. (1992) "The world's languages in crisis." *Language* 68(1), 4–10.

McCarty, T., Watahomigie, L. J., Yamamoto, A. Y., & Zepeda, O. (2001) "Indigenous educators as change agents: case studies of two language institutes." In L. Hinton & K. Hale (eds), *The Green Book of Language Revitalization in Practice*. San Diego: Academic Press (pp. 371–383).

Nettle, D. & Romaine, S. (2002) *Vanishing Voices: The Extinction of the World's Languages*. Oxford: Oxford University Press.

Stein, W. (1992) *Tribally Controlled Colleges: Making Good Medicine*. New York: Peter Lang.

Zepeda, O. & Hill, J. H. (1991) "The condition of Native American languages in the United States." In R. Robins & E. Uhlenbeck (eds), *Endangered Languages*. Oxford: Berg Publishers (pp. 135–155).

Lessons from A'aninin (White Clay) People and Fort Belknap College

Mary Eunice Romero-Little

Much of what is known and understood about indigenous language acquisition today comes from the unprecedented worldwide initiatives in indigenous mother-tongue maintenance and reclamation, such as those developed by the Māori people of Aeotearoa (New Zealand) and by Native Hawaiians, who established 'Aha Pūnana Leo, a Hawaiian immersion preschool (Kamana & Wilson, 1996; Warner, 2001). In addition to these international models, there are American Indian and Alaska Native language education models such as the Blackfeet Language Immersion School in Montana; the Ayaprun Elitnaurvik, a Yup'ik kindergarten to 6th-grade immersion school in Bethel, Alaska; and the developing A'ani Language Immersion School (ALIS) at Fort Belknap College in Harlem, Montana. The last community-tribal college partnership is a new alternative institutional relationship in the emerging Native language education paradigm in which tribal colleges, given their unique mission to provide accessible and optimal higher education to the local community, also serve as unique engines for strengthening indigenous culture, languages, values, and traditions.

Whether school- or community-based programs, indigenous heritage-language initiatives take many shapes, forms, and dimensions, but they share a common dual-challenge: developing new generations of indigenous speakers while ensuring a culturally responsive and empowering education for Native children. This requires simultaneously maintaining control over the children's education and ensuring that the curriculum incorporates the local language and culture in authentic ways (Romero & McCarty, 2006). In the case of the ALIS, its marriage with Fort Belknap College enabled the A'aninin (White Clay) communities to infuse the curriculum with local linguistic and cultural content without compromising the integrity of the language goals—the creation of new generations of A'ani speakers—and educational progress of students. Moreover, with the unwavering intellectual and fiscal support and commitment of Fort Belknap College leaders, local control was ensured and critical issues such as Native-language teacher training and certification, language assessment, and culturally appropriate language pedagogy and curricula were addressed in ways that ensured that the A'aninin community maintained their inherent rights to educate their children in the mother language and enable each child to determine his or her own future.

Lessons from language-revitalization experiences remind us to be aware of the effects of local and national policies—specifically, the sociolinguistic, educational, and political dynamics associated with what Hornberger (1996) referred to as top-down and bottom-up language planning processes. For many indigenous communities in the United States accountability measures mandated by the No Child Left Behind Act (Public Law 107–110, January 2002) requires that all students regardless of language background and educational status meet adopted academic standards as measured by standardized tests in English. Funding for schools and grade promotion are dependent on students' performance on annual academic achievement tests. Principals, teachers, students, and parents alike are aware of and concerned about the consequences of not doing well on these tests. Thus, it is no surprise that their concerns are being transformed into heightened pressure to decrease or abandon instruction in students' heritage language and to concentrate on strengthening their English-language skills. Fortunately, the leaders of the ALIS were fully cognizant of the possible effects of these kinds of external mandates and immediately took proactive steps to develop a collaborative tribal–state relationship for language learning that benefited both A'aninin and non-A'aninin students.

Anyone involved in indigenous language revitalization knows that it is hard work. As Stein-Chandler attests, it requires the main stakeholders, the members of the community, working together to plan, develop, and coordinate the overall efforts; it requires long hours, flexibility, creativity, perseverance, and a deep, undying, caring commitment to the language and children. This, combined with their knowledge of the community, makes the stakeholders highly capable and reliable leaders for the language-revitalization efforts. In my experience, successful efforts require such people in partnerships and/or relationships because no one person can renew a language alone. It especially requires leaders/planners to support each other so that there is no "burn out" or "push out."

Finally, as the wisdom from Alaska Native elders tell us, "[T]o keep a language going, we must use it in our daily activities at home and in the community so that it is transmitted and acquired naturally" (Assembly of Alaska Native Educators, 1998, p. 1) by children in early childhood. In order to do this, a community's language efforts must consider the dynamics of individual, familial, and communal language attitudes, ideologies, and practices—all intangible yet vital social and affective aspects of language learning. For indigenous families and communities this requires a reclaiming of socialization and child-rearing practices through intergenerational *indigenous*-language learning.

In the evolution of the ALIS, the tribal college served a supportive role by providing a language-immersion context that strengthened intergenerational language use, valued the knowledge and linguistic contributions of the elders, and supported the cultural pedagogies for teaching the A'ani language and for the unique language-learning needs of their children. Their ensuing challenge is to foster intergenerational language learning beyond the safe and comfortable context of the tribal college into new domains in which language will thrive naturally on its own.

References

Assembly of Alaska Native Educators (AANE) (1998) *Guidelines for Preparing Culturally Responsive Teachers for Alaska's Schools*. Anchorage: Alaska Native Knowledge Network.

Hornberger, N. H. (1996) *Indigenous Literacies in the Americas: Language Planning from the Bottom Up*. Berlin: Mouton de Gruyter.

Kamana, K. & Wilson, W. H. (1996) "Hawaiian language programs." In G. Cantoni (ed.), *Stabilizing Indigenous Languages*. Flagstaff: Northern Arizona University Center for Excellence in Education, 153–156.

Romero, M. E. & McCarty, T. L. (2006) *Language Planning Challenges and Possibilities in Native American Communities and Schools*. Tempe: Arizona State University Educational Policy Analysis Laboratory, College of Education.

Warner, S. L. N. (2001) "The movement to revitalize Hawaiian language and culture." In L. Hinton & K. Hale (eds), *The Green Book of Language Revitalization in Practice*. San Diego: Academic Press, (pp. 133–144).

Reflections on the Case: An Edited Interview with Lynette Stein-Chandler and Katie Cherrington

Kate Cherrington

Language in any culture, in any country, is viable. Language reflects the culture and identity of any given peoples. Total-immersion language education praxis emphasizes the value of identity and recognizes the need for learners to have security in their sense of place and in their sense of self. An identity intact and known can provide learners with a sense of purpose that not only serves to feed their personal development but also contributes to the communities with which they identify.

Ideally, when starting an immersion school, there should be enough resources to make tangible the vision and purpose the community has created for the school. This includes not only well-appointed and well-resourced buildings and technology but teachers and support staff who are continually building on their profession, are being utilized for their strengths, and are strong in the praxis of the Native language-immersion school, including 120 percent commitment to the regeneration of their Native language. In all honesty, if the vision is shared by the community, if the community is dedicated to investing time and money (communal responsibility), then you can slap up a sign on the shed in the back of your yard and say, "This is our school," and just get started! Many of the successful language initiatives in New Zealand have started with strong conviction and the guts to just "Get out there and do it!"

Aotearoa has a range of immersion schools, with many of the successful examples based in the Waikato region of the North Island. Ngā Taiatea is a total-immersion high school based in Hamilton. It was opened in 2004 and is an example of tribal, community, and government organizations working together. We also have three tribal colleges that are examples of community vision and have wonderful Native pedagogy that flows through the day-to-day operations of their campuses: *Te Wananga o Aotearoa, Te Wananga o Raukawa, Te Whare Wananga o Awanuiarangi.*

Lynette Stein-Chandler

Before opening a Native language-immersion school, there should be fluent or at least semi-fluent speakers of the Native language who are able to teach. At minimum, the school should have several partnerships in place, to include (a) support from at least one fluent-speaking elder, (b) support from parents (financial and volunteering time/resources), (c) support from local public schools or tribal programs, and (d) support from local and/or tribal services, such as family and health services. A reliable funding stream needs to be secured that supports teachers and the school director, and budgets for school supplies and operating costs (which might include a physical facility).

To get started, I would recommend first and foremost a visit to New Zealand (Aoteroa) to learn how the Māori have formed and operated their schools. I would also visit schools in Hawai'i as their language-immersion programs operate within the U.S. school system. I would also suggest visiting the Piegan Institute and taking one of Darrell Kipp's seminars on "How to Start a Language Immersion School." Fort Belknap College presents a different model of partnership. I believe that tribal colleges will soon be supporting language-immersion programs in their communities. There are also other language-immersion models, such as the Canadian and French models, and surprisingly, those of the Hutterite colonies. The Hutterite colonies are maintaining a culture and way of life as well as language for their community that is based in total immersion.

Kate Cherrington

Why language immersion? Power and self-determination affect the definition of success in a Native-based educational context. To define one's world is to actualize power (Alfred, 1999, as cited in Harris & Wasilewski, 2004). Not only are students educated in Native-based programs bilingual, and therefore call on multiple intelligences in their everyday lives, but their subsequent successes are based on the knowing of who they are and from where they come. For example, many studies in Kaupapa Māori (Smith, 1999; Skerrett White, 2003) include discussions on identity and its importance to Māori in determining their successful transition through education into full and positive lifestyles (Durie, 2003).

The success stories from within the Total Immersion Māori movement are highly documented. There are some debates about the lack of choice within curriculum areas in Native-based programs as a result of the need for more resources and teachers. However, learners who graduate from these programs possess the self-assurance and confidence to strive to attain the goals they have set for themselves. In a practical sense, the Native-based schools in Aotearoa remain closely aligned to the state education system and ensure that learners have access to a variety of vocational and tertiary options on completion of their secondary schooling.

Native schools prepare students for further education simply by expecting them to achieve to their fullest potential within a community of support and celebration of what these students represent—their language, culture, lands, and genealogy.

Lynette Stein-Chandler

To sustain an immersion school requires planning and strategic action. First, it is essential to have a good grant writer. Immersion schools need to find grants that will sustain their activities to enhance their programs. A network with private philanthropic foundations can be very helpful because private money often comes with fewer ideological strings attached. Again, it is essential to have active parents—that is, parents who can support fundraising activities, provide resources and services to ensure the daily operation of the school as well as enhance learning experiences, and are available to paint, do spring cleaning, or perform yard work! We also have a symbolic tuition of $100 a month, which we have found increases family ownership in their child's learning. Families can choose to pay for their tuition by volunteering in our school. Nothing is free. We must be willing to work hard to retain our languages.

Kate Cherrington

From my experience, the only way to sustain a vision is to continue to feed and share it with community. I have witnessed the interference and occupation of Native organizations by governments and authorities, and I have seen, when all appears set to be lost, the people (community) rally and reconnect to their vision and hold on. A shared vision, carefully nurtured and actualized, will enable Native immersion schools to continue to live Native language and produce learners committed to their culture and communities for generations to come. Use the resources available to you such as curriculum, tapes, archival material, and most important, those still speaking the language who live in your community.

I would like to point out again that the value of identity is not exclusive to those committed to language regeneration in communities. Universal reverence is attached to this value, exemplified by the saying "know thyself"[1] from the Greek gods and written in the temple of Delphi. Skerrett White (2005) offers the following definition of *tūrangawaewae* (identity) that also serves to highlight the overall importance and status of identity in relation to total-immersion education and community advancement:

> The relationships between language and culture can be merged into visions and aspirations of what it is to lead a meaningful life (indexical relationship); to live a life where one's culture is accessible and intact (cultural relationship); and a life where one's identity is whole, one's right and ability to live with good health, spirit and a sense of well-being in place, and one's *rangatiratanga* is intact (a symbolic relationship); a *tūrangawaewae*.
>
> (p. 20)

References

Durie, M. (2001) "A framework for considering Māori educational advancement." Opening address at Hui Taumata Matauranga, Taupo, New Zealand, February.

Durie, M. (2003) "Māori educational advancement at the interface between tea o Māori and tea o whanui." Address at the Hui Taumata Matauranga Tuatoru, Taupo, New Zealand, March.

Fishman, J. A. (2000) "Reversing language shift: RLS theory and practice revisited." In G. Kindell & M. L. Lewis (eds), *Assessing Ethnolinguistic Vitality: Theory and Practice. Selected Papers from the Third International Language Assessment Conference.* Dallas: SIL International, (pp. 1–25).

Harris, L., & Wasilewski J. (2004) "Indigeneity, an alternative worldview—sharing the journey towards conscious evolution." *Systems Research Journal: ISSS Yearbook Dedicated to the Wisdom of the People, Fall.*

---

[1]   The Oxford Dictionary of Quotations (1975).

Keahi, S. (2000) "Advocating for a stimulating and language based education." In M. Benham & J. E. Cooper (ed.), *Indigenous Educational Models for Contemporary Practice: In Our Mother's Voice*. Hillsdale, NJ: Erlbaum.

Skerrett White, M. N. (2003) *Kia mate ra ano a Tama-nui-te-ra: Reversing language shift in Kohanaga Reo*. Unpublished doctoral thesis, Te Whare Wananga o Waikato, New Zealand.

Skerrett White, M. N. (2005) "Kia mate ra ano a Tama-nui-te-ra." Māori medium research seminar. Iterative Best Evidence Synthesis Programme. Wellington, New Zealand, October.

Smith, L. (1999) *Decolonizing Methodologies: Research and Indigenous Peoples*. New York: Zed Books.

TRIBAL NATION COMMUNITY AND MAINSTREAM INSTITUTION PARTNERSHIPS

Matthew VanAlstine (Mentor: Wayne Stein)

Introduction

Partnerships between mainstream institutions and tribal nations are becoming increasingly common in higher education. Both entities have much to gain through partnerships, but in many cases tribal communities are not receiving their share of the benefit. The following is a story about a fictional university with fictional events, but the issues involved are indeed current and real. This story is about a mainstream institution's partnership with a tribal community and what can be lost, forgotten, and distorted as a result of such a partnership.

Town Hall Meeting

The story unfolds on the campus of Northern Technology University (NTU) at an emergency town hall meeting stirred by a recent state mandate. The board of trustees and the president of NTU, along with the leader and members of the tribal council of the Eastern River Tribe of Indians (ERTI), are fielding questions concerning their embattled partnership. A young Native American female student walks through the doors accompanied by her grandmother and approaches the microphone to ask a question.

Background on NTU/ERTI Relations

NTU is located in the northeastern part of the United States; it opened in 1843 as a technical school for men. Currently, NTU is a public research university for both men and women that enrolls about 35,000 students per year. From its inception, NTU's athletic teams were known as the Natives. The nickname was chosen by the first class of students at

NTU and is said to have been inspired by the many Native American tribes located near the school. However, the first class of students viewed Native Americans as savages and ruthless warriors; thus, by choosing the team name *Natives* they hoped to instill fear in their sporting opponents. NTU is a member of a major sports organization that generates significant revenue and gains national exposure from its sports teams. NTU's campus is replete with a variety of Native American insignias, ranging from feathers, to arrows, to dream catchers, but mostly the mascot chief "Old One." Periodically through the years at NTU, some tension has arisen concerning the university's nickname and mascot.

The people of the ERTI reservation have a rich culture, language, and history that have been passed down from generation to generation. The people of the ERTI reservation have four sacred values:

1. To live with courage.
2. To seek knowledge.
3. To be of service to the community.
4. To leave the world a better place for future generations.

Although the people of the ERTI reservation have been ravaged by a variety of assimilation policies and boarding schools, they have been able to survive and persevere with their culture intact. The ERTI reservation was established in 1808 and is situated within 80 miles of NTU's campus. The ERTI reservation has a history of supporting Native American cultural events held on the campus of NTU.

Despite having four reservations within 150 miles of its campus, NTU has only 250 Native American students, which equals less than 1 percent of the overall student population. At that, the statistic of 250 Native American students is slightly inflated because many of the students listed as Native American are not Native American at all. NTU requires only self-identification of ethnicity, and many students misread the Identity box and some check Native American only because they hope to gain certain perceived benefits. NTU's Native American population is slightly below average in comparison to other schools in the state and to schools out of state with similar size and circumstances. There has never been a formal study on the experiences of Native American students at NTU, nor has any research been conducted on why more Native American students are not attending NTU. In addition, there are few Native

American faculty and staff at the university to support Native American students.

The campus climate at NTU for Native American students currently is contentious, but in general, American Indian students' concerns have been ignored. For instance, Native American students and community members have informally reported several racially motivated incidents. Most of the complaints center on NTU's use of the *Natives* nickname. Students and alumni of NTU are notorious for misrepresenting Native American culture and sacred items at sporting events. Native American students have been taunted with name calling and stereotyping, and have been the subject of inaccurate depictions of their Native American history by faculty, students, and alumni. Native American students and Native American community members believe that the racial incidents have been fueled and heightened by the university's nickname. When NTU plays the Eastern University European Immigrants, numerous posters are displayed showing a Native "scalping" an Immigrant. Moreover, the Native American students believe that a majority of the campus's knowledge about their people comes from the school's culturally erroneous and offensive mascot. However, the students' complaints continually have been dismissed, undermined, and ignored by university officials.

The Native American faculty and staff at NTU are pressured both informally and formally to support the nickname. The Native American faculty and staff who do not work with the Native students or community are the people who are most likely to support the nickname. In contrast, the Native American faculty and staff who work closely with the Native community and feel a strong tie to their culture oppose the nickname. NTU administrators favor the Native American faculty who support the nickname by giving them university grants and institutional support. Moreover, any diversity committees, public relations articles, or special task forces on the Native American nickname are filled only with the voices of faculty who support the nickname. The appearance of dissent about the Native American nickname issue on the part of Native American faculty and staff constantly is used against those who favor banishing the nickname.

Adding to the stress between the Native American community and NTU administration is the heavy influence exerted by several wealthy donors. NTU has considered changing its nickname several times, but these attempts quickly have been denounced by the institution's large alumni base. The alumni are very powerful at NTU and threaten to withhold donations the moment anyone mentions changing the nickname. Whenever the issue of changing the nickname arises, the student newspaper is flooded with letters containing an array of such comments as: "What's next—the animal right groups will want to change nicknames?" "It's an honor!" "Native Americans still exist?" "If it wasn't for the nickname, who would even remember Native Americans?" The current student body and alumni think that the *Native* nickname is a school tradition and worth keeping.

A state ruling on Native American nicknames has propelled the NTU campus into a state of chaos, with students and alumni worried about what is going to happen next. The progressive governor of the state decided to endorse a mandate that would forbid all public schools to use Native American nicknames. The governor and supporters of the mandate believed that the time had come to stop using nicknames that had been chosen out of ignorance and insensitivity. The mandate called for the immediate elimination of all Native American nicknames and mascots, effective the following school year. The only recourse for schools wanting to keep their Native American nicknames was to form a partnership with and be endorsed by one of the state's twelve Tribal Nations. After conversing with and being turned down by several of the state's tribal nations because of concerns about the effect of these nicknames on youths and their potential to fuel racism, NTU was able to establish a partnership with the Eastern River Tribe of Indians.

The NTU/ERTI partnership agreement was formed shortly after the state ruling and had several important components. NTU agreed to make Native American education a priority by supporting cultural events on campus and working with the ERTI community. In addition, NTU decided to send out a Fact of the Week about Native American heritage over the campus e-mail system. NTU pledged to put more money into the annual powwow and Native American cultural events held on campus. In addition, the athletic department at NTU agreed to host an annual weeklong sports camp for all the Native American tribal nations in the state.

The Eastern River tribe's role in the partnership is to fully support NTU's use of the *Natives* nickname and work with the university on various research projects. By supporting the nickname, ERTI allows

NTU to carry on its tradition and continue earning millions of dollars using the mascot logo. Furthermore, the NTU/ERTI partnership opened up the possibility for various departments to conduct research about the ERTI community and its members living on the reservation. NTU worked out a volunteer and internship exchange program for their students to work with ERTI's tribal departments. The ERTI tribal council decided to partner with NTU in the hope that more of their youths would be recruited and encouraged to pursue a higher education. Although many tribal members agreed with the NTU partnership, a substantial number of members disagreed with it.

Back to the Town Hall Meeting

The young female student, who identified herself as Emily, began to speak as her grandmother stood by her side.

> I am a member of the Eastern River Tribe of Indians, and I am also a student here at NTU. I have brought my grandmother here with me for strength, wisdom, and encouragement. I have spoken with her on many occasions about what is going on here, and it is with her permission that I am speaking out against this partnership. The nickname and mascot is perpetuating stereotypes, and it is impacting all Native students here on campus and elsewhere. As Native students we already have a hard time, but with the nickname things have been getting increasingly more difficult. Nobody is listening to us [students], and nobody is thinking about the impact on our self-esteem as Native youth. Our history and culture is not dependent on a nickname; it is dependent on our concern with preserving "traditional" culture and language. We are not animals, nor is our culture a joke or here for your entertainment. You can say all you want about being politically correct, or how there are bigger issues in the world, or how you can find Native people to support your opinion, or how we are just being the vocal minority, but the fact is I've been harassed, threatened, and verbally abused just because I'm against the use of the nickname. If the nickname doesn't matter then why all the outrage? Why do you care if it gets changed? Aren't there bigger issues for you to concern yourselves with? This partnership is making it harder on Native American communities who are trying to get rid of stereotypes. Now every mainstream school is using this partnership as an example of why they should be allowed to have Native American nicknames. Why can't this school put Native American education at the forefront without using the *Natives* nickname? I can see what NTU gets out of

this partnership, but what does the Eastern Tribe get? And at what cost? I ask that the ERTI tribal values prevail and that this partnership ends. My grandmother has passed on the tribal values to me, and it is time as a community that we pass this information to the next generation. Thank you.

Lessons We Learn: Commentaries from Scholar-Practitioners

Reflections on University "Partnerships"

Bryan McKinley Jones Brayboy

I am truly honored and humbled to respond to Matthew VanAlstine's essay regarding partnerships between tribal nations and institutions of higher education and the ways that the use of an indigenous mascot, symbol, or imagery complicates these partnerships. As a commentator, I have been asked to offer some words that speak directly to the case and the challenges raised by it, and the lessons learned, as well as the implications of the case and what we—scholars, practitioners, and administrators—might do next regarding the issues raised. In my brief response, I intend to take these charges in order. The case offered here feels all too real; similar events occurred at my former institution, and I was one of many people who lobbied to end the use of an indigenous symbol in my former institution's athletic program. Ultimately, the tribal nation decided to back the use of the symbol, and the National Collegiate Athletic Association released the university from probation. At the heart of my own experiences and those outlined in this essay are the tensions between tribal self-determination—namely, the right to approve the use of a mascot or symbol—and the costs to students and the tribal nation in the long run when indigenous imagery is used.

Challenges of the Case

The case presents several challenges, although I believe the primary one is the fact that this partnership is not really a partnership at all. The way I think of a partnership is as an ongoing relationship that is based on shared cooperation and responsibility. In most cases, a partnership is one in which both parties benefit in ways that address their needs. In this case, it is clear that NTU benefits in ways that the ERTI does not. The use of the mascot assists the institution in generating millions of dollars in sports revenues, and royalties from the sale of clothing and other items that have the Native mascot on them. NTU agrees to make education for its indigenous students a priority by funding cultural events, sending out educational facts via e-mail, and hosting a sports camp for indigenous children. However, what is missing from the partnership is a commitment to increase the number of indigenous students at the university. Investing in cultural events and having a university presence in the community are nice contributions, but they address neither the campus climate nor the underrepresentation of Native students on campus. Indeed, NTU has never conducted a study to examine why there are so few Native students in attendance at the institution. The challenge, then, is that NTU wants to keep the mascot and needs the ERTI to keep it. In so doing, however, it becomes apparent that the only Native the institution wants around is one in a mascot form. Having smart, capable, outspoken, engaged indigenous students is not a priority. If it were, the relationship would be one built on increasing the attendance of indigenous students at the institution, rather than offering pennies on the dollar to support cultural events. I do not want to be misunderstood here; cultural events are important, but they must be paired with the presence and retention of indigenous students.

There is one other challenge presented for researchers, practitioners, and administrators that I want to address. The presence of indigenous imagery, mascots, and symbols highlights the contested and contentious nature of the conversations surrounding their use. Not all community members may agree with or fight against the use of this imagery. In this case, we see that there are tribal members who do not see an issue with the use of the mascots and still others who might argue that our indigenous communities have bigger, more pressing issues with which to be concerned. It is not uncommon, for example, to see a drum group or young men on a reservation wearing caps and shirts that are emblazoned with a Native mascot. Few of these individuals, I would imagine, are aware of the findings of psychologists outlined in a recent American Psychological Association (APA 2005) press release. Much of the research cited was conducted by indigenous scholars and their allies. Much of what the APA found might be best viewed through a lens of colonialism and its devastating effects not only on our indigenous communities, but on most of the United States as well. In the release, the

APA stated that the use of the mascots is racist, that their use "undermines the educational experiences of members of all communities—especially those who have had little or no contact with Indigenous peoples," that their use "appears to have a negative impact on the self-esteem of American Indian children," that the use of these symbols does not allow a space for indigenous peoples to present themselves in meaningful ways, that the use of this imagery may lead to "negative relations between groups," that their use is disrespectful of spiritual beliefs, and that their use may be a violation of indigenous peoples' civil rights.

These findings point to a challenge that may be viewed as a public relations problem; that is, many people who argue for and utilize these symbols in our indigenous communities may not be aware of their effects on individuals and communities. Many of the young men who wear these symbols might have been convinced that the shirts are a source of pride and honor. My point here is not to say that these young men, and others, are wrong and the psychologists are right; rather, the research points to the influence of colonialism, and these effects manifest themselves in the "larger issues" that many indigenous people say our communities should focus on. There is a connection, I believe, between the "larger issues" and the use of these mascots as highlighted by the APA's release.

Lessons Learned

There are several important ideas and lessons to take away from this case. Perhaps the most important lesson in this is that partnerships that link predominantly white institutions of higher education and tribal nations require, in most cases, groups and institutions with very different agendas, epistemologies, and ontologies to come together in ways that will benefit both parties. The epistemic and ontological clashes have to be recognized, named, and proactively addressed in order for the partnership to work. In the case presented here, it may have served the partnership well if the institution had agreed not only to help tribal community members obtain their education from NTU, but also to support research training for indigenous researchers so that these community members would be in a position to conduct research in their own communities. In this way, the institution of higher education assists the community in its own form of self-determination. In terms of a partnership, this appears to be more in line with a way in which both groups benefit in profound ways. This is one way that clashing epistemologies may be reconciled for the benefit of both partners.

The case also points to the danger inherent in the use of indigenous imagery, mascots, and symbols. Indeed, in this case, the use of paint and feathers—items that hold sacred value for many indigenous peoples— makes the sacred profane. Any mascots that bear what some might call "traditional" Native symbols (paint, feathers, drums, or pipes) or sports fans who imitate the mascot or symbol denigrate religious, sacred items. It is unclear how indigenous communities and peoples benefit when others take up sacred items to display a commitment to a sports team.

The use of these mascots, symbols, and imagery creates and substantiates false and misleading histories of indigenous peoples. Indeed, the image of the fierce warrior who instills fear in others fails to recognize the rich history and legacies that indigenous people have as farmers, cartographers, scientists, inventors, and doctors.[1] In the case represented, NTU attempted to rectify these misunderstandings by e-mailing educational facts to its students, staff, and faculty. However, these e-mails can simply be ignored or deleted without being read; the correspondence does little to actively work against a stereotype that is reified daily in the campus bookstore and on the athletic field.

One final lesson that I intend to address in this brief response is the ways that larger racist beliefs, policies, and procedures work in this partnership. If we dig deeper into the agreement presented, it becomes clear that NTU is happy to have indigenous people present in the form of a mascot, but they appear to be unwilling to explore why these people are invisible as students, staff, and faculty. We learn that no studies have been conducted to explore why there are so few Native students on campus

---

[1] There is, of course, a long legacy of indigenous peoples serving the United States in the armed forces. In every armed conflict since the Revolutionary War, Indigenous peoples have bravely served and many of our communities honor veterans at every public gathering. My point here is to neither deny the importance of these individuals, nor to ignore their service. Rather, my point is to trouble the portrayal of mascots as fierce, war-mongering people who scalp their victims and instill fear in everyone they see. The history of the United States points to the fact that the U.S. Army brutalized many Indigenous peoples and notably massacred groups of women, children, and unarmed elderly people. If we are going to explore and interrogate savagery, we might examine the Sand Creek Massacre, Wounded Knee, and Bear River.

and that the needs of those students who are present are largely ignored by the institution. The presence (or lack thereof) of real, live indigenous people on campus is a clear indication of the values and priorities of the institution. The lack of Native students, staff, and faculty on campus can be instructive, however. I now turn my attention to what might be done next in this case and what institutions might do if they are truly interested in having partnerships with tribal nations.

The "So What?" Question and Some Responses

For partnerships to work, all sides of the partnership must benefit in tangible ways; symbolic benefits are important, but tangible ones are what create good will and longevity. In the case presented on the previous pages, I am left with thinking about the ways that NTU could be a real partner to the ERTI in productive ways. In order to achieve this, NTU must examine the partnership and agreement and ask itself: how and in what ways does the community benefit from the partnership, and how can we benefit from this partnership in better ways? As it turns out, there do not appear to be any real, tangible benefits for the community itself. NTU could explore the dearth of Native students on campus as the first way to address the partnership. The institution may find that its policies and procedures are constructed in ways that fail to welcome indigenous peoples, and that these same policies and procedures push those who are present away from the institution.

This problem sets up some obvious solutions for the institution that benefit both parties. NTU could send recruiting officers to the tribe's elementary, middle, and high schools to begin early recruiting and offer college preparatory courses for these students, staff, faculty, and community members. The admissions office could hire its own Native recruiter to assist in the process. The very presence of an indigenous admissions officer and recruiter speaks volumes regarding an institution's commitment to indigenous students and communities.

Preparing teachers and guidance counselors for the local schools would assist in the long-term recruitment of indigenous students in meaningful and proactive ways. Relatedly, NTU would agree to conduct research in the ERTI community. The institution and the community would be well served to prepare indigenous researchers, from the community, to engage in this work and to engage in research on the experiences of indigenous students, staff, and faculty at NTU. The institution increases its Native enrollment and positions itself to obtain funding to conduct the research and opens doors of access to research projects, while the community engages in the research as partners and it is community members who are part of the data collection and analyses. In too many cases, institutions want to collect data in communities, but they do not truly engage in a partnership around the data collection. Perhaps one of the most straightforward, productive ways to engage in real partnerships is to prepare indigenous researchers who listen to community members' needs and desires and assist the tribal nations in the project of self-determination. That is, the tribal nation defines the research problems, and the institution and its (indigenous) researchers address the problem. This creates a "win–win" relationship that is at the core of productive partnerships.

Matthew VanAlstine has given us much to consider and contemplate. Emily, with the presence and backing of her grandmother, offers us a glimpse of the ways that clashing epistemologies may come together to produce courageous, thoughtful, engaged scholars and tribal citizens. Those of us who teach at predominantly white institutions and who are citizens of indigenous nations and communities crave opportunities to bridge the competing discourse between Emily's ways of knowing and being to assist young people like Emily in being productive community members. I suspect, from reading Mr. VanAlstine's essay, that he is precisely the kind of individual whom a partnership between an institution and a community might assist in recognizing his power as a cultural being and as an intellect.

Reference

American Psychological Association (2005) www.iresist.org/pdf-files/apa.pdf (last accessed 17 July 2007).

Reflections on University "partnerships"

Paul Johnson

Across the nation many colleges, like NTU, continue to use Native American images as their mascots despite continuing calls by Native communities to curtail the practice. Attempts to change these mascots have not always been successful because of the deep support these mascots and images have fostered. From my participation on a number of "mascot review" committees, I have listened to and debated against the various justifications given for using Native American images as mascots. Native educators continually describe the negative effects of the continued use of these mascots, and urge action to effect change that is educationally, politically, and culturally sound for Native people, but they have had limited success.

National organizations such as the National Indian Education Association, the National Education Association, the National Congress of American Indians, the American Indian Movement, the National Association for the Advancement of Colored People, the National Collegiate Athletic Association (NCAA) Minority Opportunities and Interests Committee, and the U.S. Commission on Civil Rights have passed resolutions calling for a ban on using Native names, mascots, and logos. Even with this organizational support, we continue to meet resistance to changing this practice.

The NTU case study describes a typical situation and discusses the various justifications given for the continued use of Native American images. It describes the methods used to ensure their continued use, and suggests the necessity for change and action to effect change that is educationally, politically, and culturally appropriate for our communities.

The argument supporting the use of Native Americans as mascots falls into two narrow categories: tradition and money. Individuals who favor using Native mascots argue that these mascots honor and celebrate Indians. Supporters believe that their mascot is part of the school's tradition, and that changing the mascot is simply giving in to "politically correct" pressure groups. Others argue, and I agree, supporting the use of Native mascots, like other examples of stereotyping, is also linked to emotional and economic arguments and a long history of institutional racism.

A common assumption is that to take a mascot away is to undermine the traditions that have been developed over the years. The same people who make that assumption argue that the origins of these mascots were harmless or unintentional. Regardless, the effects, whether intentional or unwitting, are the same, and that is that Native people are subjected to the effects of institutional racism. In NTU's case, Native students comprise less than 1 percent of the overall student population, yet the University gains wealth from marketing the Native image.

Media illustrations and educational misrepresentations contribute to widespread stereotyping about Native American peoples. A primary driving force behind such stereotyping is NTU's athletic department. This is not an atypical situation because for coaches and players the idea that they could be "braves" or "chiefs" is important. College athletics is now a multimillion-dollar business and a great marketing tool for the institution. Unfortunately, stereotypes can be seen in the dance, the music, and the symbols used by these athletic department mascots. More often than not, these depictions lead to unnecessary contentious behavior on campus and, more important, the overall negative effect on Native students' self-esteem.

The dominant culture in the United States has long sanctioned racially harmful behaviors toward Native Americans. Vine Deloria's *Custer Died for Your Sins* provides many examples from America's history, including the savage-Indian image that was used to facilitate the removal of Indians. Portraying Native Americans as savages, heathens, or "less than human" allowed early Americans to create a feeling that Indians were "less worthy." These images gained the support of the majority of Americans for our removal. This technique has been perfected in America. The intentional stereotyping and exaggerations about our cultures and other indigenous cultures continue.

Alumni argue that changing the institution's mascot has the potential of negatively affecting their giving of funds to the college or university. The argument is that any change that can be perceived as having the potential to interfere with alumni giving must be approached with extreme caution. Colleges and universities are dependent on alumni giving, so curtailment of giving could harm students, staff, and faculty alike. In my experience, the "tradition" argument is not as solid as supporters would have us believe. The high schools and colleges in Michigan that have given up their Native mascots have met with little reprisal from their alumni or donors.

Economically, mascots make it easy to sell goods because their Native American symbols appeal to alumni, students, and community supporters. The logos and related goods make use of the mascot, and "spin-offs" on the Native American motif are easily manipulated to continually develop new products to sell. Other university departments, such as the admissions, alumni, and development offices, tie into these images quite easily. I believe that when the spiritual knowledge, rituals, and objects of tribal cultures are transformed into commodities, economic and political power merge to reinforce institutional racism. This is a blatant form of oppression exerted by a dominant society on other cultures, and typically is a source of economic profit. The marketing of Native American cultural imagery by a college or university solidifies the process of institutional racism.

There is no doubt that the marketing of Native Americans is a profitable venture, except when Natives attempt to get a fair market value for their products. In Michigan, where the budgets of higher education institutions are underfunded, any attempt to change their marketing efforts is met with resistance. This becomes *the* major issue. Institutions ask our communities, "What do we do with the thousands of t-shirts, sweatshirts, towels, and other trinkets displaying our logo?" "Who will cover our losses?" Once again, they place the onus on the victim.

People who support Native mascots claim that the mascots honor Indians, with no appreciation expressed for tribal customs or reality. Schools such as NTU have created their own image of the "Indian" or the "Old One." That it is an exaggerated image never enters the minds of spectators, because it simply reinforces the stereotype they learned about in classrooms and textbooks. Spectators who witness the mascot accept the mascot unconditionally because it reinforces their labeling. Further, because this labeling is subconscious, attempts to unlearn it and confront it are met with defensiveness, hostility, and an unwillingness to consider the possibility that the image may result in racist or biased behavior. All of these exaggerated images prevent the dominant culture from understanding the historical and current culture of indigenous people. Because the mascot image simply reinforces or affirms their stereotype, the image must have been implanted earlier in our lives.

I believe that, given the educational mission of colleges and universities, people who work at them cannot ignore this use of oppressive images. The costs are too high. There are several ways that educational professionals can protest the use of Indian mascots. First, they must educate themselves and then act in the best interest of students, as well as other faculty and staff. Their concern should be the community, institutional, and racist effects of using Native Americans as mascots. As individuals, they need to stop lending their support to the continued use of such mascots. They should avoid wearing clothing with Indian images as logos, displaying the mascots in their offices, or using them for publicity.

The institutions must commit "hard dollars" to supporting the recruitment and retention of Native staff and faculty. They should invite the local Native community to become an active partner in the development of Native programming at the college. Neither educational professionals nor Native people should participate in culturally demeaning actions such as the tomahawk chop or "war chants." Those who are responsible for educational programming on campus can make use of local resources or invite guest speakers from the local community to teach students about this issue. These are steps all of us can take, whether or not we work at a school with an Indian mascot. The use of school mascots is an issue that needs to be addressed by all college and university departments; now is the time to do so.

For this to be a real partnership, NTU must embrace the guiding principles of the ERTI people. NTU must incorporate into their educational process these values: to live with courage, to seek knowledge, to be of service to the community, and to leave the world a better place for future generations.

Reference

Deloria, Vine Jr. (1969, 1988) *Custer Died for Your Sins: An Indian Manifesto.* New York: Macmillan.

Reflections on the Story: An Edited Interview with Matthew VanAlstine and Wayne Stein

On the Topic of the "Mascot" Issue

Wayne Stein

The practice of using American Indian tribal names and/or slang words as a mascot symbol is well over a hundred years old. Originally, mascots were chosen to portray the sports team as fierce, brutal, and a force to fear. At the time this practice took hold, in the nineteenth and early twentieth centuries, American Indians were viewed as dangerous barbarians with little human character or integrity. It is clear that these depictions of American Indians were a form of cognitive dissonance used by the early colonists and later their descendants to justify the economically motivated stealing of American Indians' lands, and the killing of them if necessary. It is ironic that cognitive dissonance continues to be used in current-day struggles between American Indian communities and a handful of postsecondary institutions that are clinging to their outdated, and often offensive, mascots.

Today mainstream institutions of higher education that still use American Indians as mascot symbols are caught between being politically correct (or just plain civil) and offending their powerful alumni who have embraced their institution's mascot symbol as a semi-sacred icon. The claim is made that this practice honors American Indians. In the end, money and institutional politics will win out almost every time. Being civil and changing an offending mascot that makes the institution much money and has powerful political supporters is very difficult to do, even for an enlightened institution of higher education.

Matthew VanAlstine

There are multiple ways to view the importance and meaning of the Native American nickname and mascot issue. Unfortunately, the indigenous perspective is too often ignored and patronized by mainstream media and the general population. Supporters of Native American nicknames and mascots are very good at selling the idea of indigenous communities being honored, and any issues that arise come from the vocal minority. The general population of the United States, having grown up with Native American nicknames and mascots, are engrained with the notion that it is a nonissue and a valued tradition. In addition, indigenous communities have been exposed to the idea and images of Native American nicknames and mascots as common and inoffensive. Although there are multiple viewpoints on the mascot issue, an imbalance in power between indigenous and mainstream institutions often leaves the indigenous voice in the margins.

The problem with the Native American nickname and mascot issue in Indian Country is that there are other important and more pressing issues to be resolved. There are many indigenous people who are not opposed to the use of Native American nicknames and mascots because of their own lack of knowledge and understanding of the effects and messages which these things convey. The dilemma in Indian Country is developing a cohesive voice against the use of Native American nicknames among all tribal nations and people. If one tribal nation supports the use of Native American nicknames, that automatically weakens the legitimacy of indigenous peoples' objection to their use in the minds of the mainstream population. Indigenous voices are dependent on unity, and any dissonance will result in a loss of meaning and impact. Those who understand the hostile and stereotypical educational environment that schools with Native American nicknames and mascots produce need to continue with their message to mainstream and indigenous communities.

On the Topic of Partnerships

Matthew VanAlstine

The fundamental differences between indigenous and traditional (Western) higher education institutions is a commitment to cultural values and creating communities that are spiritually, physically, and mentally healthy. Indigenous institutions are guided by cultural communities whose focus is on sustaining their ancient language and cultural values that have been passed down through many generations. Western institutions are guided by capitalism and knowledge that is grounded in science rather than spirituality.

In the case study, the Western institution and indigenous community enter into a partnership with different goals in mind. The Western institution is focused on preserving its money-making nickname and pleasing its powerful and influential alumni. The indigenous community is entering the partnership with the idea of making the experience of higher education more attainable and relevant for current and future indigenous students. The indigenous community is entering the partnership with the intention of benefiting all indigenous communities, whereas the Western institution is entering the partnership with the sole intention of benefiting itself. Indigenous communities, following their cultural values, are often willing to share their resources, but sometimes they need to consider whether the outside communities have authentic intentions.

The problem for indigenous communities in partnerships with Western institutions is that they do not always know what they are giving up in relation to what they are receiving. The indigenous community in the case study stands to benefit from the partnership with a Western institution, but at the same time it gets the short end of the stick. It is important for indigenous communities to have cultural brokers with indigenous hearts at the Western institutions with which they build partnerships to ensure that those institutions have authentic intentions. In addition, when entering partnerships with Western institutions, members of indigenous communities need to keep their cultural values and identity close at hand when making decisions that affect their own future and those of current indigenous students.

Wayne Stein

There are some fundamental differences between indigenous and mainstream institutions of higher education. Conversely, they also have many goals in common; the trick is to find the shared goals and proceed from there to develop an effective partnership. Some of the most common problems the two types of higher education institution have when trying to form a partnership to serve indigenous (American Indian) students are: (a) mainstream institutions often do not understand the wide cultural gap that exists when indigenous students leave their homeland to attend a mainstream institution, (b) indigenous students must often do a substantial amount of catching up in certain academic areas such as math and writing skills, (c) indigenous students often come to the mainstream institution from communities that are economically impoverished, (d) trust between the two institutions must be developed over time, and (e) if the mainstream institution is using an indigenous (American Indian) tribal name or slang word for its sports teams, the challenges of maintaining partnerships and serving American Indian students become more difficult to address.

The above-mentioned potential problems between indigenous and mainstream institutions can be solved if both sides are willing to work on solutions that indigenous students and their communities can embrace.

1. The cultural gap, once recognized, can be fixed by the mainstream institution's creating a space on its campus designated as a gathering spot for indigenous students. Indigenous schools can help narrow the cultural gap that their students will encounter once they leave those institutions

by providing workshops on how to survive the coming new educational experience.

2. The mainstream institution must provide academic and financial assistance specifically for indigenous students from the moment they arrive on campus. This assistance will send a powerful message to indigenous students, their community, and the indigenous institution—that the mainstream institution wants indigenous students on campus. This commitment starts at the top of mainstream institution, in the president's office, and takes the will of the rest of the institution to make it work.

3. Trust is a tough one; only honest dealings between the indigenous institution and the mainstream institution over time can create trust.

4. The mascot issue is complex and can divide the personnel of the mainstream institution as well as people from the indigenous community. If mainstream institutions really value indigenous students and the communities from which they come these institutions will take into consideration what the majority of those indigenous people think about their mascot and act accordingly.

Matthew VanAlstine

A partnership between two institutions should include a sense of trustworthiness and shared meaning. Indigenous institutions, when negotiating with mainstream institutions, need to evaluate their own needs and the strengths that they bring to the partnership. Cultural integrity is immeasurably valuable and should not be compromised for the sake of instant gratification. What I hope that people learn from this case study is that indigenous communities are closely related, and what happens in one community affects other communities. Although indigenous nations are unique and independent of one another, they are at the same time interdependent.

"YOUNG MAN ... TURN THAT CAMERA ON ..." STORIES OF CROSS-CULTURAL CONNECTIONS

Francisco Guajardo (Mentees: Lai-Lani Ovalles and Edyael Casaperalta)

To Record, Or Not . . .

As 20-some-year-old Chaney Bell sat across from an elder at the Flathead Reservation in rural western Montana, he fumbled through his gear— handling video cassettes, stripping a tripod out of its bag, and pulling out a digital video camera, microphone, and the obligatory headphones. He seemed nervous, exceedingly cautious, yet displayed a demeanor of great respect as he prepared to speak with a tribal elder. The source of Chaney's anxiety was the presence of the camera and other technology. Although the elder had agreed to be interviewed, Chaney wasn't certain whether the technology would be a distraction to the conversation, or whether that same equipment would be a symbol of disrespect to the elder or his stories, which Chaney so passionately wanted to capture on videotape.

Chaney's apprehension was rooted partly in history, which points to research as an invasive practice in indigenous communities. Smith (2002) and others have suggested that Native communities historically have viewed research as yet another strategy through which to extend the colonization process. On the other hand, Smith cited storytelling and oral history as decolonizing research methods through which indigenous people can own their own research and stories.

> As he gathered the equipment, Chaney addressed his interviewee: "Elder, may I have your permission to videotape this interview, because . . ."
>
> Before Chaney completed his question, the elder interrupted, sensing young Chaney's anxiety, but also determined to make a point. "Young man," he said, "you better turn that camera on because if you don't, my stories may die forever."

And with that, Chaney Bell began to document the stories of elders in Flathead.

241

The Context

This story is about how Chaney Bell and members of other tribal communities across the country worked closely with the Llano Grande Center, a nonprofit organization based in Edcouch-Elsa High School in rural south Texas, in order to strengthen young people's storytelling ability through digital media. Our story is also about cross-cultural connections between the Center, which is operated largely by Latino youths and educators who live in a rural place along the Texas–Mexico border, and Native American communities from Flathead in Montana, Lummi in Washington, and Laguna in Eastern Cibola County, New Mexico. But the connections are also more expansive because they tend to be about youths and adults working together in respectful ways—and in a manner in which they purposefully reflect on issues of history, culture, identity, and power. These cross-cultural and cross-generational relationships were facilitated through a national leadership initiative called Kellogg Leadership for Community Change (KLCC), the W. K. Kellogg Foundation's earnest attempt to move leadership development from an individual-based model to a collective or community leadership framework.

The communities came together as participants in KLCC's first two sessions, which focused on teaching and learning, as well as youth–adult partnerships. As the early leadership-development work unfolded in 2003, the Llano Grande Center strategically videotaped its work, both locally and nationally, when the Center's leadership Fellows participated in national meetings. The Center used the video data for evaluation and program-development purposes. In addition, the Center produced edited videos to show conference participants the possibilities of using videos for reflection, evaluation, and teaching and learning opportunities. As youths and adults from Llano Grande produced these videos, which we call digital stories, participants from other KLCC communities expressed an interest in learning how to use video technology to produce their own digital stories. And so, the Llano Grande Center launched its digital-storytelling workshop series.

The origin of the Center's video work is found in its oral-history project initiated in the mid-1990s. As youths and teachers ventured into the community to engage elders in conversation, or as elders traveled to the local high school to share their personal narratives, the Center carefully video-recorded these oral histories. The video work, however, is of secondary value. Of primary importance is building a relationship between youths and elders, and on learning from elders' life stories. The Center employed video recording to document these stories, but only after several years of collecting stories by using much more rudimentary technology, such as paper and pencil at first, then audio recording. But the faces of the elders were too compelling not to capture on video, and the grace, vigor, and stories they wore on their faces had to be recorded. The old technology could not capture those qualities; video could, so the Center purchased cameras and began to convert oral histories into digital stories.

The Center uses this technology to enhance its leadership-development work, which follows a model of participatory and collaborative processes. Contrary to the mainstream model of individual leadership practice and development, the Center operates on a collective-leadership model, in part because it allows more people to participate in decision-making and power-sharing experiences, but also because collective leadership is much more consistent with the history and culture of our Latino community along the Texas–Mexico border. Our elders teach us through oral histories and through present-day conversations that families and relationships are central to how we build leaders in our communities. The individual leadership model, or the "Lone Ranger" model, as one elder called it, is not consistent with the history of our communities.

The Connections

The Center began convening digital-storytelling workshops in south Texas during the summer of 2005, but it also organized training sessions at different sites across the country. Chaney and others from Flathead came to south Texas in 2005, but Fellows from other KLCC sites received training at their home sites. As these sessions developed, so did a strong cross-cultural connection between members of Native American communities and members of the Llano Grande Center, a community of people not traditionally viewed as indigenous.

As an organization informed by community- and family-based Latino epistemologies, the Llano Grande Center is anchored by its work on finding, cultivating, and celebrating personal, family, and community stories. To be sure, the people who populate the Center have undeniable indigenous roots, but those roots largely have been lost as a result of centuries of political displacement, immigration, and other historical forces. The identity of the Center is thus consistent with the Mexican immigrant and the Latino experience in the United States. Anzaldúa's (1987) notion of the "lost" indigenous identity of Chicano(a) people is a direct product of a history of conquest, colonization, and oppression, particularly in the physical spaces along the "borderlands." In addition, many of the immigrant children who continue to populate schools along the border originate from indigenous communities in Mexico, although the children and parents themselves are largely unaware of their indigenous roots. The historical forces of oppression, the persistent lack of knowing of one's origins, and the silencing of people and communities shape important parts of the Llano Grande Center's vision and work. Thus, the curricular focus on oral histories, place-based pedagogy, and digital stories is a strategic attempt to help youths and others cultivate a clearer sense of history, culture, and identity. Digital storytelling emerges from this teaching and learning spirit.

A Sampling of Stories

One cool morning, 15-year-old Joseph sat in the back of a classroom in a Laguna Department of Education building. Llano Grande youths and teachers had traveled to the Laguna Reservation in the open lands of eastern New Mexico to deliver a digital-storytelling workshop. A typical Llano Grande team includes youths and adults working as co-trainers and co-creators. Adults take responsibility for youths, and youths understand that power is to be shared and negotiated in a respectful and democratic manner by adults and youths alike; this is a central tenet of the work of Llano Grande (Guajardo et al., 2006). On this morning on the reservation, Llano Grande staff found ten eager participants ready to learn the art of digital storytelling. The eleventh, Joseph, presented a challenge. To be sure, the challenge did not appear rooted in cultural differences, i.e. Native versus Latino; rather, Joseph seemed more like a normal teenager who was not captivated by what seemed to him a traditional workshop.

"Joseph," asked one of the facilitators, "what story might you want to tell?"
"I don't know," responded Joseph disinterestedly. "Well, what are your interests, what do you like to do?" continued the interviewer. "I don't

know," echoed Joseph. "Hmmm," said the facilitator, at an apparent loss for words.

This pattern continued for a couple of minutes, with little or no apparent connection made between Joseph and the facilitator. Facilitators, both youths and adults, asked questions, but Joseph sat silently and without expression. But a turning point in the conversation occurred when the facilitator asked Joseph about his family. His response was rather mundane, but he perked up a bit. The facilitator then posed follow-up questions, which led to fuller responses, and soon thereafter Joseph was engaged. After 30 minutes of exploration, Joseph had his story, and he went on to produce an emotionally riveting digital story that featured at least a dozen immediate family members who had fought in foreign wars for the United States of America.

"My Uncle Frank," he said, "served in Vietnam, but I don't know much about his stories. But my grandma does . . . maybe we can go talk to her."

So off we went, in a borrowed van, to Joseph's 93-year-old grandmother's house on the Laguna Reservation. The conversation with his grandmother was a historic event—for Joseph, for the accompanying guests, and for Uncle Frank, whom Grandma summoned to her house some time during the second hour of the visit. The emotional intensity heightened when Uncle Frank arrived, as he expressed both joy and great pain in reliving his Vietnam stories.

Joseph produced a beautiful digital story that he titled "Native Americans in War," and he did it by initiating conversations with his grandmother, his uncle, and others as he explored the family narrative deeply and authentically. Although he initially appeared isolated, Joseph emerged as an engaged listener and processor of stories. Collective leadership development is fundamentally connected to the conversations and to the process of people working and building together, as opposed to the individual leadership model in which the leader is more apt to create and act by him/herself. Joseph exemplifies the emergence of collective leadership, grounded in conversation and community, and creating together.

The last report we heard at the Llano Grande Center is that Joseph is interested in pursuing a film career.

Other stories produced by youths from the local middle school addressed issues that appeared to be of great urgency to them. As they conducted research for their stories, they interviewed the school principal and selected teachers, and then crafted their own narratives to complement the voices of interviewees. The stories had an impact. They alerted school leaders, who feared the digital stories' going public, to think more deeply about issues such as discipline, more responsive teaching, and the need for greater youth voice in the school. The youths succeeded in raising awareness, while they built storytelling, technology, and advocacy skills. The middle school storytellers worked collaboratively to produce their story. Rather than the single moviemaker producing a story that alarms an intended audience, this group of youths worked together, built skills together, and approached the school principal together. In that process, they felt more supported as their collective leadership behavior took shape.

Other digital storytellers produced pieces that were equally important. A group from the Lummi Reservation told the story of the Cedar Project in the lush timber region of northern Washington state, on the edge of the Pacific Ocean, where nature, tradition, and spirit intersect in ways that celebrate the past, the present, and the future. Yet another Lummi group featured the symbolic value and vitality of the totem pole. The Lummi work around digital storytelling, and storytelling in general, offers a compelling example of how youths and adult members of a community have come to share power. Through a commitment to explore the roles of youths in leadership roles on the reservation, Lummi elders have modeled exceptional power-sharing behavior, and in so doing have enlisted the talents and energies of emerging youth leaders. The digital-storytelling exercises were but one mode through which this relationship was manifested. The formation of collective leadership development is on display on the Lummi Reservation, and the stories of that kind of leadership will continue to emerge. Indeed, there is no shortage of stories emanating from Flathead, Laguna, and Lummi.

Making Cross-Cultural Connections

The purpose of the Llano Grande Center's digital-storytelling workshop was to probe our new friends from tribal communities—to challenge them to tell their stories through a distinctly digital mode. The work began years ago by focusing on personal storytelling for identity formation, and it has since evolved into storytelling for collective leadership for community change. Beyond that, the work has allowed one largely Latino community located along the Texas–Mexico border to build deep cross-cultural connections with Native American communities across the country.

The epistemologies that inform Llano Grande's leadership-development work are shaped by *platicas*, or dialogues, as well as by the stories youth researchers and teachers collect and put to use. This dialogical and storytelling method, which is consistent with Smith's decolonizing methodologies, finds a deep degree of compatibility in the leadership-development work of Native American communities, such as Chaney's. The conversational and storytelling modes emerge as a center-piece of collective-leadership formation, and begin to define a leadership model dependent on groups of people engaging in *platicas* as a foundational part of this brand of leadership for community change (Guajardo & Guajardo, 2004).

The Llano Grande Center finds connection and affinity with the groundedness and richness of Native cultures. Moreover, as historian Rodolfo Acuña (1988) suggested, the history of Mexican American people in the United States is one of conquest and colonization—two historical processes that have plagued Native communities most pro-foundly. In this socio-historical context, honor, respect, value for elders, family, land, spirituality, and the narrative form are important qualities shared by Native communities and those who work with the Llano Grande Center. They are qualities essential for the healthy development and existence of Latino families and Native American communities alike. Indeed, they may be essential for the healthy development of all human groups.

Closing Reflection

"Thank you, young man. Thank you for recording this. It's a good way to make sure my stories, and the stories of other elders, stay alive," said the elder to Chaney.

"It is my privilege," said Chaney, "I take this very seriously. And thank you for helping me keep your stories."

References

Acuña, R. (1988) *Occupied America: A history of Chicanos*. New York: Harper & Row.

Anzaldúa, G. (1987) *Borderlands/La frontera*. San Francisco: Aunt Lute Books.

Guajardo, F. & Guajardo, M. (2004) "The impact of brown on the brown of South Texas: a micropolitical perspective on the education of Mexican Americans in a rural South Texas community." *American Educational Research Journal*, 41(3), 501–526.

Guajardo, F., Perez, D., Ozuna, J., Guajardo, M., Davila, E., & Casaperalta, N. (2006) "Youth voice and the Llano Grande Center." *International Journal of Leadership in Education*, 9(4), 359–362.

Smith, L. (2002) *Decolonizing Methodologies: Research and Indigenous Peoples*. London: Zed Books.

Lessons We Learn: Commentaries From Scholar-Practitioners

Commentary: Cultivating Native Leadership Through the Pedagogy of Multiple Literacies

Teresa L. McCarty

It was a warm June day when my colleague, Fred Bia, and I drove out to the red-rock mesas near Rough Rock, Arizona, to interview community elder Bit'ahnii Yée Be'esdzáán. Like Chaney Bell in Francisco Guajardo's account, Fred and I were both 20-something and at work on an oral history project for the local community and school. Like Chaney Bell, we felt some apprehension about the interview; as the only non-Native member of our oral history team, I expect I was much more apprehensive than Fred, who had grown up at Rough Rock and who would conduct the interview in his native Navajo. Also like Chaney Bell and the Llano Grande team, we shared a passion for this work, having felt the excitement of discovery and the appreciation for human experience.

We found Bit'ahnii Yée Be'esdzáán sitting on a narrow bed under a juniper-covered shade house next to her *hooghan* (a traditional dwelling), a gray kitten curled up beside her. She was perhaps 90 years old at the time. She had lived all her life near Tsé Ch'izhí—Rough Rock— a small community in the interior of the Navajo Nation. After exchanging introductions and courtesies, including the expected protocol of identifying kin and clan relationships, we asked her to tell us how people had settled the local area. Her words took us back to a time of great hope and despair.

Bit'ahnii Yée Be'esdzáán's mother had been born in captivity at a place Navajo people (Diné) call Hwéeldi, and which the U.S. government named Fort Sumner, New Mexico. In the autumn of 1863, Colonel Kit Carson led a scorched-earth campaign through the valley just east of Rough Rock, burning fields and homes and slaughtering the families' herds of sheep. Over the course of that winter, having only berries and piñon nuts to eat, Bit'ahnii Yée Be'esdzáán's grandmother, along with several thousand other Diné, surrendered to U.S. forces at Fort Defiance, Arizona. From there they were marched 300 miles across wintry plains to a concentration camp at Fort Sumner. Not knowing where they were being sent, with little clothing or blankets to keep them warm, and the women carrying infants on their backs, some 8,000 Navajo people eventually made it to Fort Sumner. What came to be called the Long Walk claimed hundreds of Navajo lives. At Hwéeldi, over 2,000 more would die of starvation, diarrhea due to poor food quality, and Anglo-introduced disease before a peace treaty was signed in 1868.[1]

"My mother's name was K'é Hoonibah," Bit'ahnii Yée Be'esdzáán related. "She was born at Hwéeldi."

> When my mother was being born, a group of soldiers came up over the hill carrying swords. My mother's grandmother was afraid. "What are they going to do to us this time?" she thought. But all this time, the soldiers had only come to discuss peace with the *naat'áanii* [Navajo leaders]. . . . Then all of a sudden, there were a lot of people talking up there over the hill. There was peace [*k'é*].

Surely there was hope in the naming of Bit'ahnii Yée Be'esdzáán's mother. K'é Hoonibah means "Peace Finally Found You" or "Peace Arrived." "After my mother was born," Bit'ahnii Yée Be'esdzáán recalled, "they moved back near Rough Rock. My grandmother used to tell me this story."[2]

---

[1] Additional oral histories on the Long Walk and Hwéeldi can be found in Ruth Roessel's (1973) *Navajo Stories of the Long Walk Period*.

[2] Excerpts from this oral history interview can be found in McCarty (2002, pp. 22–23), and in McCarty and Zepeda (1999, pp. 200–201).

I have situated this commentary on Llano Grande's storytelling project within another "storytelling story" to highlight the broader lessons that can be learned from this work. First and foremost, oral history projects such as these challenge us to critique dominant narratives of indigenous experience and Native–White relations. They call into question what Māori researcher Linda Tuhiwai Smith (1999) called "research through imperial eyes" (p. 8). As Guajardo writes, this is decolonizing research through which "indigenous people can own their own . . . stories." Indigenous community-based oral history is an act of resistance against established academic practices, but just as assuredly it is a proactive epistemic stance on the value of indigenous knowledge and ways of knowing.

By reclaiming and privileging local narratives of experience, the *products* of this research debunk limited and often erroneous portrayals by outsiders. But as we learn from the Llano Grande case, and as we found at Rough Rock, the *process* underlying this work is equally significant. Indeed, Guajardo writes that although video documentation is essential to preserve precious knowledge that might otherwise be lost, of primary importance is the "building [of] relationship[s] between youths and elders, and . . . learning from elders' life stories." This process brings together young and old and those in between, joining them in shared storying and strengthening intergenerational ties. Symbolically and concretely, this process *creates* community. This is tellingly illustrated in Guajardo's account of Joseph, his grandmother, and Uncle Frank, whose dialogue about his Vietnam War experiences transformed young Joseph from a disinterested bystander to an "engaged listener and processor of stories." As Guajardo notes, this "exemplifies the emergence of collective leadership grounded in conversation and community."

The Llano Grande case contains yet another lesson not explicitly addressed by Guajardo, but latent in his account nonetheless. In the modernist arena of schooling, much has been said and written about— and innumerable policies have been devised to ameliorate—the presumed literacy "deficiencies" of students of color, their families and communities. Consider, however, the rich and variegated literacy events co-constructed by Chaney Bell and Joseph, and the complex literacy practices in which they and their interview participants engage. Consider the depth and breadth of historical knowledge contained in the narratives of Flathead and Lummi and Laguna and Rough Rock elders, and in the narratives that constitute the oral traditions of any indigenous people. Consider the multiple literacies acquired and displayed in the negotiation of such narratives by teachers (elders) and learners (youths). In these multiple-literacy engagements, "the textual is also related to the visual, the audio, the spatial, [and] the behavioral," including multi-media (The New London Group, 1996, p. 64).[3] These intricately textured, cross-generational transactions are the epitome of what literacy theorist James Gee (2004) called "situated language learning." They are also manifest-ations of the abundant "funds of knowledge" in Native families and communities, the "historically accumulated and culturally developed bodies of knowledge and skills" essential for individual, family, and communal functioning and well-being (Moll *et al.*, 2005, p. 72). Finally, these narrative engagements are expressions of distinctly indigenous lit-eracies framed within primarily oral intellectual and cultural traditions, including, as Cochiti scholar Mary Eunice Romero-Little (2006) pointed out, indigenous "ways of knowing, learning, and teaching" (p. 400).

Having "listened" through the printed word to the story of Llano Grande, what might our next steps as educators, scholars, community members, policymakers, and citizens be? Certainly the Llano Grande experience can be adapted by other schools and community organiza-tions. It is a curricular and pedagogical design ripe with transformative possibilities. Although Llano Grande's cross-cultural breadth may be more ambitious than many schools can attempt, the model of cross-community and cross-generational partnerships is a compelling and emi-nently feasible one. At Rough Rock, oral histories became the basis for the development of bilingual texts in which students not only acquired interdisciplinary knowledge and skills through local content, but also came to see their parents and grandparents as published authors. Another oral history project there involved high school students as videographers for interviews with elders about the origins of their

---

[3] "Multiliteracies" and "multiliteracy pedagogy" are terms associated with The New London Group, a consortium of ten literacy scholars named after the place where the group first met, in New London, New Hampshire. They describe multiliteracies as encompassing a "multiplicity of communications channels and media, and the increas-ing saliency of cultural and linguistic diversity" (The New London Group, 1996, p. 63). The role of pedagogy, they continue, "is to develop an epistemology of pluralism that provides access without people having to erase or leave behind" who they are (1996, p. 72).

bilingual-bicultural community school. "The students think it's wonderful," their teacher reported. "They're really excited. They've written questions. They want to be part of it" (McCarty, 2002, p. 4).

Finding meaningful ways to affirm Native youths in being a central "part of" community building may be the most important lesson these projects hold. As Guajardo observes, oral history affords a vehicle for reaching across generations and enlisting "the capable talents and energies of emerging youth leaders." A powerful part of this process is a pedagogy that activates the multiple linguistic resources within indigenous communities, nurturing and articulating oral, written, visual, and even digital modalities. This pedagogy also makes use of Native languages, a domain in which elders play a pivotal role. Yet if indigenous languages are to survive as viable means of transmitting culture, it is also a domain in which youths must be supported as language learners.

The cultivation of multiple literacies, including oral traditions and Native languages, can foster new forms of indigenous community empowerment and leadership. By honoring and reinvigorating those traditions and multiple literacies, Llano Grande and projects like it are charting the way.

References

Gee, J. P. (2004) *Situated Language and Learning: A Critique of Traditional Schooling*. New York: Routledge.

McCarty, T. L. (2002) *A Place to be Navajo: Rough Rock and the Struggle for Self-determination in Indigenous Schooling*. Mahwah, NJ: Lawrence Erlbaum.

McCarty, T. L. & Zepeda, O. (1999) "Amerindians." In J. A. Fishman (ed.), *Handbook of Language and Ethnic Identity*. New York: Oxford University Press, (pp. 197–210).

Moll, L., Amanti, C., Neff, D., & González, N. (2005) "Funds of knowledge for teaching: using a qualitative approach to connect homes and classrooms." In N. González, L. C. Moll, & C. Amanti (eds), *Funds of Knowledge: Theorizing Practices in Households, Communities, and Classrooms*. Mahwah, NJ: Lawrence Erlbaum, pp. 71–87.

Roessel, R. (ed.) (1973) *Navajo Stories of the Long Walk Period*. Tsaile, AZ: Navajo Community College Press.

Romero-Little, M. E. (2006) "Honoring our own: rethinking indigenous languages and literacy." *Anthropology and Education Quarterly*, 37(4), 399–402.

Smith, L. T. (1999) *Decolonizing Methodologies: Research and Indigenous Peoples.* London: Zed Books.

The New London Group (1996) "A pedagogy of multiliteracies: designing social futures." *Harvard Educational Review*, 66(1), 60–92.

Commentary: The Subtleties of Cross-Cultural Partnerships

J. Kehaulani Kauanui

In the case study offered by Francisco Guajardo, in collaboration with Lai-Lani Ovalles and Edyael Casaperalta, readers learn about the subtle dynamics involved in cross-cultural partnerships. In the first case, the Llano Grande Center sponsored a project to convene digital-storytelling workshops and sent a Latino male student in his 20s who was from a rural Texas borderland to interview a Flathead male elder on a rural reservation in western Montana. In this intergenerational exchange, we see the protocols involved in securing informed consent and permission to document indigenous knowledge, as we also learn about place-based pedagogy.

One thing that was immediately striking was the student Chaney's apprehension about the technology involved in the project and the elder's possibly seeing the camera as a sign of disrespect or something that could possibly get in the way of the conversation. Yes, the elder responded favourably, and explicitly stated his reason for agreement— because time was of the essence in terms of documenting the stories he wished to tell, which he feared otherwise would probably die when he does.

One thing to consider here are the reasons why one might assume that indigenous elders would be apprehensive about the technology involved, especially given the long history of exploitation by nonindigenous researchers, as well as the ways in which those who are part of the dominant society have often used technology for less than philanthropic ends. What we might also consider is that indigenous communities have often taken technologies imposed by colonial and neocolonial forces and used them to their own benefit, within their own cultural logics, and for their own agendas. In this case, the purpose is to advance cultural perpetuity in documenting the story. In terms of the documentation of stories in digital form, we might consider the various methods peoples have used to record their oral histories in ways that promote various kinds of cultural literacy. It seems that digital stories are not conversions per se, but are another way (among others) to record indigenous knowledge.

What we do not know exactly is how the youths and elders were chosen to be paired and by whom. How might the factors used in pairing people for intergenerational and crossracial exchange instruct us when considering what it takes to make a productive team who have mutual interests? The key here seems to be the mutual respect necessary for participatory and collaborative practices that involve power sharing, and how they can be maintained in ways that do not breach cultural mandates that might demand hierarchy.

In the second case, the writers turn to the Laguna Reservation and 15-year-old Joseph. Here, at first, we see a student who seems alienated and distant in the classroom. Instead of ignoring his seeming indifference, the instructor helps cultivate a point of entry so he can enter the discussion and clarify his own interests and investments. He probes his own family history of military service in foreign wars. This story serves as an example of how to create opportunities for intergenerational exchanges and promote the continuity within families for sharing history and knowledge. This case exemplifies the possibilities of building collective leadership—here, collaboration between Joseph and his grandmother and uncle. Moreover, the case shows how to pursue youth development without instructors imposing their own interests or agendas onto students.

Reflections on the Case: An Edited Interview with Francisco Guajardo, Lai-Lani Ovalles, and Edyael Casaperalta

Lai-Lani Ovalles

Stories are meant to be shared. The use of digital media to tell and share stories can build upon the traditions of oral storytelling in indigenous communities. Much of the media to which we are exposed on a daily basis comes from corporations that profit from the proliferation of racism, sexism, and consumerism. By engaging youths and adults in digital storytelling, the opportunity to take responsibility for what, how, and why stories get told becomes an empowerment tool. Instead of an "outsider" looking in and telling you what your worldview is, you get to tell the world how you view life.

Francisco Guajardo

The Llano Grande brand of digital storytelling is guided by dialogue—between facilitator and storyteller, but also through the internal dialogical process. These introspective and interpersonal exchanges allow storyteller and facilitator to share stories—often very personal, formative stories. Through this story-sharing process, Llano Grande facilitators have been able to build friendships and deep relationships with people from other cultural groups. In this context, bonds have been formed between people from Native American communities and Llano Grande youths and adults. This peculiar bond is characterized by the formation of trust shaped through the story engagement process; it is a trust that might not have been formed in the absence of dialogues focused on personal stories.

A preponderance of the stories created through this digital storytelling work have centered on personal transformations; in addition, the process of creating the story has changed the storytellers themselves. This change typically is a result of the storyteller's gaining a deeper understanding of his or her lived experience and particular story. This transformation then becomes the root for community change, and when people from different cultural groups share the experience, it becomes the root for greater cross-cultural understanding.

Edyael Casaperalta

Profound learning is intimate; it is tangible, it is felt, a physical connection. When I learn about myself, I expand beyond my corporeal limits, my spirit grows, I gain a sense of space, and I feel. Because I understand the power of my story, I become aware of the power of other stories. So, instead of denouncing them, or confining myself to just one story, my own story takes hold of me and demands that I recognize and respect the stories of others. My story(ies) teaches me to listen to the multiple stories living inside me and inside others, to create spaces where they can be heard (physically and spiritually) and honored.

Digital storytelling is a tool that facilitates this process. Students who engage in the (re)writing of their own stories learn about others' stories and find common grounds with other members of their community, across cultures, languages, and so on. The first indigenous president of Mexico, Benito Juarez, said, "El respeto al derecho ajeno es la paz"—that is, "Respect for others' rights is peace." By respecting our own and others' stories, we begin to create spaces in which we can create peace.

Francisco Guajardo

Many indigenous communities (schools) will be interested in this engaging process. However, they must remember to address authorship (ownership of traditional knowledge) and cultural appropriateness (what can be shared with a broader audience and the manner in which it is shared). Any digital storytelling process must respect stories, both individual and community stories. Those who assist the storytellers may be cultural workers, they may be technical-assistance providers, or they may be both, but they are not owners or authors of the stories. Rather, storytellers from the indigenous communities own the stories.

Therefore, our Llano Grande brand of digital storytelling is rooted in dialogical processes; that is, we have conversations out of which values, stories, and cultural imperatives emerge. Conversations teach us that certain stories are appropriate for a particular community, whereas other stories might not be. Identification and development of stories come out of this dialogical experience. Hence, we learn about cultural appropriateness through conversations.

Edyael Casaperalta

I would say that a digital story is, by default, respectful of traditional knowledge because it is precisely this knowledge that inspires it. The community creating the digital story is the best judge of who should be credited, what to share, and how to share it with the intended audience. If the digital story is, in fact, created in the spirit of traditional knowledge, relationships, and collectivity, the result will be a story that honors the ways of knowing of that community.

Francisco Guajardo

Regarding the affordability of digital storytelling, well, anyone can be a Spielberg today. There was a time when moviemakers needed to invest more than $100,000 in technology to make a movie. Today, anyone can make a movie with an investment of $2,000 to $3,000. A digital storyteller needs a computer with digital video editing software, a digital video camera, good audio equipment, and a videocassette. The most critical element, however, is a good story, and you really can't put a price on that.

PART V

CHALLENGE TO ALL INDIGENOUS SCHOLAR-PRACTITIONERS

Henrietta Mann

The following is excerpted from Dr. Henrietta Mann's *Reflections on the Day*, presented at the 2005 World Indigenous Peoples Conference, Hamilton, New Zealand.

My 70+ years here on this good earth, relatively speaking, have been but a brief journey to date. I look back and I ask, *What have I done?* I can say only that I have spent more than three decades teaching in higher education, enjoying a fulfilling job, and taking care of my tiny space in the big circle of life. Like many of you, I am working in the trenches. As professors and teachers, we're digging the trenches and we have laid them across the oceans to intersect different cultures. What I see you as educators and researchers doing is creating what I like to call a "peaceful revolution." That's the journey we are on in our classrooms. We are regenerating old knowledge from our traditions in a different place and time so that we can repatriate

259

ourselves through revitalizing our cultures and our languages. We are taking back the indigenous traditions that have been shaped by our lands. We are making ancestral teachings vital and dynamic so as to be congruent with the time in which we live. Succinctly stated, we are repatriating our very spirits through education in peaceful ways.

Elders need to be ever mindful of hope. Young people give me hope when they speak our Native tongues. They give me hope when they go back to the mountain to acquire new teachings and share them with all who care to learn. Just as every generation that has preceded us has done, we also need to learn and teach our languages and our cultures. Our elders have taught us that each of us has been given a purpose in life with equally great responsibilities. You have much work ahead of you, and it may appear daunting! You can, however, acknowledge that what goes on in the world of the spirit can be replicated here on earth and that you can draw on that power. Through your efforts, all children can become aware of who they are as powerfully indigenous.

The knowledge that has been generated here is absolutely phenomenal. One of the seven common characteristics of prayer for indigenous peoples is that we all have and can develop great minds—great minds that are respectful, loving, kind, and inclusive. We are creative peoples. I appreciate the new songs that have been created: songs of courage, songs that are contemporary, and songs that unify us. We need to have our indigenous researchers present our work and publish it. We need to show that our research is valid and that our own scholars can do this work in a sensitive and respectful way. We need to communicate our learning to the world because we have much to teach.

As indigenous researchers *we* are the researchers of our respective homelands. *We* need to bridge the gap between theory and practice. *We* need to add the dimension of culture to what is researched and produced so that it benefits our communities and families. *We* need to hear the voices of children and elders and, most important, the voices of our interpreters across cultures. We are obligated to our communities to do the work, and to engage in research that helps to sustain our ways of life.

This work captures dreams, aspirations, and love. This work will ensure that our children are happy and can laugh and that they are complete and whole beings. My humble self believes in what you do and can do. *Hahoo!* Thank you for the gift of hope. I forever hold you in my prayers and in my heart.

About the Editor and Contributing Authors

Makalapua Alencastre, a Native Hawaiian educator, has focused her life's work on the reestablishment of Hawaiian as the primary language of the home, education, cultural and recreational activities. Her professional and research interests are inspired by her commitment and love for the Hawaiian language and culture and include language acquisition, immersion education-program planning and evaluation, resource development (teachers and curriculum), video-documentation, and educational reform. Makalapua established and directed a P–12 indigenous immersion program on Oʻahu and is currently the Associate Director of Kahuawaiola Indigenous Teacher Education Program for the Ka Haka Ula O Keʻelikolani College of Hawaiian language at the University of Hawaiʻi at Hilo. (Contributing author)

Maenette Kapeʻahiokalani Padeken Ah Nee-Benham, Kanaka Maoli (Native Hawaiian) scholar and teacher, is a Professor in the Educational Administration Department at Michigan State University. She teaches graduate level courses in school leadership, organizational theory, research methods, and school–family–community relations. As a scholar, mentor, and teacher, her inquiry centers on the nature of engaged educational leadership; the wisdom of knowing and praxis of social justice envisioned and enacted by community based leaders; and educational policy and practices for indigenous communities (family and children/ youth). She is the author of numerous articles and books on these topics. Maenette has taught preK–12. (Lead IOMV Scholar)

Bryan McKinley Jones Brayboy, Lumbee, is a visiting President's Professor of Education at the University of Alaska-Fairbanks. An educational anthropologist, he focuses much of his work on American Indians in higher education, peer groups, and minorities and schooling. His recent work in support of the American Indian Teacher Training program at the University of Utah, has presented important queries for indigenous educational policy makers to address. He works tirelessly to support the development of American Indian centers of study at post-secondary institutions. (Contributing author)

Edyael Del Carmen Casaperalta was born and raised in Durango, Mexico. At the age of 12, her family immigrated to South Texas. This formative experience inspires her interest in researching the "psychology of immigration." Her participation in community development, youth leadership, and higher education projects with the Llano Grande Center for Research and Development since 1998 has been of great importance in shaping her professional goals. Edyael recently graduated from Occidental College with a Bachelor of Arts in Psychology, and is currently pursuing a Master's in International Affairs with a focus on Latin American Studies at Ohio University. She hopes to improve the mental health opportunities available to immigrant communities across the country through research and advocacy. She also loves to practice Portuguese and dance Salsa! (IOMV Emerging Scholar)

Kate Cherrington's tribal affiliations are Ngati Hine, Ngati Wai, and Pakeha. Currently Kate is raising her two children at home, and studying. She is madly and deeply in love with her husband Bentham Ohia and together they are committed to the advancement of all peoples and the celebration of indigeneity. Much of this work has been achieved through work and association with Te Wananga o Aotearoa. Her other passions include her roles as Vice President of the Advancement of Māori Opportunity (AMO) and serves on the board of Americans for Indian Opportunity (AIO). Kate has been a founding member of Rangimarie Māori Cultural group that also serves as a vehicle to community advancement and the promotion of peace. Some of Kate's roles have included a Māori Liaison for Te Tauihu o nga Wananga— the National Wananga Association, including assisting the management of the World Indigenous Nations Higher Education Consortium (WINHEC) inaugural accreditation and audit applications in 2004, WIPCE Academic committee member (2004), Kohanga Reo mother and teacher, and kapa haka teacher for a children's community group. (IOMV I Scholar and Contributing author)

Susan C. Faircloth, an enrolled member of the Coharie Tribe, is an assistant professor of Educational Leadership and Special Education at The Pennsylvania State University. She is also affiliated with Penn State's American Indian Leadership Program through which she earned her doctoral degree in December 2000. Susan's research centers on the education of American Indian and Alaskan Native students with disabilities and the ethical dilemmas and administrative challenges school leaders face in implementing federal education policies. Prior to joining the faculty at Penn State, she served as the Director of Policy Analysis and Research with the American Indian Higher Education Consortium (AIHEC). (IOMV Scholar)

Jeremy Garcia is a member of the Hopi/Tewa Tribes of Arizona. He is a Curriculum and Instruction doctoral student at the Purdue University Graduate School of Education. He is involved with the development of a Native American Cultural Center, and the recruitment and retention of Native American graduate students at Purdue University. He received his Master's in Curriculum and Instruction from Michigan State University (2000) and his BS in Elementary Education from Northern Arizona University (1997). His prior work with Salt River Pima-Maricopa Indian Community included teaching, and the development of a Parent and Community Involvement Program. Emphasis of the program incorporated partnerships among parent, community, university, Tribal departments, and business ownership in student achievement. Jeremy has also worked with pre-service teaching programs at Northern Arizona University, Arizona State University, and Purdue University. He has special interest in Parent and Community Involvement, Culturally Responsive Pedagogy, and Teachers as Leaders. (IOMV Emerging Scholar)

Francisco Guajardo is assistant professor in the Department of Educational Leadership at the University of Texas Pan American in the U.S.–Mexican border town of Edinburg, Texas. At UTPA he teaches courses in curriculum development, instructional leadership, socio-cultural contexts of education, and research methods. Between 1990 and 2002 he was a teacher and high school administrator at Edcouch-Elsa High School, where he also founded the Llano Grande Center for Research and Development, a school based nonprofit organization focused on building community youth leadership. Out of the Center he leads initiatives on digital storytelling, oral histories, and civic engagement. (IOMV Scholar)

Alohalani Housman is an assistant professor of the Hawaiian Language College located at the University of Hawai'i at Hilo. She has been involved with Hawaiian language medium education for over 23 years; first as a parent, then as a teacher in the classroom for 14 years, and currently as a curriculum developer and teacher trainer for 9 years. In 1987 she was recruited to become the teacher in one of the two first Hawaiian language immersion classes in the Hawai'i public school system. She is a mother of four Hawaiian-speaking children, two of whom have graduated from Nawahiokalaniopuu School and from the university. She is also a grandmother of four Hawaiian-speaking children. Alohalani is a pre-service and in-service teacher trainer for K–2 Hawaiian medium schools. She is the developer of Hawaiian literacy materials for elementary schools, with a focus on modernization of the traditional Hawaiian syllabic approach for initial reading beginning in preschool and kindergarten. (Contributing author)

Theresa Jackson is a member of the Saginaw Chippewa Indian Tribe of Michigan. She is currently a full time student at Saginaw Chippewa Tribal College pursuing a degree. Theresa writes that she is most importantly, "a spouse, mother of four, and full of life's experiences from my community." (IOMV Emerging Scholar)

Paul Johnson, Ojibway, has been a student, a student athlete, a coach, a teacher, a program analyst, a professional development consultant, and is currently semi-retired. In 1995, Mr. Johnson began a new career of service. He has begun to give back to his community and now shares his skills with the Saginaw Chippewa Tribe of Michigan. Currently he is the President of the Board of Regents of the Saginaw Chippewa Tribal College. Formerly he worked as the planner for the new Ziibiwing Cultural Center and is currently the lead planner for a new 13 million dollar Elders Complex being constructed for the Saginaw Chippewa Tribal Community. Mr. Johnson continues his commitment to improving the educational outcomes of Native students. (IOMV I Scholar and Contributing author)

Kū Kahakalau is a native Hawaiian practitioner, educator, researcher, song-writer and community activist, residing on the Island of Hawai'i. As founder and president of the Kanu o ka 'Āina Learning 'Ohana, Kū has created and oversees an innovative family of programs that are community-based, family-oriented and culturally-driven and serve thousands of native Hawaiians from infants to elders. All programs are grounded in a *Pedagogy of Aloha*, developed as a result of decades of indigenous heuristic action research. This *Pedagogy of Aloha* is at once ancient and modern, and presents unprecedented potential to address the distinctive needs of Hawai'i's native population. (Contributing author)

Julie Kaomea is a Native Hawaiian associate professor in the Department of Curriculum Studies at the University of Hawai'i at Mānoa. Julie's educational research utilizes critical, post-structuralist methods and draws from postcolonial theories in analyzing the interface of culture and education with an emphasis on the enduring effects of colonialism in Native Hawaiian and other (post)colonial, indigenous educational communities. (Contributing author)

Keiki Kawai'ae'a is the Director of the Kahuawaiola Indigenous Teacher Education Program, and the Hale Kuamo'o Hawaiian Language Center for the Ka Haka Ula O Ke'elikōlani College of Hawaiian language at the University of Hawai'i at Hilo. She is a pioneer in the Hawaiian language revitalization movement spanning some 25 years as a Hawaiian language immersion parent and teacher, curriculum developer, teacher trainer and administrator. She has been an invited speaker and panelist at national and international gatherings addressing Indigenous education, language and culture revitalization and native teacher education. Keiki has also been instrumental in the development of the Na Honua Mauli Ola Hawai'i Guidelines that have an impact on the education of learners in culturally healthy and responsive ways. (IOMV Scholar)

J. Kehaulani Kauanui (Kanaka Maoli) is an Associate Professor in Anthropology and American Studies at the Center for the Americas, at Wesleyan University in Connecticut, where she teaches courses on indigenous sovereignty politics, nationalism, race, and citizenship, as well as gender and sexuality. She earned her Ph.D. in History of Consciousness at the University of California, Santa Cruz. Her published essays can be found in the following journals: *The Contemporary Pacific, Political and Legal Anthropology Review, Social Text, Amerasia Journal, American Studies, Comparative American Studies, Women's Studies International Forum,* and *Pacific Studies.* Her first book *Hawaiian Blood,* examines the legal construction of Hawaiian indigeneity relating to race and colonial land dispossession (Duke University Press, forthcoming). Her second book focuses on Native Hawaiian feminist decolonization (in progress). She is currently co-editing a book, *Native Feminisms Without Apology,* with Andrea Lee Smith. (Contributing author)

Noelani Lee, a Native Hawaiian, is the Executive Director for the 501(c)3 non-profit, Ka Honua Momona International (the bountiful earth), on the island of Moloka'i. She received her BA from Princeton University in Anthropology, having written her thesis on Hawaiian Sovereignty, and her MA from the University of Hawai'i, Manoa in Pacific Islands Studies. In an effort to push the boundaries of the University's acceptance of indigenous knowledge, Ms. Lee was the first person at the University of Hawai'i to dance and chant her Master's thesis, "Mai Home Hawai'i: Hawaiian Diaspora and the Return of Hawaiians from the Diaspora." (IOMV Emerging Scholar)

Teresa Magnuson is a member of the Pokagon Band of Potawatomi and the turtle clan. She is a graduate student in Higher, Adult, & Lifelong Education (HALE) at Michigan State University and owner of Red Paint Printing. Teresa received her BS in Sociology from Michigan State University in 2003. Her academic career is driven by the desire to contribute to indigenous language preservation and revitalization efforts. Upon completion of her graduate schooling, Teresa looks forward to developing Anishnabemowin language immersion programs for adult and youth learners. (IOMV Emerging Scholar)

Henri[etta] Mann, a Cheyenne educator, is the Special Assistant to the President of Montana State University—Bozeman. She is Professor

Emeritus in Native American Studies at Montana State where she taught American Indian Religions and Philosophical Thought, American Indian Literatures, and a graduate seminar. She has written primarily in the field of American Indian education and she lectures on topics concerned with the discipline of Native American Studies. (*In Our Mother's Voice*, Elder)

Teresa L. McCarty is the Alice Wiley Snell Professor of Education Policy Studies at Arizona State University, where she also directs a large-scale study of Native American language shift and retention. Her research, teaching, and service focus on Indigenous education, language planning and policy, and ethnographic methods in education. Her recent books include *"To Remain an Indian": Lessons in Democracy from a Century of Native American Education* (with K. Tsianina Lomawaima, Teachers College Press, 2006), *Language, Literacy, and Power in Schooling* (Erlbaum, 2005), and *A Place To Be Navajo: Rough Rock and the Struggle for Self-Determination in Indigenous Schooling* (Erlbaum, 2002). (Contributing author)

Mindy Morgan is an assistant professor of Anthropology at Michigan State University and is affiliated with the American Indian Studies Program. Her work centers on how indigenous communities both view and use language as a symbol of cultural persistence and tribal identity within the U.S. as well as the impact of federal policy on indigenous language maintenance. In 1996–1997 she served as the curriculum coordinator for a Nakoda language project at Fort Belknap College funded by the National Endowment for the Humanities. In the fall of 2003, she began a new research project regarding Ojibwe language maintenance and revitalization programs. She teaches courses concerning Language and Culture as well as contemporary Native communities for the Department of Anthropology. (Contributing author)

Lai-Lani Ovalles, worked with The Institute for Community Leadership (ICL), a nonviolence and social justice based organization in Seattle, WA. She facilitates ICL's dynamic literacy-based curriculum with diverse groups of youth in public schools that confronts racism, sexism, militarism and consumerism. As the Outreach Director for ICL, Lai-Lani builds relationships with groups, colleges and universities, and individuals who have a thirst for social justice. She organizes and speaks on issues of multi-racial unity, sovereignty, youth leadership and addressing the academic achievement gap in schools. She believes in the power of culture, creativity and indigenous knowledge to guide the creation of a just and peaceful world. (IOMV Emerging Scholar)

CHiXapkaid (**Michael Pavel**) a Skokomish Tribal member and traditional bearer, is an Associate Professor of Higher Education in the Department of Educational Leadership and Counseling Psychology at Washington State University. He teaches graduate level courses in the higher education areas of history, administration, law, teaching and learning, student development, multicultural issues, and politics. CHiXapkaid's research interests focus on Indigenous students' experiences with K–12 academic achievement and educational attainment, postsecondary access and achievement, and blending traditional cultural training with modern day educational experiences. (IOMV Scholar)

Tamarah Pfeiffer is of the To'dichinii (Bitterwater) people born for the Metal Hat Clan (Beesh Bichai) and an enrolled member of the Navajo Nation. Dr. Pfeiffer earned her doctorate at Penn State University in the area of Educational Administration and was closely affiliated with the American Indian Leadership Program at Penn State. Currently Dr. Pfeiffer works both as an adjunct faculty for Arizona State University with their Principalship program teaching courses in research design and as a High School Principal at Rough Rock Community School in the heart of Navajo Country. Dr. Pfeiffer is a strong advocate for bilingual, bicultural, bi-literate education and has devoted her educational career to building strong educational settings for Navajo students. (Contributing author)

Iris PrettyPaint, an enrolled member of the Blackfeet Tribe in Browning, Montana, serves as Co-Director of Research Opportunities in Science for Native Americans (ROSNA) at the University of Montana where she works to enrich and establish connections between UM women scientists and Native American women scientists and students. She received her B.S.W. in Social Work from the University of Kansas in 1978 and her M.S.W. in Social Work from the University of Minnesota in 1996. (Contributing author)

Troy Richardson (NC Tuscarora/Saponi) is an assistant professor in education and American Indian studies at Cornell University. He is also director of education for the Transboundary Indigenous Waters Program in the American Indian Program. (Contributing author)

Mary Eunice Romero-Little (Cochiti Pueblo), Assistant Professor in the Curriculum and Instruction Division at Arizona State University, earned her Ph.D. in Education from the University of California at Berkeley, and is the recipient of the American Indian Leadership Fellowship from the W. K. Kellogg-UC Berkeley Partnership and the Katrin H. Lamon Resident Scholar Fellowship from the School of American Research, a center for advanced study in Anthropology, the Humanities, and Native American Art located in Santa Fe, New Mexico. She is currently serving as a co-principal investigator for the Native Language Shift and Retention Project, a three-year research study funded by the United States Institute of Educational Sciences (IES) and sponsored by the Arizona State University and a Junior Faculty Research Training Fellow at the American Indian and Alaska Native Head Start Research Center at the University of Colorado at Denver and Health Sciences Center. Her research interests are Indigenous languages, American Indian education, second language learning, and the socialization of Native children. (Contributing author)

Kalena Silva is a Professor of Hawaiian Studies and the Director of Ka Haka ʻUla O Keʻelikōlani College, the first college to focus on an indigenous language of the United States. Through the medium of Hawaiian, he teaches undergraduate and graduate courses in Hawaiian performing arts, language and literature. Together with his colleagues, Dr. Silva has pioneered a P–20 Hawaiian medium education system founded upon a Hawaiian cultural world view to provide learners with educational opportunities enabling them to become fully-engaged citizens of the world. (IOMV I Scholar and Contributing author)

Wayne J. Stein is a Professor of Native American Studies and Higher Education Studies at Montana State University in Bozeman, Montana. He works closely with the seven tribal colleges (TCU) of Montana and several others around the country. He has also consulted with several tribes interested in starting their own TCU. His teaching responsibilities in the College of Letters and Science focuses on undergrad Native American Studies in literature and contemporary issues of American Indians; while his focus in the NAS Master's graduate studies program are TCU's, minorities in higher education, and contemporary issues of American Indians. His area of scholarship and publishing has focused primarily on TCUs, but he has done some research and writing in the areas of Indian gaming and faculty of color in higher education. Dr. Stein has formally served as President of Sitting Bull College and Vice-President of Academic Affairs at Ft. Berthold Community College. Dr. Stein's tribal affiliation is Turtle Mountain Chippewa. (Contributing author)

Lynette Stein-Chandler, a White Clay scholar and teacher, is founder and director of the White Clay Immersion School and faculty in the Native American Studies Department at Fort Belknap College in Montana. She teaches elementary students in the White Clay language and also teaches Native American Studies courses in Education, Cinema and White Clay language. She is living her dream of restoring an educating education while revitalizing the White Clay language and philosophy teaching to all ages of community members. The White Clay Language Immersion Elementary School is unique in that it is based at a tribal college and will be the next important movement in Indian Education and tribal colleges, educating all generations of our people. (IOMV Emerging Scholar)

Samuel Suina is a Native American from the Pueblo of Cochiti in New Mexico. He has served in many tribal officer positions for his tribe and is a composer of Indian songs for his people. Suina is currently serving as the Director of the New Mexico Tribal Extension Task Force at New Mexico State University (NMSU). The Tribal Extension project is a statewide initiative that involves the collaborative effort of NMSU, all 22 New Mexico Tribes, and the three New Mexico 1994 tribal college land grant institutions. The goal of the Task Force is to establish eight Tribal Extension Centers throughout New Mexico. Dr. Suina has served as an adjunct professor at the University of New Mexico, New Mexico Highlands University, and the Santa Fe Community College. Undergraduate and graduate courses that Dr. Suina has taught include: Indian Education Issues, Native American Agricultural Issues, Indigenous Peoples of North America, Indigenous Peoples of the Southwest, Impact of U.S. Federal Indian Policies on Indian Tribes in North America, and

Indigenous Practices to Resolving Conflicts. Suina has a Ph.D. in Higher Education/Sociology from the Pennsylvania State University, an M.A. in Guidance and Counseling from the University of New Mexico, a B.A. in Psychology from Fort Lewis College, and a high school diploma from the Institute of American Indian Arts in Santa Fe, New Mexico. (*In Our Mother's Voice*, Elder)

Katherine A. Tibbetts, Ph.D., Research Analyst. Kathy has over twenty years' experience in evaluation at Kamehameha Schools. Her current role at KS includes technical support to KS program staff for program monitoring and evaluation, technical assistance to Hawaiian culture-based charter schools, research related to the well-being of native Hawaiian students in the public school system, and work on an instrument to describe the developmental assets of Hawaiian youth. Kathy previously served as one of six facilitators for the 2000–2015 KS Strategic Plan. She is a long-term board member for Hawai'i's first public charter school, and is one of the founders of the Indigenous Peoples in Evaluation TIG for the American Evaluation Association. She is also an active member of the Hawai'i affiliates of the American Educational Research Association and American Evaluation Association. Her dissertation in Educational Psychology on the stability of test scores and their use in school evaluation was awarded second place by Division H (School Evaluation and Program Development) of the American Educational Research Association in 2005. (IOMV Scholar)

Shelly Valdez is a member of the Pueblo of Laguna Tribe, located in central New Mexico, and of Hispanic descent. Shelly's educational background includes a Bachelor of Arts degree in Elementary Education, Master of Arts in Elementary Education, and Ph.D. in Multicultural Teacher Education focusing on research in the area of Science Education. Shelly has worked in the area of education for 26+ years and currently owns and manages an educational consulting business, *Native Pathways, Inc. (NaPs)*, located in New Mexico. Through her business she has been afforded opportunities to work with programs, corporations and institutions, targeting education initiatives that have a vested interest in embracing cultural relevancy in education at various levels. (Contributing author)

Matthew VanAlstine is an enrolled member of the Grand Traverse Bay Band of Ottawa and Chippewa Indians. He is a doctoral student in the Higher, Adult, & Lifelong Education (HALE) program at Michigan State University. Currently, Matthew is the Director of Native American Programs at Central Michigan University where his main focus is the recruitment, retention, and success of Native American Students. In his spare time he is an adjunct faculty member for the Saginaw Chippewa Tribal College where he has taught developmental courses and Native American Law and Policy. Matthew is committed to helping Native American students realize their potential and life goals. (IOMV Emerging Scholar)

Malia Villegas is Alutiiq/Sugpiaq with family from the Aleutian Islands of Kodiak and Afognak and the Hawaiian Island of Oʻahu. She is a doctoral student in Communities and Schools at the Harvard Graduate School of Education (HGSE). Her primary research interests include: community-based indigenous education, rural education, teacher recruitment and retention, and education policy. Malia's current research centers on Alaska Native community leaders, perspectives on defining student success, "what does it mean to be a successful Alaska Native student?" She is completing the first phase of this work with the Alaska Native Policy Center and First Alaskans Institute. She holds undergraduate degrees from Stanford University, as well as a Master's degree from HGSE. In her spare time, she enjoys singing karaoke, fishing, and working on her first Œhumbling, Alutiiq basket weaving project. (IOMV Emerging Scholar)

Lawrence E. Wheeler, enrolled member of the Walker River Paiute Tribe (Nevada) with Seneca, Cayuga and Navajo ancestral roots, has been a lifelong resident of Cattaraugus Seneca Territory in Western New York. Mr. Wheeler considers himself an "eager student" of the Seneca Language. Mr. Wheeler holds both a Master of Science degree in Mathematics (1998) and a Master of Science degree in Mathematics Education (2001) both earned at Syracuse University in Central New York. As a teaching assistant at Syracuse University and later a member of the adjunct faculty at SUNY Fredonia, Mr. Wheeler enjoyed teaching undergraduate Mathematics at the university level. Mr. Wheeler completed his secondary teaching certification and taught Mathematics at the secondary level for three years. Mr. Wheeler currently coordinates K–12 programs and studies the effects of said programming on Native American learning for the Seneca Nation of Indians in Western New York. (IOMV Emerging Scholar)

Nālani Wilson is a doctoral candidate and teaching fellow in Akoranga Whakakori, the School of Physical Education at the University of Otago in Dunedin, New Zealand. Her work focuses on incorporating Pacific epistemologies, specifically Kānaka Maoli and Māori, into outdoor, experiential and environmental education. (Contributing author)

Tarajean Yazzie-Mintz is interested in the way in which language and culture shape classroom instruction and school policy. Her primary research is focused on American Indian Education, particularly documenting the way in which teachers who teach Native children conceptualize what is a culturally appropriate curriculum and pedagogy. Recent work includes professional development and research with urban teachers in schools serving students who are English language learners. Assistant Professor, Indiana University, School of Education. (IOMV Scholar)

Valorie Johnson is employed in her "dream job" as a program director in the area of youth and education at the W. K. Kellogg Foundation of Battle Creek, Michigan. In this role, she manages and monitors active projects, including the "Capturing the Dream" Native American Higher Education Initiative and reviews and assesses new proposals. Previously, Val was director of Native American Affairs for the State of Michigan's Department of Social Services (DSS) in Lansing. She coordinated the activities of 20 outreach staff throughout the state, and led the development of a range of programs and services, which served Native American children, families, and communities. Val began her career as a human relation's executive with the National Education Association in Washington, D.C. She earned her Ph.D. in educational administration from Michigan State University, M.Ed. in educational psychology, and B.S. in Human Development from the University of Hawai'i. As a consultant, Val has advised human service and educational institutions across the United States including the U.S Health and Human Services department,

Washington, D.C. She also served as a guidance counselor at the Institute of American Indian Arts in Santa Fe, New Mexico, and the Kamehameha Schools in Honolulu, Hawai'i. From 1989 to 1992, Val was a Fellow in Group X of the Kellogg National Fellowship Program. She formerly served on the Board of Regents for Bay Mills Community College and now serves on the Board of Americans for Indian Opportunity. Val is married to Paul Johnson (Ojibwe) and has four sons—Stephen, Christopher, Derek Nyagwai, and Dustin Owl. (*In Our Mother's Voice* Mentor)

Name index

Subject index